Louise Chandler Moulton

Lazy Tours in Spain and elsewhere

Louise Chandler Moulton

Lazy Tours in Spain and elsewhere

ISBN/EAN: 9783337225490

Printed in Europe, USA, Canada, Australia, Japan

Cover: Foto ©Andreas Hilbeck / pixelio.de

More available books at **www.hansebooks.com**

LAZY TOURS

IN SPAIN AND ELSEWHERE

BY

LOUISE CHANDLER MOULTON
Author of
"SWALLOW FLIGHTS," "IN THE GARDEN OF DREAMS," "RANDOM
RAMBLES," "BED-TIME STORIES," "SOME
WOMEN'S HEARTS," ETC.

BOSTON
ROBERTS BROTHERS
1897

TO

SIR BRUCE AND LADY SETON,

THE WELL-BELOVED FRIENDS AND FREQUENT HOSTS OF
THIS LAZY TOURIST,

I INSCRIBE THESE PAGES.

L. C. M.

SHALL a Lazy Tourist apologize for laziness? Then forgive me, kind readers, that I have travelled in pursuit of pleasure, or of health, rather than of "very hard facts;" that I have recorded impressions more often than details, and that I have not even the saving grace to be ashamed of having been a vagrant.

L. C. M.

CONTENTS.

	PAGE
I. A LAZY TOUR IN SPAIN	1
II. IN SOUTHERN ITALY	49
AT NAPLES	51
IN PURSUIT OF VESUVIUS	60
SORRENTO DAYS	67
POMPEII, AMALFI, AND PAESTUM	76
III. IN AND ABOUT ROME	85
ALL ROADS LEAD TO ROME	87
MOST ROMAN PART OF ROME	97
AMONG STATUES AND PICTURES	107
AMONG THE MANY CHURCHES OF THE ETERNAL CITY	116
SOME ROMAN VILLAS	130
IV. FLORENCE THE FAIR	139
FLORENCE THE FAIR	141
FROM FLORENCE TO PARIS	154
V. PARIS AND PICTURES	163
VI. RAMBLES IN SWITZERLAND	191
IN SWITZERLAND: AT LUCERNE	193
TO, AND IN, GENEVA	200
CHAMOUNY AND THE MER DE GLACE	213
OVER THE TÊTE NOIRE, TO CHILLON	220
A POSTSCRIPT: AT RAGATZ	228

CONTENTS.

		PAGE
VII.	CERTAIN FRENCH CURES	235
	At Aix-les-Bains	237
	Brides-les-Bains	254
	Lights and Shades of Travelling in Savoie	264
	Les Voirons: A Paradise on a Hill-Top	270
VIII.	HOW THEY CURE THEMSELVES IN GERMANY	277
	Marienbad and Nuremberg	279
	To, and at, Carlsbad	296
	From Carlsbad to Paris	313
IX.	AT WIESBADEN, AND AFTER	323
	What one does at Wiesbaden	325
	To Paris, by way of Frankfort and Metz	248
X.	AN ENGLISH "CURE," AND A GLIMPSE OF YORKSHIRE	357
	Tunbridge Wells	359
	In Yorkshire	866

A LAZY TOUR IN SPAIN.

LAZY TOURS.

A LAZY TOUR IN SPAIN.

THE only bit of real estate I ever owned was "a Castle in Spain." I have long been familiar with its aspect. I have seen its shining turrets in the crimson of sunset skies. I have heard faint music, on winds blowing from the East, which I felt sure was caught from harps in its high windows; and mysterious scents have reached me now and then, wafted, doubtless, from its far-off gardens.

From my childhood I had longed to visit my Spanish estates as pertinaciously as Columbus longed to set forth from those shores of Spain to discover this far-off new world in which I thus discontentedly abode. But tales of expense, difficulty, and danger have been rife about the pleasant paths of Spain.

"You will find it such a fatiguing journey," said one. "The hotels are poor, the railway trains crawl, and you'll be poisoned with garlic."

"And you'll not be free from danger," said another. "Bandits have been banished from the rest of the civilized world to survive in Spain. They may take possession of your train any fine day. You'll still find the 'robber purse,' which Washington Irving speaks of, a necessary precaution."

"And then the expense," croaked a third. "You can't go without a courier, and he'll pillage you right and left."

"And then you'll never find your castle, you know." But it was only Mrs. Gradgrind who said that; and I did not mind Mrs. Gradgrind.

Suddenly, in Paris, I made up my mind to go. Four other rash ladies came to the same resolution; and we looked about for a courier. We chose him at last for his pious face. He was the Vicar of Wakefield, in German, — at least, that is how he impressed me; but the Wise Woman of our party said he was a Sunday-school superintendent off home duty, and disposed to treat us with a sort of paternal care, as if we had been the lambs of his flock.

It was a frowning October morning when we left Paris, and by the time we got to Tours it rained most spitefully. We defied the rain, however, and drove about the town, and back and forth across the beautiful river, which flows through Tours as the Arno flows through Florence. We went to the cathedral, and lingered under the great tent-like cedar of Lebanon in the Archbishop's garden, and then drove out through the sullen rain to that Plessis la Tour which the readers of "Quentin Durward" know.

The next day it rained still, and it rained all day long, while on we journeyed. We drove through a pouring rain at night to our hotel in Bordeaux, and started away from it the next morning in the same cheerful condition of the weather. But the sky had cleared before we got to Biarritz; and after that the sun shone on us for seven weeks to come, with only one brief and appropriate interruption.

Biarritz the beautiful! No wonder the Empress Eugenie built her villa there in the days of her glory. Part of that villa is a restaurant now, and looks like "a banquet hall deserted,"—or it did in the late October when the Biarritz season was coming to an end; but there is hardly a more superb view in Europe than can be seen from its windows. Biarritz, like Tours, is a place to go back to; but we had little time to linger there. Were we not *en route* for Spain, the country of beauty and of bandits, of love and of fear?

On the 26th of October we entered our promised land. We went through the custom-house at Irun. We had been forewarned that the examination would be rigorous and disagreeable, and that our papers especially would be subjected to the closest scrutiny. On the contrary, not a paper was examined, and nothing could have been more perfunctory than the whole performance. The officers consulted somewhat over a seal-skin cloak belonging to the Nut-brown Maid; but whether they were admiring or condemning we could not tell. They folded it up respectfully at last, and marked the box that contained it as passed.

It was on this occasion that the Nut-brown Maid confided to me that she had a passport which had cost her time and trouble and a national bank-note for five dollars; and of which, therefore, she was extremely desirous to make use. The officers of the customs grieved her by not asking for it; and I must mention here that for a lady travelling in Spain a passport is as unnecessary as a marriage certificate.

We journeyed on from Irun through the lovely Basque country. The Wise Woman grieved that we were thus hurrying through the abode of these gentle, serious, handsome Basque folk, whose language, they claim, is the oldest in Europe. But the rest of us were happy, if only there had not been so many tunnels to shut out from our view the wonderful mountain scenery. The railway from Irun to Burgos is said to be a masterpiece of engineering. Shall I ever forget how that afternoon sped on, leading us from beauty to beauty, until at last the royal Spanish sunset came, kindling the skies to crimson, and touching the hill-tops with a baptism of blood and fire? And then we saw visions. Down one western slope we were sure we saw Don Quixote ride, and on the hill-top opposite it was a true giant, and not a windmill, that confronted the faithful knight. And in the heart of that western glory surely we saw a castle,

"With its battlements high in the hush of the air,
And the turrets thereon,"

and each woman of us believed herself its rightful châtelaine.

We were tired enough when we got to Burgos, at a late hour in the evening; and I fear we grumbled unduly as we jolted on through the rough streets the long, long way to the hotel. Why it is that all over Spain the railway stations have gone into the country on a vacation, and you have to drive a Sabbath day's journey before you get into town and find your hotel, I have not yet been informed; but, even here, I have faith in the good intentions of the Spanish people.

Our Vicar of Wakefield had telegraphed for rooms for us beforehand; and on arriving, chilled to the bone, at the Fonda del Norte, we found a bright fire burning, and we found Matéo. Matéo was our chambermaid; and for good-humor, brightness, and black eyes, it would be hard to name her peer. She and the fire consoled us. The beds were clean and soft, and we laughed at the idea of Spanish discomforts until breakfast. But the breakfast, oh, the breakfast! The tea was bad; the eggs deserved respect only for their age; the bread was sour; and the butter,— it is a horror to remember. All over Spain the butter is vile, on account, I imagine, of the sterility of the soil; but in most places the food, as a whole, is good. We took the worst first, in the matter of provisions, in taking Burgos. But when our rather forlorn breakfast was over, and we went out of doors, it mattered little that to break our fast had been a penance. Here we were, in Spain, in Spain!

Had we been taken up blindfolded by some of the genii that did transport duty in the time of the Arabian Nights, and set down in Burgos without a word of forewarning, we could not have mistaken our locality. Here were the dark-eyed señoras of our long dreams; here "the stately Spanish men;" and here, above all, were the beggars, the gentle, persistent, picturesque Spanish beggars, and it was escorted by a troop, a throng of them, that we moved on to the cathedral, that cathedral of which De Amicis speaks as a miracle of boldness, genius, and labor, producing "the effect upon you of a superhuman voice which cries 'I AM.'" What vastness of space, what splendor of design, what lavishness of ornamentation, what superb expression altogether of man's faith and worship! One grieves only that the grandeur of the vistas should be broken by the choir, which is almost a church within a church.

Burgos is the town of the Cid, — the Homer of Spain. Everywhere you come upon traces of him. One favorite excursion is to his tomb. On the way you pause at the Convent of Miraflores, built by Isabella the Catholic in memory of her father and mother, and containing their monument. It is a desolate road that leads from Miraflores to San Pedro de Cerdeña, the beloved home of the Cid, whither, when he was dying at Valencia, he begged with his latest breath to be taken. Thither was he borne, when all was over, upon his faithful horse Bavieca, who is said to have wept at his deathbed. Upon Bavieca was the dead Cid set upright, clad in his armor, and with that good sword Tibona in his hand, with which, though dead, he yet struck down a Jew who audaciously plucked him by the beard. At San Pedro de Cerdeña was Bavieca buried, as the will of the Cid commanded. "When ye bury Bavieca," he wrote, " dig deep, for shameful thing it were that he should be eaten by curs, who hath trampled down so much currish flesh of Moors." The Cid is no longer buried in his own tomb, which is in the centre of the convent chapel. Here, indeed, are the marble effigies of himself and of his faithful wife, Ximena; but their bones are in a casket, with a glass top, in the town hall at Burgos, where my own eyes have beheld them.

It would be a mistake to leave Burgos without seeing the beautiful Cistercian Convent of Las Huelgas, founded by the wife of Alonzo VIII. as a refuge for unmarried women of noble families. Through the grating that shuts off the choir in the church of this convent we saw some of these white-robed Cistercians at their prayers. Was I wrong in pitying them, I wonder? Some were young and beautiful now, and others had been so long ago; but here they all were, women of noble race, with their ardent Spanish eyes and their pleasure-loving Spanish lips; full, when they came here, of all girlhood's restless dreams and longings, and yet condemned by family pride and family poverty to this life of seclusion; this finality of all things, which has nothing beyond it save death.

The Wise Woman of our party decreed that our next stopping-place should be Valladolid; so we made the journey thither from Burgos in an evening, found a comfortable French hotel, slept the sleep of the weary, and awoke next morning ready for a day of sight-seeing in Valladolid. It was a very satisfying day to me, for it satisfied me that I never want to go there again. The cathedral is grand in its outlines, but so white and bare and cold that I shiver to remember it. The interests of Valladolid are all in the past tense. In the fifteenth century it was the home of kings. Charles V. adorned it with noble edifices, and his son, Philip II., was born here. Cervantes lived here once, but I believe that Cervantes was a melancholy man. You are taken to his humble house, and his "statue watches it from the square." Here the great man worked, making clothes for the king and his nobles, and thinking, meanwhile, his immortal thoughts. You go also to see the house where Columbus died; the university, and a whole list of other things,—among them the convent built by Torquemada, the terrible confessor of Isabella the Catholic, and the Plaza Mayor, where, under his influence, heretics used to be burned for the glory of the Lord. The court was at Valladolid then, and the court used to go to see an auto-da-fé as now in Madrid it goes to see a bull-fight; and the poor heretics, arrayed in yellow shirts painted all over with flames and figures of devils, made much amusement for the fine folk.

The Museo of Valladolid has received more praise than it deserves, for it is largely given over to rubbish. It contains a few good pictures, however,— Rubens's "St. Anthony of Padua" among them; and some wonderful statues in wood from the two greatest wood sculptors Spain has ever known,— Juan de Juni, who delighted in using his art to depict the morbid and the terrible, and the gentle Gregorio Hernandez, who, like Fra Angelico, never began his task without first saying his prayers.

In the afternoon we drove all about the dreary, desolate town, which looks as if some caprice of fate had set it down in the midst of a desert, and which we were thankful enough to leave in the gray of the next morning.

Our destiny that day was the Escorial, and on our way we passed Medina, where Isabella the Catholic died in 1504, and Avila, where her only son, Prince Juan, was buried. Juan was a young prince of very noble qualities, and had been most carefully educated by his royal parents. In his twentieth year he was married to the beautiful Princess Margaret, daughter of the Emperor Maximilian, whom he loved as well as if they had not been the children of kings. Leaving him thus, just married, and with every prospect of happiness, Ferdinand and Isabella hastened away to another marriage, that of their daughter Isabella to the King of Portugal. Meantime Prince Juan was taken suddenly ill. King Ferdinand, by travelling rapidly, managed to reach his death-bed; but Queen Isabella, who was forced to journey more slowly, only arrived after all was over. When the young prince was near his end, his father strove to cheer him with hopes of his recovery, but he lifted his eyes as toward some vision of glory that others could not behold, and said that he was ready to leave a world which at the best was so full of vanity and trouble; and he prayed only that the loved ones from whom he parted might be as resigned to part with him as he was ready to go.

There, in Avila, his sorrowing parents built his monument, and placed on it the semblance of his sleeping figure, "lying as he had smiled,"—the most touching of all sepulchral effigies. From the carven stalls which they occupied at Mass the stricken father and mother used, thenceforth, to look down on their best-beloved sleeping below, and the sad eyes of one would seek the sad eyes of the other, and the silent tears would start.

Avila is still surrounded by its perfect wall, and is scarcely changed at all since the time of Santa Teresa, who was born there in 1815. The Roman Catholic Church regarded Santa Teresa as especially raised up by Heaven to breathe new life into their religion. She was born of noble parents, who were also very pious; only, biographers say, that the mother was given too much to the reading of romances, and it was no doubt from her that Santa Teresa inherited her strong bent to the romantic, as well as to the mystical. From her earliest childhood she was constantly reading the lives of the saints and martyrs, and at eight years of age she set off from home with her little brother to find the country of the Moors, in the hope of being martyred by them, but was captured and brought back by a hard-hearted and unromantic uncle.

When she was twelve years old her mother died, and Teresa got possession of the deceased lady's beloved library of romances, the consequence of which was that the student of her character finds in her a curious blending of religion and romance, personal vanity and personal piety. One noble saying of hers deserves to be remembered: "I conceive," said she, "that the misery of damned souls in hell consists in the impossibility of their loving God or man." She believed that when she was twenty she was caught up into heaven, and shown a plan for reformed convents, which she returned to earth to carry out. She founded seventeen nunneries and fifteen monasteries, in different parts of Spain, beside her own especial Convent of St. Joseph at Avila. She arrived at Toledo, with only four ducats to found a convent, and when people exclaimed at this she said, calmly, —

"Teresa and four ducats can do nothing; but God, Teresa, and four ducats can do anything."

She died in her sixty-eighth year, in her own convent at Avila. Roman Catholic legends assert that the spirits of ten thousand martyrs were present at her death-bed, and the Lord Jesus came in person to convey her to her heavenly home. Even now, in her convent chapel, the nuns sit during Mass upon the steps, rather than in the stalls carved for their use, because they believe that in Teresa's life-time angels used to come down to occupy these seats, and they wish still to leave them free for the possible grace of such high visitants.

From Avila the railway climbs toilsomely along the mountains up to the Escorial, passing through sixteen enormous tunnels on the way. Just before we reached the Escorial it began to rain. This was the only rain that diversified our seven weeks of brilliant Spanish sunshine. Somehow it seemed fitting that it should rain then and there. In the morning we went across to that palace so gloomy that, as Théophile Gautier in his "Voyage en Espagne" suggests, one can, after seeing it, always console himself, whatever the trouble of his life may be, by thinking that he might be at the Escorial, and is not.

From far away you can see the gloomy pile, so massive that it stands out from the mighty hills behind it, and confronts you in all its stately ugliness. It was built in the form of a gridiron, in honor of St. Laurence.

Do you know his story, with its touch of grim humor? He was broiled on a gridiron, in the year 261, over a very slow fire. He bore the grilling, while his life "held out to burn," with scornful composure, and when one side of him was well-done, he told his cooks that it was time to turn him; and suggested that they should taste him, and see if he was most palatable well-done or under-done. In memory, then, of this grim saint, on whom he had called for aid during the battle of St. Quentin, Philip II. resolved that the Escorial should be built.

The first stone was laid in 1563, but the erection was not finished until 1584; and in 1598 its founder, Philip II., died here, where for fourteen years he had lived, more as a monk than as a monarch, though he boasted that he was ruling the world, with a bit of paper, from under a hill. This mighty gray pile seems almost a part of the strong hills; and Ford says of it, that, cold as the gray eye and granite heart of its founder, it would have been out of keeping if placed amid the flowers and sunshine of a happy valley. The largest number of the priceless pictures that used to adorn it have been removed to the gallery at Madrid, though many still remain; and there are rooms on rooms hung with tapestry that it is worth a journey to see; also the noble library is full of interest, and the chapel is a miracle of stately simplicity.

Yet it is none of these which chiefly moves you, but rather the all-pervading memory of one thin-lipped, implacable man, who built this place for his home and his tomb, — who lived here mournfully, and died here awfully.

As you move on from place to place, you feel that you are treading in his footsteps. I sat in the very seat where he was sitting when news was brought to him of the destruction of the Spanish Armada; and there was something right royal in the way he received these tidings. Not a muscle of his face moved, we are told; and he said quietly, "I thank God for having given me the means of bearing such a loss without embarrassment. A stream can afford to waste some water when its source is not dried up."

The little inner room in which Philip II. died opens into the chapel, and at this opening the king's face used to be seen, during his last illness, following the prayers with a sort of desperation. It seems that at the end he was haunted by awful doubts whether his bigotry and his persecutions, by which he had thought he was doing God service, had not, after all, been a crime. The story of his death, with all its terrible details, came back to us as we looked from the little room which had witnessed his agonies into the stately chapel where his effigy, in gilt robes, kneels forever beside the high altar.

Then we followed him down into the Panteon, that place of sepulture for kings and the mothers of kings, where he sleeps peacefully, let us hope, in that coffin of gilt bronze for which, with almost his latest breath, he ordered a white satin lining and a plentiful supply of gilt nails. This Panteon seems to have possessed a singular attraction for the Spanish sovereigns. They have not been distinguished for holiness of life, yet they have been wont, while living, to haunt the Panteon, and look at their future resting-places. Maria Louisa scratched her name upon her empty urn with a pair of scissors, and Philip IV. used to sit in his niche often during his lifetime to hear Mass.

The whole Escorial is pervaded by a sense of almost supernatural gloom. You can hardly breathe freely there, or speak in an ordinary tone of voice; and to get away from the place, and move on to Madrid, is a relief.

The situation of Madrid is as little attractive as it well can be. It was chosen for the capital of Spain because that vandal, Charles V., had the gout. The city is two thousand four hundred feet above the level of the sea, and its stimulating air so helped the royal great toes that the august Charles exclaimed, "Here shall be the only Court!" And here it is to this day. It is a fascinating city, notwithstanding, with its great plazas, its park, its prado, and its fine out-of-doors statues, of which, perhaps, the best is that of Philip IV., in the Plaza del Oriente, in front of the royal palace which Velasquez himself designed. From the windows of the royal palace — one of the grandest royal residences in the world — you can look off to the snow-capped Guadarramas, and, beholding their icy splendors, forget the pitiful little play-river near at hand, the Manzanares, concerning which some joker suggested to one of the kings that he should either sell his bridge or buy a river.

Whatever fault may be found with Madrid as to its situation, it must be conceded that it has one of the finest picture galleries in the world. One of the finest, did I say? I pause to ask myself if I ever received as much pleasure from any other. It should have volumes written about it instead of a mere brief mention in the uncritical diary of a lazy tourist. Here Titian and Coello and Velasquez have handed down to us such living portraits of the Spanish sovereigns of the House of Austria that we know them all by heart, beginning with Charles V. and his dog. To have lived in this world and to die without having ever seen the pictures of Velasquez, — that, truly, were an evil fate. You can see Raphael, Titian, and even Murillo to excellent advantage in many other galleries; but here in this Museo at Madrid is almost the entire work of Velasquez.

What is the sombre, splendid charm of this wonderful Andalusian? Partly, I think, that he dared to tell the truth as no other man has told it before or since. What other painter of royal portraits ever made them as revealing as the Day of Judgment? Here they are, these kings and queens, weak when they were weak, sensual when they were sensual; so human that you almost see the blood throb in their veins. These buffoons are the court fools of all time: this Æsop, — what is there in his face, with its sensitive humility, its innocent shrewdness, its pathetic patience, that I cannot look at it except through a mist? I do not like Velasquez in the few instances when he paints religious subjects. He was a realist, not an idealist; and he should have left the holy people to Murillo, who has so depicted the girlish sweetness of her whom the Spirit of God overshadowed that it is no wonder Spain gave him the name of the Painter of Conceptions.

I knew little of Goya until I found him in this gallery. He was the painter of bull-fights, and peasants, and Spanish ladies who flirted behind their fans, — a fiery Aragonese, whose delight in bull-fights was so great that, during the latest years of his life, while residing at Bordeaux, he would go once a week to Madrid to see a bull-fight, and return without stopping even to salute his old friends.

What is this cruel, fascinating sport, that it can have taken such a hold on the Spanish people, we asked ourselves; and then we began to say diffidently to each other that, being here, perhaps it would be well to see it for ourselves. The Wise Woman had protested against it with such lofty scorn that, for dear consistency's sake, as I think, she stayed at home; but the rest of us went, and with us our Vicar of Wakefield with his bland and patriarchal smile.

The amphitheatre is an immense place, round like the Roman Colosseum, and the ring is surrounded by "terraced granite," and crowned with galleries. Six bulls were doomed to die for our entertainment, but I only out-stayed the taking off of three of them. It was the last grand bullfight of the season, and the audience was a brilliant one. The young king and queen looked down from their box of state; old Isabella was there with her daughters; and adjacent boxes were occupied by lords and ladies of high degree.

The first bull was very meek. His sole desire seemed to be to be let alone. The picadores, or mounted spearsmen, pricked him with their lances, and he looked at them with an injured air, as if he would fain have said: "How can you? I am a well-intentioned bull, and I deserve nothing of this sort." One was divided between disgust at his want of spirit and indignation that a creature so harmless and kindly should be foredoomed to death. He waked up slightly when the banderilleros came in with their darts and their gay cloaks; but, all through, one felt that he was being butchered to make a Spanish holiday, without at all taking his own part;

and even the matador, whose office it was to give him his death-wound, performed his task a little scornfully, as if it were hardly worth the trouble.

The second bull was a different fellow altogether. As a young American on my left expressed it, he was "all there." He had a sullen, determined, desperate nature. He gored two horses to death, literally in an instant, just uplifting them and running them through with his mighty horns. He made sullen plunges at the banderilleros, and he pushed the great matador himself to the end of his resources; but at last he lay there dead, and the team of mules dragged him out of the arena. He was as black as an undertaker's horse; and he had been solemn and indignant and scornfully defiant all the way through.

The third bull was a little red one, as fiery and aggressive a creature as can possibly be imagined. He did not chance to hurt the horses, but he made swift plunges at the cloaked banderilleros, which it took all their skill to escape; and once he even leaped the barrier, and caused a precious consternation among the audience for a moment. This brilliant creature made hot work for the banderilleros, and held even the matador for a long time at bay; but at last he gamely died, and the black mules dragged him away, as they had done his brothers before him.

By this time I thought I knew enough about bull-fights, and I left the king and queen and their court to behold the other three combats without me, and went away to walk on the prado and reflect. My sympathies were all with the bulls. They were the only creatures who had no least show of fair play. They alone were doomed with absolute certainty from the start. Even the horses might escape; and at worst their torture was but for a moment. The men were only in just enough danger to make the thing exciting, and there were ninety-nine chances out of a hundred that they would come off scathless; but the bull, let him bear himself never so bravely, was to be made an end of.

There was one feature of the spectacle that was so picturesque that, at the risk of being called inhuman, I must own to enjoying it. When the banderilleros came in with their gay cloaks and their darts, it was a pretty sight to see their encounter with the bull. They would give him a little prick, just enough to attract his attention, and he would turn to attack them. One second they were there, behind their satin cloaks, and the next they were safely over the barrier, and their enemy, making his plunge against them, found nothing. And then, if you had seen his contempt for such artful dodging! "Surely," he said to himself, "this butterfly-looking creature, all green and gold, *was* here, and where *is* he?" And then he would look round, and see another gorgeous mantle, and make another vain spring against the empty air. There is no denying that the grace and agility of these men was a pretty sight. Their figures were faultless. Their dazzling costumes glittered in the sun; and their movements were grace itself. I kept thinking of a line of Harriet Spofford's, —

"Ye riders bronze your airy motion,"—

and I thought if but these motions could be bronzed, we should have such a group of statues as the world has not yet seen.

But I was glad to leave it all behind me, — the heat, and the noise, and the confusion, and the cruelty, — and go out into the tranquil afternoon. It was pleasant, later on, to drive in the Buen Retiro, the Hyde Park of Madrid, to meet the sunset. The king and queen had seen the last bull killed, and were placidly driving together, and there, in the park, you met all the beauty and fashion of Madrid. What a French fashion it was! We had left señoras in mantillas at Burgos; here we found Spanish belles in Worth gowns and Rue de la Paix bonnets. I had seen just such costumes a month before in the Bois de Boulogne.

We went to the opera while we were in Madrid. The Madrid Opera-House is one of the finest in the world, and the performance is nearly always good. Only the best singing will be tolerated by a Madrid audience, — a fact of which I saw an illustration that was almost tragic. A young American had come there, much heralded, and under an engagement for six nights. She had already sung one night before I heard her, and had failed to please. For this evening another prima donna had been announced, but she had been taken ill, and the American girl unexpectedly appeared in her stead. The rest of the company was as good as could be desired, and met with a hearty welcome. When the American sang, she was quietly disregarded, save when, now and then, a distinct hiss would come from some of the least fashionable portions of the house. How I pitied her as I saw her stand there, with all those hostile eyes looking her over, all that sea of scornful faces turned toward her! How could she go on? But not to do so would have been to forfeit her engagement, and lose all that was her due. Upheld by I know not what sense of stern necessity, she steadily sang her part through. When a scene was applauded, she stood aside, with her pale face and her set lips, knowing that no share in the applause was for her. Not one expression of Spanish approval or encouragement sustained her from beginning to end. I felt that no gladiator fighting in an arena ever displayed a more dauntless courage.

From Madrid we made an excursion to imperial Toledo, — Toledo of the Romans, of the Goths, of the Moors, of the Christians! We were full of enthusiasm as we started from Madrid in the early — too early — morning to find it.

The train seemed nearly empty. We could almost fancy it crawled on for our sakes only; but crawl it did. I suppose that even a snail gets somewhere at last, and at last we came in sight of Toledo, grandly rising from the yellow Tagus, crowned by its Alcazar, and with its irregular towers, its battlemented walls, and all its solemn, stately, desolate beauty.

The Tagus girdles the town, leaving only one landward approach, which is fortified by Moorish towers and walls.

Like Rome, Toledo stands upon seven hills, and like Rome, everything about it is venerable. No mushroom place this, built in hot haste, as solace for a monarch's gout. All here is substantial and ancient.

For three hundred and fifty years the Moors held sway in Toledo, and you see Moorish remains at every step. It was the Moors who built the noble gates, of which the finest is the Puerta del Sol, with the horseshoe-shaped arches which distinguish Moorish architecture.

Externally, nothing could be more imposing than Toledo; but when fairly within it, one realizes that all is desolate, forsaken, going to decay. It once had two hundred thousand inhabitants; it has twenty thousand now.

But how fascinating it is, even yet! The narrow, illy-paved streets wind up and down and in and out, and lead you from wonder to wonder of interest and of beauty.

If one had space in which to speak fully of the various Spanish cathedrals, one must needs linger long with that of Toledo. The Virgin herself is said to have descended from heaven to assist at a Mass here, and no wonder.

The carving of the stalls in the cathedral choir is so beautiful that I should like to study it every day for a year, and the stained-glass windows are among the finest in the world.

They sparkle as with jewels, and throw their parti-colored reflections on the eighty-eight columns which uplift the gorgeous ceiling. There are noble pictures and glorious tombs, — a collection of works of art, in short, which might be the sufficient goal of any pilgrimage.

The Church of St. John of the Kings must not be forgotten, or its lovely cloister, with its richly clustered pillars on three sides, and its perfect Gothic arches. This cloister is being slowly restored, but meantime the undisciplined roses have their way in it. We gathered great bunches of them.

Outside this church hang chains which were suspended there as votive offerings by captives who had been delivered from the power of the Moorish infidel.

Two synagogues yet remain to attest the former importance of the Jews in Toledo. The ceiling of one of these synagogues was made of beams from the cedars of Lebanon.

Legends say that Toledo was the place of refuge of the Jews when Jerusalem was taken by Nebuchadnezzar. So ancient is it that you can believe anything, from the tale that ascribes its foundation to Hercules to that other solemnly enforced and detailed account which asserts that Tubal began to build it one hundred and forty-three years, to a day, after the Deluge.

It looks old enough to have been begun even before the Deluge, and it is certain that, when the Moors first took it, it was largely populated by Hebrews.

You feel as if nothing there ever had been or ever could be young, until you look up to some vine-wreathed balcony, and meet the dark eyes of some Spanish beauty, smiling coquettishly from under her lace mantilla; and then, suddenly, the old, old world seems eternally young, with love and hope and smiles springing up like flowers in the sun of every summer.

When the Christians recovered Toledo from the Moors they set a heavy tax upon every Jewish head; but the Jews were allowed to retain their synagogues, on the plea that they had not consented to the death of the Saviour. When Christ was brought to judgment, they said, the votes of the tribes had been taken, and one tribe had voted for His acquittal, and from this tribe were the Jews of Toledo descended!

Can you fancy at all this quaint old town, high, high above its yellow river, with its substantial Moorish architecture, its narrow streets which wind and climb through the desolate city where two hundred thousand people used to make merry, and where its poor twenty thousand live now as quietly as if they were all holding their breath, in order not to wake the echoes of some long-dead past?

Can you fancy, in this solemn, silent place, possessed by ghosts of Romans, Goths, Jews, Moors, and Christians, red roses flaunting their brightness in the warm south wind, and young cheeks glowing with new joys and hopes as if no one had ever died?

Two days later on we left Madrid, and went for consolation to Cordova. Cordova, like Toledo, is a city which has been, and is not, — which belongs more to the dead than to the living; for the gay days are past when it used to be called "The city of the thirty suburbs and the three hundred mosques."

Here, as in Toledo, are *patios;* and though I have heard them called courtyards, a *patio* is not precisely a courtyard, nor yet is it a garden or a room, but it is a delicious combination of all three.

A small vestibule is usually between it and the street. On its four sides rise slender columns, which support a gallery. It is paved with marble. In the centre there is often a fountain. Palms grow in these *patios*, flowers blossom there, ivy climbs round the graceful little pillars; here are statues, perhaps, or busts or graceful urns.

The *patio* is the heart of the home, — the place where you go to sip after-dinner coffee, to chat, to lounge, to dream.

Cordova was of importance in Cæsar's time; he

half destroyed it because it sided with Pompey. "The Great Captain," who was born there, used to say that other towns might be better to live in, but the place in which one should be born was certainly Cordova. Cordova was renowned, in those farthest off days, for its men of letters, whose wisdom astonished even the Romans.

Roman Cordova yielded to the Goths. But the Goths were conquered in turn by the Moors, and Cordova became the capital of Moorish Spain. It saw, under the Moors, the days of its greatest glory.

In the tenth century it contained nearly a million of inhabitants, three hundred mosques, nine hundred baths, and six hundred inns. How is the mighty fallen! It is said to have some fifty thousand inhabitants now; but looking back to a sojourn of some days there, I can scarcely remember to have met any one in the streets save tourists and beggars.

Its narrow paths are so roughly paved that it is a penance to walk in them; and its houses — whitewashed once a year — dazzle your aching eyes. Carriages are not allowed to enter the busy streets, and only the omnipresent donkey disputes your right of way. As night comes on you see young men clinging to the iron railings of the balconies of the lower windows, and holding interminable talks with their sweethearts inside them. This is a recognized method of courtship, and he who failed to adopt it would be deemed but an indifferent wooer. There are beautiful suburbs, with orange orchards and olive groves, to tempt one beyond the range of shops and streets. There are a thousand things quaint and strange for the traveller's delight; but to me Cordova means two things, two which I would gladly cross sea and land to find once more, — the Mosque Cathedral (La Mezquita) and the Sultana's Garden.

How shall one picture in words the wonders of La Mezquita? Its exterior gives no hint of what awaits you, for it is surrounded by walls from thirty to sixty feet in height; but once you have entered, through the Gate of Pardon, the Court of the Orange-Trees, the enchantment begins.

It means so little to say, in set phrase, that there are a thousand columns, surmounted by the Moorish horseshoe arches; and that some of these columns are of jasper, some of porphyry, some of verd-antique, and no two alike! You do not stop to think of these details; you wander on and on, as among the countless trees of a forest. You lose yourself in this divine immensity. It is like nothing else on earth.

Look where you will, the interminable vista stretches out beyond, and allures your tireless footsteps.

The stained glass of the windows, when the sun strikes it, throws patches of vivid color against the marbles. The place is so vast that you scarcely think about the cathedral church, which that royal vandal, Charles V., allowed to be engrafted in its centre in 1523, — a piece of barbarity which even he had the grace to regret when he came to see it later.

There is one tiny chapel, with a roof like a shell, which is adorned with mosaics sent from Constantinople. These mosaics are said to be the finest in the world. This is the Ceca, or Mihrab, the Holy of Holies, where the Koran used to be kept on a stand which cost a sum equal to five millions of dollars; and around this spot the very marble was worn in a circular hollow by the faithful Mussulmans, who used to crawl around it on their hands and knees.

But I feel, as I write, the commonplace insufficiency of these bare details. What mere words could fitly picture even the roofed-in forest of pillars, the countless Moorish arches, the exquisite tracery of the carvings? It is like nothing else in the world. You wander on as among the trees of a spacious grove; and yet you feel that you are in a temple. Perhaps some sudden sound of holy music breaks the stillness. The sentiment of worship, the love of beauty, the memories of a stately past, — how they all sway you at once; and you kneel with the rest, and — is it a low wind breathing through this strange forest, or the wings of some unseen presence, or the beating of your own half-choked heart, which so thrills you that whether in the body or out of the body you hardly know?

I have passed long afternoons in La Mezquita,

wandering up and down among the aisles of this wonderful forest, recalling the old legends which cluster about the spot, kneeling with the faithful at their prayers, or kneeling alone in some far-off corner, and listening to the remote sound of the holy music, half able to fancy that I was in some outer court of heaven. It is at close of such an afternoon as this that one fain would gather roses in the Sultana's Garden, and be brought back thus to the simpler joys of our human life.

How long ago did the Sultan make this garden for his love? I do not remember how many hundred years have passed since the dark-eyed beauty gathered its first roses; but still they freight the soft wind with their breath, and still the fairy ferns grow green, and the oranges ripen in the sun, and the solemn old carp are happy in the fish-pool.

We went there when the day was wearing late, and found the place as full of fragrant beauty as when she lived for whose pleasure it had been made. And as the ghost of Philip II. had possessed the grim Escorial, so the shade of that dark-eyed beauty for whom its first rose-tree had been planted still held sway in this garden. It was November; yet the carp were happy, and the lavish ferns were green, and the riotous roses intoxicated the autumn air with their summer breath; and under the trees she seemed to glide, — a presence felt rather than seen. One almost felt it a sacrilege to pluck her flowers; and yet she heeded not the trespass. She is as dead as Cordova.

We went to Granada to console ourselves for leaving Cordova. There seems to be a silent, unspeakable feud between the railway stations and the hotels all over Spain. They keep as far away from each other as possible.

The station is usually quite *out* of town, and the hotel very much *in*. But at Granada the station is far out from the city's heart in one direction, and the hotel where we were to stop still farther out in another. It was between eleven and twelve at night when we drove thus the whole length of the unsleeping town.

Save in Toledo and Cordova, — where everything sleeps all the time, except the beggers, — a true Spanish town sleeps only at high noon. All night long the lights burn; all night long you see the people busily idle, idly busy.

On through the town we went, glancing in at open doors as we passed, until suddenly stillness, broken only by the flow of murmuring waters, was about us, and a soft gloom through which the high moon could hardly pierce.

We had entered the enclosure of the Alhambra, and the elms the Duke of Wellington planted were arching thickly over our heads. And our hearts beat fast, and we whispered to each other, "We are here at last!"

We drove on up the height, and everywhere the water murmured beside us, and the moon peered at us through the trees, and it was a dream in which we moved, and yet no dream, for here we were in front of Hotel Washington Irving, and when we said, hardly knowing that we spoke, —

"Is it the Alhambra?" the one-eyed landlord answered, in good English, —

"Yes, ladies, and your rooms are ready."

If only it had been May, instead of the late November, then would all the Duke's elms have been full of the nightingales who pair and build and brood there in the May, and set the night mad with the passion of their singing. But when we woke next morning, we were sure that no time of year could have been lovelier. The air was soft as in June, — a young, unexhausted air, which it was a delight to breathe.

Our windows looked out into a garden, where fountains bubbled and roses bloomed, and down under the trees sat happy pilgrims sipping their coffee.

The town of Granada reposes in the Vega, a lovely valley thirty miles in length, which the system of irrigation so skilfully arranged by the Moors has turned into a veritable Garden of Eden. Round this happy valley circle frowning mountains, whose snow-crowned tops are ten thousand feet above the sea-level, — the Sierra Nevadas.

From the postern gate of the Siete Suelos, Boabdil, the last Moorish king, took his departure after the conquest of Granada. But still the Moors rule the Alhambra, for their memory possesses it.

Their red towers guard the heights as of yore, and the snowy Sierra Nevadas look down to see what manner of people walk through the old haunts now. From the outside you can form no idea of the beauty or grandeur of the place. You go in by the Gate of Justice, and skirt the impertinent, unfinished palace of Charles V., and suddenly you perceive that you are in the real, yet unreal palace of your dreams. You wander on, from court to court, from charm to charm. The creamy, pinkish walls are covered with a tracery as delicate as frost-work. You are in the land of Faery. You do not think of size, or strength, or any commonplace attribute whatever. As solidity was the ideal of Egyptian architecture, so lightness was that of the Moors. They turned their tent-poles into marble pillars, and sculptured their stucco with the delicate traceries of the Cachemire hangings with which they had draped their tents.

From the windows of one court you look forth to the haughty mountains, and from another at busy Granada down in the valley, and from others at the hills, mined with the caves where the gypsies burrow. One of the quaint inscriptions, being interpreted, says, "Look attentively at my elegance;" but in a first visit to the Alhambra you cannot look attentively at anything. A sort of intoxication seizes you. You are impelled by a wild desire to see everything at once, and you hurry from place to place, fearful lest night should surprise you before you have beheld the whole.

I am half inclined to think that the Court of the Lions is the loveliest spot of all. Before I saw it I had fancied I should find there lions as grand as the lion kings Thorvaldsen sculptured; but the lions of the Alhambra are like nothing on earth or in heaven. Their feet are as clumsy as bed-posts, the alabaster basin of the fountain rests on their patient backs, and its waters spout through their open mouths. The charm of the Court is not in its lions, but in the group of slender pillars and the exquisite arches that spring from them. Standing here you seem to be in the very heart of the enchanted place. On one side is the Hall of the Abencerrages, where the blood-stains from the dripping blood of the warriors slain there are still pointed out, and their unappeased ghosts moan on through desolate midnights.

After our first day there, we went back again at night, the moon being full; and with what words dare one attempt to paint the transcendent, ethereal vision? Delicate columns, cobweb traceries of carving, perfect arches, and over all the high moon's enchantment! Even when I write of it the old tightening of the breath comes back, — the almost fear to take one step farther on, lest the whole dream-like fabric should dissolve.

"Do you believe in ghosts?" some one asks at my elbow.

"I *see* them," I whisper back, and there they are. The dark Moors group themselves under the slender pillars of the Court of the Lions; the murdered, unappeased Abencerrages moan in the hall where they were slain, and the revealing moon points out the spots where their blood stained the white marble. It was Boabdil who shed their blood; and he was cruel enough to kill, but not brave enough to conquer, and his turn came to go mournfully out of the Alhambra, with his mother's scornful words in his ears, — "It is well that you should weep as a woman for what you could not defend as a man."

And his ghost came also, with bowed, shameful head, and from her Mirador the swart sultana looked forth and smiled, triumphant possessor still; and, in her garden, Lindaraya walked as of old among her myrtles and her roses.

When one reads of the charm of the Alhambra by moonlight, one believes that it must be exaggerated; but when you stand there under the pale moon, amid ghosts and glories, you know it would be as impossible to exaggerate as to describe it.

You go back again, the second day, prepared to look more coolly; and then you perceive the exquisiteness of all the details, — the delicate, infinitely varied traceries of the walls, with their ceilings, as if a sudden, large-flaked snow-shower had been turned to stone; the slender pillars that seem fit only to serve for temples in fairyland, the wonderful, inexhaustible beauty that surrounds you everywhere. And every spot has its own legend. From the tower of La Cantiva a Christian captive flung herself down to death, rather than live to be the bride of the Moorish king. In the Hall of the Ambassadors, Ayeshah, the mother of Boabdil, girt her son with a sacred sword, and sent him forth for his vain struggle to repel the invaders; but on his way he broke his lance against the gate-way, and his young sultana wept and called him "The Unlucky One." And in 1492 — the very year in which Columbus discovered America — conquered Boabdil surrendered his sacred sword, and departed forever from the gate of the Siete Suelos.

I must not forget the Torre de la Vela, or watch-tower, from which we used to watch the sunset, as it burnt the west with its fiery splendors, while the snow-crowned Sierra Nevadas reflected the western glory.

The Alhambra *is* Granada, and yet if the Alhambra were not there, how much else there would be!

There is the Generaliffe, with its lovely tropical garden, its old pictures, its superb view; and down in the town there are churches and convents, and the grand Cathedral where Isabella the Catholic, — the great Isabella who sent Columbus forth to find our new world, — lies buried, with her husband, King Ferdinand, beside her. Sumptuous indeed is their tomb, with their effigies resting side by side upon the lofty marble sarcophagus. Near by is the tomb of their daughter, Queen Juana, with her handsome, worthless husband, Philip of

Burgundy, and in the vault beneath, the four royal coffins may be seen.

The coffin of Philip is that very one which his crazed, fond wife kept with her wherever she went during the forty-seven long years of her widowhood.

The Cathedral is the haunt of beggars who call themselves guides, and who get in your way till you are glad to give them your last penny to be rid of them. It was in this way I met a ragged son of Spain, about twelve years old, and so beautiful that I could no more forget him than I could forget the Alhambra. He was the very raggedest of the whole crew, but, oh, how fascinating he was, with the smooth oval of his dark cheeks, and with his eyes so deep, so melting, so pathetic, that they almost brought the tears to mine. He thought that he spoke English, and this was the manner of his speaking: "Antigua house, see, missis." With pennies I bribed him to learn to say, "I am a very bad little boy." He said the words slowly and solemnly, as if they were an incantation, without the most distant idea of their meaning; and I heard of him, weeks afterward, startling subsequent visitors to the Cathedral with this formula.

Granada is a thoroughly living city, and not a dead one, like Toledo or Cordova, though in place of its former population of four hundred thousand, it has only seventy-five thousand now, exclusive of the gypsies, who herd like outlaws in their holes in the hill-sides. These live in the dirt and wear rags, and lie and steal, and tell fortunes; but some of them are handsome, and if you bribe them sufficiently, they will put on clean finery and come into town and dance for you, and promise you luck, while they look as if they would take pleasure in cutting your throat.

We saw a gypsy dance while we were in Granada; but we saw one to better advantage later on in Seville.

I wish we had gone first to Seville, because Seville is so beautiful that it should be an unqualified delight to visit it, and there can be no unqualified delight for those who have banished themselves from the Alhambra. The journey from Granada to Seville is an easy one, except that your train starts from Granada at five o'clock in the morning. I think it was not much more than half-past three when the fatherly voice of our Vicar of Wakefield was heard at each lady's door calling on us to arise. Half an hour afterward we sat at breakfast in the dining-room, and he came in and surveyed us with a bland smile. "Don't over-precipitate yourselves, ladies," he said tranquilly; "there is plenty of time."

We reached Seville at about three in the afternoon. From far away we could see its Giralda climbing toward the flawless sky. The air of the late November was like summer. Roses were blooming everywhere. Orange trees bore flowers and fruit; bananas and dates and figs hung temptingly within reach, and such grapes as no northern sun could ripen were there for our gathering. Our hotel was most comfortable, and a sense of *bien être* diffused itself tranquilly over our spirits, marred only by regrets that we could not have stayed on in Granada until spring, when all the elms would be homes of nightingales. Seville, however, was full of seductive consolations. It is a place in which to linger long. I can imagine a happy life divided between the Alhambra and Seville. I would go to the Alhambra in time to hear the nightingales thrill the soul of the spring with song. I would stay there through the summer and the autumn, and then come to Seville for the brief, bright, southern winter.

Here the cathedral is the largest in the world except St. Peter's in Rome, and far more interesting than St. Peter's. The Giralda, or bell-tower, was built by the Moors. You ascend it by an inclined plane, up which horses can easily be ridden. From this Moorish-built Giralda twenty-two Christian bells call the faithful to prayers. In the cathedral below you find a wonderful museum of arts: stained glass hardly equalled anywhere else; pictures by Murillo, Campaña, and Morales; emblazoned *retablos;* everything, in short, with which munificent piety could adorn a church. There are three pictures that stand out from the rest in one's memory. I should put first Murillo's "St. Anthony of Padua." The saint kneels in his humble cell, tranced in worship, looking up toward the child Jesus, radiant with the supernatural light He himself creates, and surrounded by throngs of angels. Murillo's "Guardian Angel" is almost equally beautiful, if less grand. A glorious, strong-winged seraph leads a trustful child by the hand, and points him beyond the earth to the light of heaven. The third of the three pictures that so hold my memory is "The Deposition from the Cross," by Pedro de Campaña. Before this picture Murillo, by his own desire, was buried, and before it he used to stand for long hours in his lifetime, waiting, as he said, "till those holy men had finished their work." In the chapter-house of the cathedral is a Conception by Murillo, which it seemed to me was almost the loveliest of his innumerable pictures of this subject.

What a contrast is Seville, full of bustle and activity, to Cordova, in whose solemn old streets reigns almost the stillness of death. The gay Sevillians seem all life and joy. The streets are so narrow that in many of them two carriages could not by any possibility pass each other, and carriages are not allowed to intrude on the most crowded shopping-streets at all. Here, as in Cordova, young men cling to the iron railings of the balconies and whisper ardent nothings to the dark-eyed darlings within. And you hear blood-curdling tales of the swift, murderous use of the long Albucete knives, when a lover finds some interloper at the window of his chosen before him. Don Pedro the Cruel set an example of this use of the Albucete knife, and his ardent countrymen have not been slow to follow it.

Pedro the Cruel seems to pervade Seville, somewhat as Philip II. does the Escorial. His mother fled to its Alcazar with him when he was a child, and when he came to be king he in great part rebuilt it. It was here that he lived with his beautiful morganatic wife, Maria de Padilla. Here he received the Red King of Granada, and then murdered him for the sake of his jewels, one of which, "the fair ruby, great like a racket ball," even now adorns the crown of England. He had pleasant little pastimes peculiar to himself, this Don Pedro, one of which was to have the heads of people whom he did not like cut off and hung over the door of his dressing-room. He and his victims were dust long ago, but the lovely garden of the Alcazar at Seville still keeps his unlovely memory fragrant. The garden was improved afterward by Charles V., who built there the most fascinating summer-house in the world; but it was Don Pedro who planned it and arranged the magical fountains, which, when a key is turned somewhere, spring up all along the paths, and shower the walks and the blossoms, and make rainbows in the sunshine. Orange trees that cruel Pedro's hands planted still drop their golden balls upon the ground, and the very flowers are the far-off descendants of those the wicked king used to gather for his beautiful, sad love.

The Alcazar itself is a wonderful palace; thoroughly Moorish, fresher in color and gilding than the Alhambra, but so well kept and so frequently inhabited that it altogether lacks the poetic charm which silence and solitude have woven about the other. St. Elmo, the palace of the Duke de Montpensier, has a fine gallery of Spanish masters, including the "Madonna della Faja" of Murillo, and two Spanish girls by Goya, looking over the balcony of a theatre, so alive that one never could forget them. The house of Pontius Pilate is another show-place. It dates from the sixteenth century, is Saracenic in its architecture, and has the most beautiful tiles I have ever seen, which flash in the light like jewels. The government tobacco manufactory, where three thousand Spanish girls and women are employed, stares with its many plebeian windows into the stately pleasure gardens of the Duke de Montpensier, and not far off rises the Torre del Oro, so named from the gilded tiles which roofed it in in the old days when it used to be the prison-house for Don Pedro's cast-off sweethearts.

From the Torre del Oro along the Guadalquivir stretches for two or three miles the pleasant drive and promenade of Las Delicios (The Delights), the afternoon haunt of the beauty and fashion of Seville, as the Buen Retiro is for Madrid. Nowhere can you see finer horses than in these two pleasure places, and Spanish horsemanship is a thing to dream of. There are objects of interest enough in Seville to keep the most energetic of tourists busy for many a day. In the chapel of the Hospital of the Caridad you see six Murillos, among them the two great pictures of "Moses Striking the Water from the Rock," and the "Miracle of the Loaves and Fishes." The Museo is still more rich in Murillos, and you find there also beautiful examples of other Spanish masters, though not one of Velasquez, Sevillian as he was by birth.

One must not fail to visit the gypsy quarter, or the pottery manufactory, or the Roman ruins at Italica; and if there be ever a spare hour, unfailing entertainment awaits us in the streets, with their life as different from our own as is the sunny southern country from our "land of mist and snow." You get really fond of the handsome, wheedling beggar children, and you make friends with the peddlers of small wares in the narrow streets. And every day and all the days you stroll into the cathedral with its ever-varying charm.

It was Thanksgiving Day at home while we were at Seville, and we put our heads together and discussed in what way we could make festival of it. And lo! our Vicar of Wakefield confided in the manager of the hotel, and he gave us a Thanksgiving dinner that rivalled the feasts of home, with the loveliest flowers for every lady; and then, for the evening, he arranged a gypsy dance. Think of a gypsy dance in honor of a Puritan Thanksgiving! Not only ourselves, but all the Americans in Seville were present, and various English and Spanish people besides.

Behold! here is the announcement of the gypsy chief, printed on bright yellow paper, and this is his "English as she was written":—

Don Francisco de la Barrera have the honor to inform to the visitors that to-night will be held ball, at nine o'clock precisely.

Tragano Street, No. 10.

The ball shall be composed as under specified.

Then followed the programme of the dances, and what dances they were,—languid, sensuous, voluptuous. In one of them was embodied a whole drama of love and wooing. I have never seen on any stage anything to equal the coquetry of the girl who danced away from her lover, and tormented and mocked at and eluded him, only to be won, at the end, and yield her lips to his swift and triumphant kiss; and the Vicar of Wakefield looked on with that preternaturally pious face of his, and his lips, keeping time to the music, seemed to be saying, "Bless you, my children!"

Why did we ever leave Seville? That is the question I have been asking myself ever since. Our party divided there. The Wise Woman and the Nut-brown Maid and the Lady Anna went on to Italy, and the Sweet Singer and I came home. But why? Why, even, should one go to Italy who might stay in Spain? And, above all, why should one come home to the east winds, when the oranges are ripening in sunny Seville, and the roses are waiting to be gathered?

We went early to the station to take the night express for Madrid. One always goes to a Spanish railway station an hour in advance, and then has only time enough to buy a ticket, and get a basket-trunk weighed and registered, since every employé in Spain makes it the business of his life to move more slowly than every other one. We said good-bye with wet eyes, when we left the others at the hotel, and hid the quiver of our lips behind the great bunches of roses the kindly hotel manager gave us to cheer our departing way. The sky was aflame with a wonderful red sunset, glowing up to the very zenith. Against it the graceful Giralda rose ; and there, in the dear old town, the happy, careless, gay, out-of-doors life went on, and we went off — was it forever ?

We reached Madrid the next morning, and found again our Velasquez-painted men and women, our Murillos, our vivid Canos, and our strong, sad Riberas. We ruined ourselves in photographs, drove in the Buen Retiro, and then, after a day and a night, started for Bordeaux. We had left Seville on a Tuesday evening ; on Saturday we ate our dinner at the hotel in Paris, from which we had departed eight weeks before. We had had few discomforts and no perils. The bright eyes of the Sweet Singer had done no more harm than bright eyes must, and we were safe and prosperous, but not quite happy, for we had left Spain, and, after all, neither of us had found her Castle.

IN SOUTHERN ITALY.

AT NAPLES.

TO go from Venice straight to Naples is the strangest transition. Surely Venice, with her winding water-ways, is the stillest city in the whole world, and surely Naples is, of all cities, the most noisy.

It was ten o'clock at night when we left our hotel in Venice, and dropped down the Grand Canal to catch the eleven o'clock train for Naples. We seemed in some mystic world of shadows. Lights from the silent palaces mirrored themselves in the water, but not so much as the ghost of a sound broke the magic stillness, save the faint plash of our own oars, and once the impertinent whistle of a little steamer carrying home its party of excursionists.

I had dreaded to find the Grand Canal invaded by steam, but these little boats are not at all obtrusive. They are not even so large as the great old coal-barges which have haunted the canals of Venice from time immemorial. They seem merely like a gondola grown fat and worldly, and with a big black cigar in his mouth. The whistle of the one that met us on our transit scarcely disturbed the night's peace for a moment, and silently, through a silent world, we glided down to the railway station.

There, indeed, was noise enough, and bustle and hurry and confusion, and bad French and worse Italian; and then it was eleven o'clock, and somehow we had got into the train, and were rushing on through the night toward Naples.

Next morning we woke to see the Adriatic tossing its white caps wrathfully in the cold March sunshine, and to wonder why gentle Venetia should have chosen to wed so rough a mate.

It was again ten o'clock at night when we reached Naples; and then we drove and we drove, till it seemed as if the driver of our rattling conveyance must have been moved to show us the whole city, instead of merely taking us to Hotel Nobile, where we slept the sleep of the weary, and awoke next morning to look from our windows over the blue and shining Bay, with Capri and Sorrento and sad-fated Ischia dreaming in the sunshine.

Oh, if I could but make a picture of Naples! People who have been at Constantinople vaunt the beauty of its Golden Horn as superior even to the Bay of Naples; but for me, who have not seen the Bosphorus, the loveliness of the Queen of Southern Italy remains without peer.

High above it towers Vesuvius, — a cone of cloud by day and of fire by night; and at the feet of this watching, threatening, red-eyed monster, the town stretches along the shore of the Bay,— the great, careless, happy, sad, rich, poverty-stricken town, full of contradictions.

Along the shore of the Bay is the fashionable drive, where from four to six of a spring afternoon all Naples takes its pleasure. On one side is the blue, blessed water where the fairy islands sleep, and on the other the beautiful park, the Villa Reale, with its orange-trees heavy with fruit, its flowering almonds pink with blossoms, its gleaming statues of old gods, its temple where the merry music plays, and its motley throng of fair ladies and handsome men and picturesque priests and dark-eyed children.

When you walk in the Villa Reale it seems as if all Naples must be there; but when you turn to the long drive by the Bay, it seems as if all Naples had taken to driving. There are as grand carriages as you can see anywhere, with liveried coachmen and footmen; there are neat phaetons, drawn by dear little ponies gay with silver trappings, and in the midst of them there are plenty of the shabbiest cabs of the street, with ragged drivers, and sometimes as many as seven or eight bare-headed peasants, drawn by one pathetic pony, so small that you could almost take him up in your arms. And they are all so happy! Bright eyes, red cheeks, mouths wide with smiles,— you think of Browning's

"Bang, whang, goes the drum — tootle te tootle the fife —
Oh, a day in a city square's the gayest thing in life!"

We had all sorts of queer experiences with the little cabs we hired. Usually we looked first at the driver, to see that he should have as much coat and as few rags as might be; and having chosen him for himself, or rather for his clothes, we took our chances as to his horse.

Once we were drawn by a beast so slow that I could only fancy he must have been trained to carry criminals to execution, and give them as long a time as possible to repent on the way. Stately carriages rolled ponderously by us; mad little traps whirled along threatening to take off our wheels; other drivers looked at us mockingly, and through the surging crowd we drove at a pace so slow that an ordinary walk would have seemed frantic haste in comparison.

Another time a little horse, as white, as meek-looking, and almost as small as a sheep, took it into his head to play a tune with his hind-feet on the footboard of our phaeton. The Young Companion of our party was somewhat afraid; but I reminded her that horse and driver were both safe and sound, despite their daily association, and I had faith to believe we should get home alive. Everybody chances things in Naples, just as the town itself chances that sullen Vesuvius may get more angry than usual, some day, and turn it into a second Pompeii.

Beside this lovely drive, where fashion and folly meet along the smiling Bay, there is the long Via Roma, formerly the Toledo, on which, as Howells has said, "the magnificence of modern Naples is threaded." On each side high, well-built, respectable houses, some of them palaces, rise monotonously, with their many windows and their many balconies; and all along the streets are shops full of glittering jewels, or costly silken stuffs, or pretty trifles in the way of bric-à-brac; and because the sidewalks are narrow the foot-passengers are always crowding off them into the streets, and picking their way among the thronging vehicles.

Here is my lady's carriage, with her superb horses and imposing servants, and her own fair face looking out from the newest Paris bonnet. And here, equally at home, are the patient donkeys, each one with a load five times as big as himself, and often driven by the tail, as if that appendage were a bridle-rein. Here are the long brotherhoods of black-robed young scholar-priests, taking their sober way as if blind to the gay show around them; and here, almost always, is some imposing funeral, with a hearse, mostly of glass, looking like the van of a menagerie, and quite as gayly decorated. Inside, in each of the four corners, sits a priest "to attend the dead," and carriages on carriages follow these gay hearses, and my own impression is that, of all festivals, Neapolitans most enjoy a funeral.

Whenever we went to the National Museum, with its delights of painting and sculpture, we had to traverse this gay Via Roma, and we got to know it well. We found never-ending amusement in the narrow side streets which cross it, leading on one side down to the bay, climbing on the other to the highest heights of the far-reaching town. These streets are far too narrow and too steep for carriages; but they fairly swarm with human life, and now and then a donkey pushes his way up the long passage, jostling the crowd with his friendly little shoulders. Sometimes he carries a monstrous bundle of straw, or an enormous pannier of vegetables, and then he so fills the street that the human throng has to crowd itself into door-ways; and sometimes a swarthy, handsome peasant, all black eyes and white teeth and gay cap, rides the little beastie down, to take his pleasure with the rest below.

Very gorgeous indeed are the Naples dandies, of whom you always meet crowds in the Via Roma. Speckless in costume, dainty, dapper little men, — we used to wonder if they spent their lives in buying new gloves, and making visits to the dark-eyed signoras who looked from the balconies of the grand houses.

We walked down the Via Roma one afternoon, the Young Companion and I, in pursuit of an ice-cream. We were banished from the museum at four o'clock, as one always is. The day was warm, and we thirsted for the well-beloved Neapolitan ice, which we could have procured at any hour of the day in Boston or New York. We went into one great restaurant after another, and were told in each that the ices were not yet ready. Finally we found one, almost at the lower end of the street, where a smiling little man told us, in answer to our accustomed inquiry, —

"Oh, yees, but certainly we have of the cream."

He departed. We sat there and waited, burning with thirst and impatience, till a quarter of an hour had gone by. Then he reappeared, smiling more than ever, and spread our little round table with a white little cloth. Then we waited another quarter of an hour, and he came again, but this time, it was evident, with the sole purpose of bestowing on us a consolatory smile, which did not console us.

We suggested that half an hour earlier in the day we had asked for cream, and he had promised it to us.

"But certainly, most certainly."

Here his English failed him, but not his good-humor. He smiled, and pointed below, then turned an imaginary crank round and round, to intimate to us by this reassuring pantomime that our cream was at that very moment being concocted down there below.

Sure enough, at five of the clock our ices came, dainty and delicious, each fresh from its own little mould; and we discovered that in Naples it is a waste of time to seek for the refreshment of an ice before five o'clock in the afternoon.

You can form no complete idea of what Naples is like till you have seen it from the heights above. We learned this when we drove to San Martino.

We were all together, — the "Fräulein Professor," as they call her in Germany, the Young Companion, and I, — and the sun shone, and the birds sang, and the tree-blossoms shook out their sweet scents on the gentle wind, and it seemed a good world to live in.

Up, up, up, we went, till we came to the high hill-top which the suppressed Carthusian monastery of San Martino crowns. The church is full of art treasures, richly adorned with mosaics and frescos, and containing in its *"Tesoro"* the "Descent from the Cross" of Spagnoletto, considered his masterpiece, — a picture so sad and so powerful that its majestic sorrow must forever haunt any one who has once seen it. The ceiling of this "Tesoro" is frescoed with the story of Judith, and the whole ceiling is said to have been painted in forty-eight hours by Luca Giordano when he was in his seventy-second year, — an almost incredible feat.

I wish you could have seen, in a grotto connected with this monastery, what I think must be the greatest doll-show in the whole world. It represents the adoration by the Magi of the infant Jesus, and also the general state of the nations of the world at that epoch. There are donkeys and sheep and cattle. There are Jew traders and Arab merchants. Men are playing games, mothers are rocking their children. All the life of the world is being carried on in miniature. There are hundreds of little figures, all perfectly costumed, and more entertaining than you can possibly imagine.

We saw all the monastery's treasures; we walked through the cloisters which the feet of so many dead-and-gone monks had trodden; and then, long before we were ready, it was time to go. One more look, from the ramparts that wall the monastery round, at Naples, far down below,— the great, gay, bustling town, with its many spires, its hovels and its palaces, — and then good-by to monks and monastery, and we rattled down the vine-hung mountain, back into the busy streets.

IN PURSUIT OF VESUVIUS.

ON our way to our hotel, the night we reached Naples, we first saw the red light from far-off Vesuvius, and thereupon we resolved to make his nearer acquaintance. We saw him again when we woke in the morning, and made our arrangements to pay our respects to him the first windless day; for that the day should be profoundly still is of the first importance if you would beard a volcano in his lair.

The southern sun never shone on a lovelier morning than the one on which we finally set forth. The deep blue Italian sky arched over us; the blue waters of the Bay sparkled in the sunshine. Our horses tossed their stately heads, and would have champed their bits, no doubt, only horses are not driven with bits in Naples. Our driver was a handsome Italian, and he rejoiced our hearts with the information that he could "spik Inglis," — how well we discovered later on.

The first part of our drive took us through the wide-spreading city. The year before, cholera had mowed men down there like grass, yet it did not seem as if the place could ever have been fuller. It fairly swarmed with life. The humbler people live in rooms on the ground floors of the houses, — rooms lighted only by the doors opening into the street, and naturally it is so much gayer and brighter out of doors than in that most occupations are carried on *al fresco*. Mothers nurse their infants, or brush their children's hair, in full view of the passer-by. They cook strange messes over braziers of coals, They knit, they spin, they patch rags with rags. They rock babies — swathed precisely as are the mummies you find in the pyramids — in the queer little baskets that serve for cradles. They keep house, in short, out-of-doors.

That special day Naples was doing its washing; and as it is a city with no back-yards, all their clothes — the pitiful rags, I mean, which it pleases them to call their clothes — were hung out to dry in front of the houses, sometimes on poles thrust from the windows, sometimes on lines drawn from one window to another. In one place a regiment of soldiers was tranquilly drilling in an open space filled with just-washed clothes, and the flapping skirts they had to dodge were a droll background to their military movements.

Everything was for sale along the way. Oranges were heaped in baskets lined with long green grass. The lemon-stands were pictures; they had a sort of shrine-like aspect, — the lemons being hung from poles bent like arches and rooted in the highly decorated tables below. Here, too, was your snow-cooled lemonade, if you chose to stop for it. Wooden saw-horses were hung with macaroni drying in the sun. Small boys and girls thrust perpetual bouquets into our carriages, asking three francs to begin with, and lowering the price franc by franc, with frantic excitement, as we were whirled on beyond their reach.

The hour which it took us to get out of town seemed hardly six minutes long, instead of sixty; for queerness succeeded to queerness, and we agreed that street life in Naples is unique under the sun.

We were content, however, to lose sight of it all when once we began to climb the mountain, and could look down at the wonderful view below us of blue bay, and crowded city, with Capri and Sorrento fair in the distance. Almond-trees were pink along our paths. Pear-trees bloomed in bridal white, and the dark stone-pines gazed unmoved at these light-minded neighbors dressed as for a sylvan *fête*, — the dark stone-pines that are the offspring of the stately heights, and scorn any small tricks of adornment.

We had not climbed quite away, even yet, from the gentle bandits of to-day, who, instead of picking our pockets, besieged us with entreaties. Here were a band of wandering musicians, singing to their mandolins, and their strain seemed so like the voice of the spring day, blent so fitly with the sunshine on the laughing world and the trees in flower, that they had their will with our purses.

Then a dark-eyed little maid would start up from the roadside with bunches of yellow marigolds in her hands, and run herself breathless beside us until we pelted her away with sous. And once a boy came with a bit of carved lava to sell, — a boy so perfect that Murillo should have painted him; and when I would not buy his lava, but gave him a coin for pure delight in his faun-like beauty, darted off and gathered for me a spray of the lovely pink almond-blossoms, and then sprang away, and smiled at me from a distance, to show me that he wanted no further reward.

Old crones proffered us the rough strong wine of Vesuvius, — which we had too much respect for our sanity to drink, — while others tried to tempt us with strings of shells or of coral; and all the time the blue Bay sparkled far below, and the sun shone on busy, bustling Naples, and quiet Capri and fair Sorrento. On and on, and always up, until we had left all verdure behind us, and were traversing the black slag, — the forlorn wastes covered by deposits of lava.

It seemed as if one had entered the Inferno. It was easy to see, in the twisted lava, sad shapes whom pain had tortured until it turned them into stone, and giant tree-trunks contorted by wilder storms than ever forest knew. And still on and up, with the tranquil Bay far below, until, at last, sullen Vesuvius, smoking forever his unfriendly pipe, was near at hand.

We had been more than three hours on our

way before we reached the railway station at the foot of the highest height. We refreshed ourselves with weak coffee and strong oysters, and then we got into the train which goes up nine hundred yards toward heaven, at an angle of forty-three degrees. The ten minutes occupied in this transit might well try the strongest nerves. The road seems almost perpendicular, and if the cable should break! . . . I suppose it never has. Probably it never will; but, side by side with you goes the awful "If," and you are glad enough to step out of the car when you reach the upper station, though it be to struggle over masses of jagged lava which cut your boots to pieces and torture your unhappy feet. You will be offered clumsy chairs, fastened to poles; and panting men are ready to seize the poles, and bear you still farther upward; but having seen one venerable lady swaying about in this seat of peril, we prefer to trust to our own feet, and hobble on.

And, after all, the old giant, smoking his perpetual pipe, has little beauty to compensate you for the toil and weariness of your approach to him. You see a hole, some three or four feet in diameter, from which he belches forth heated masses of red and yellow lava. His sulphurous breath nearly stifles you, and you turn away quite ready to decline the honor of his farther acquaintance.

So you struggle back to the upper station; and then you plunge down by the same perilous railway, and again you watch the iron rope, and think, under your breath "If!" But ten minutes cannot last forever; and soon we stand once more on solid earth, and the driver touches his hat, and the handsome horses neigh their welcome, and off we start again, rattling down the mountain, with the bay shining far below, while the afternoon sun stretches across it such a path of glory that you fancy it a bridge leading into Paradise, over which Heaven's shining ones might journey.

Down, down, down, quite down at last; and busy Naples seems busier than ever. It is milking time, and everywhere you meet cows, which are driven from door to door, with bells around their necks to announce their approach. The housekeeper who wants fresh milk comes out with cup or pitcher, into which the warm, sweet milk is pressed. Or, if you like goat's milk better, here is the little herd of goats, with full udders, equally at your service.

Here is a Punch and Judy show, and all the neighbors have come out to see Punch box his wife's ears. Here, beside our carriage, is a little live bundle of laughs and rags, who turns a somersault, and expects us to pay him for standing on his head. Here are donkeys about as large as a child's rocking-horse, and with brays loud enough to be heard from one end of Naples to the other. Here are priests and peasants and dashing soldiers, and now and then a fine carriage that has strayed away from the Chaiaia; and then, once more, you are beside the Bay! And lo! all the little skiffs and fishing-boats have come home to rest, and there they are, like a flock of bright-winged birds, safe in harbor, — and we — we are safe too, and our hotel opens its friendly doors, and we go in, content that Vesuvius should smoke his pipe in a solitude we are scarcely likely again to invade.

SORRENTO DAYS.

WHO could put into words the magic of Southern Italy? "My eyes make pictures when they are shut" of a land all orange orchards and olive groves, and heights that only the stone-pines have stormed, and blue waters, and a loveliness which is as the loveliness of a dream; yet I am helpless to convey the subtle and forever elusive charm. No place mocks more utterly at description than does that Sorrento where Torquato Tasso was born, in 1544, and to which he returned, disguised as a shepherd, in 1592, — three years before his death. He died in Rome; but I think his heart was in Sorrento, and perchance his ghost still haunts his fair birthplace.

Hans Christian Andersen says, in his "Improvisatore," that "when one tries to describe the beauties of Nature, words seem to place themselves in array like loose pieces of mosaic, but they do not evoke the vision." And Nature still seemed to smile this defiance at us as we rode out of Naples on the train for Castellamare. We had a little carriage to ourselves, we three, and we sprang from side to side of it to see, on one hand, the lovely bay, and on the other the heights, with the clouds flecking them, and below, the orange orchards, where the ripe fruit lay on the ground, that glorious March day, as the apples lie at home when an autumn wind has rifled the populous trees.

The ride to Castellamare was a delight, which grew to rapture as we drove on from there to Sorrento. Still we wound along between the wooded heights above and the shining Bay below. Sometimes an orange orchard overhung us, separated only by a low wall whose clefts were gay with poppies, and sometimes the gray wall was so high that it almost shut from our vision the hills above, while always the Bay purled against the shore below us, and we could see far-off Vesuvius keeping his sullen watch over careless Naples at his feet.

We found Sorrento the quaintest of quaint places, — all oranges and olives, and narrow streets and placid peasants, and boundless content for the stranger within its gates. We drove through it at a rattling pace, just catching glimpses of shops full of gay-colored silks, and other shops full of inlaid orange-wood, — the two specialties of Sorrento. We brought up at last in the spacious courtyard of Hotel Tramontane. I had a room there with a balcony which overhung the Bay. Near at hand was Capri; farther off Vesuvius still smoked his persistent pipe; and over all, when I first took possession, lay the sunset's golden glory.

Surely, out there in the blue distance dreamed the Happy Islands; surely I had but to enter one of those little skiffs below and steer it westward, to find that unknown land which is east of the sun, and west of the moon, and which I was only restrained from going forth to seek by an impertinent dinner-bell, and the appearance on the scene of the Fräulein Professor and the Young Companion. They had a pink-and-white bower-chamber on the other side of the house, looking into an orange orchard, whence the morning birds sang to them, while the morning sun looked approvingly into their windows.

From dinner we came back to my balcony. The sunset glory had faded, but a new glory of the moon had arisen, and I was not minded to seek the Happy Islands by moonlight, for I feared lest I should find ghosts in them, as white as the moonlight and as cold. I waited, half thinking that they would walk toward me on the waters, until the spell was broken by a knock upon my door.

"Would the signoras of their good pleasure like to behold the dance of the tarantella?" Surely the signoras would like to behold it; and we descended to a gay little room, fitly frescoed with dancing-girls, and draped with red-and-blue hangings, and then,—

" The quick, sweet rasping of the fiddles
Set the dancers in the dance-room a-going."

The tarantella is — like most peasant dances — a love-story. The two who dance it approach, retreat, coquet with each other, and finally join hands in token of future union. It seemed greatly to amuse most of the spectators, but my thoughts were still sailing on the Bay, under the magic moon, keeping tryst with Shadows.

Next morning we heard the nightingale for the first time. The singer lived in a cage in Signor Tramontano's orange garden, and, enchanting as was his song, his owner said it was not his loveliest. It was pretty to hear our host describe, in his Italian English, what the nightingale's song at its best might be.

"They sing," he said, "to woo the she bird with which they are wishful to mate. One bird, he begin, and he sing, and sing, and sing, the sweetest music you could ever hear, and it seem as if his heart would break with the cry. And his love, she listen. Then another bird, far away, he begin in his turn, and his cry comes through the night, and he sing and he sing, as no man could ever sing so high, till the tree where he rests does quiver. And the love, she listen, and make a little tender, troubled sound, not knowing yet which song to choose. Then the first, he sing again, and then once more the second, he answer, and the bird-love she listen, and at last she give a low, cooing call, and fly home to him whose song has pleased her best; and so they are mated, and they make then the nest."

From Sorrento such delightful excursions invite us that one need never be at loss for a fresh pleasure. One day the Young Companion and I went to Capri by steamer, and the sail was diversified by the persistent attentions of venders of coral and of wood carving, and the gay music of an accompanying band of Italian minstrels.

After an hour or so people began to say, "Oh, there it is!" and "It" was the entrance to the famous Blue Grotto. An Italian girl stood, as if she were the warder of the place, on a narrow ledge of cliff beside the entrance, and her vivid coloring made a gay picture against the gray rocks. And then little row-boats bustled about our steamer, and everybody got into them, and the Young Companion and I were in the midst of the throng, in our own little boat. The entrance to the grotto is scarcely three feet in height, and it is barely possible for one tiny skiff to enter at a time; and to do that the passengers must lie down in the boat. Once inside, however, and the grotto is comfortably spacious.

The deep brilliant blue is almost more than the eye can endure. Fain would we have had this sapphire solitude to ourselves; but no, we were in a village of little boats. I counted seventeen which surrounded us, and I do not think I counted them all. Our boatman offered, for a franc, to dive into the blue depth of water and show us how it would turn him to silver. But the prospect of having him back again dripping from his blue bath did not attract us, and we were deaf to his beguilements.

To be alone in the Blue Grotto, — ah, that would be as if one had gone into the heart of a jewel, and the under world were revealing its secrets! As it was, half the effect was lost; but a strange vision of beauty abides in one's memory.

We went out, heads lowered, as we had come in, climbed into our steamer, and on we went to Capri proper, where we landed for rest and luncheon, which awaited us in the veranda of a quiet little hotel overlooking the bay. When luncheon was over, and we went into the courtyard of the hotel, we bade farewell to quiet. A crowd of donkeys and their drivers blocked our way. The women wore the gay peasant costume, with long glittering ear-rings and bright kerchiefs, and, oh, they had such tongues!

"*Would* we ride?" they all clamored at once. We *must* ride! I half thought we should be torn in pieces among them, and I took refuge on one donkey, and the Young Companion followed on another. A little girl led each donkey, and a woman — stick in hand — walked beside it, and a young man who seemed to consider himself a professor of English tagged along; and thus our procession marched on up the hill toward Villa Tiberius. My driver was such a pretty young woman that I asked her if she were married. No, she was not married, but she was promised, — yes, promised to an American. "Ah," said I, "I am American!" Her face beamed with pleasure. She patted the donkey on which I was riding, and said in a cheerful tone, as if she took pleasure in presenting to me a countryman in a foreign land, "This donkey, *he* American, too. Good donkey, — Americano!" Since then my fellow pilgrims speak of all the donkeys as my relations. At any rate, the one I rode was a good little beast, and bore me on and up very patiently.

Strangely lovely is the site of the villa where wicked old Tiberius lived and sinned, and threw his slaves and sometimes his friends and guests into the sea for pastime. I wonder where his evil shade is now, and whether it haunts the old scenes still! I fancied he was walking beside us as we made our way back to the shore and the steamer, and we were glad to sail away from him across the sea aglow with the sunset toward fair Sorrento.

Next day we drove from Sorrento to Masso, and on to the old convent, La Deserta, which has been turned now into an orphanage for boys. As we drove towards the convent, schools of young priests met us, taking their solemn walk, breviary in hand; but, all around, the world was gay. Over our heads the heavy-laden orange and lemon trees bent with their weight of fruit. Poppies and daisies nodded to us from the clefts of the rocks, and adventurous roses climbed the walls and flaunted their pink blossoms from the heights. Below — between us and the shining bay — were groves of olive-trees, with their gnarled trunks and little gray leaves; and sometimes the young spring-green of the just-leaved larch flashed like a jewel among the sombre gray of the olives, and seemed like the youth and age of the tree-world, strangely allied.

From the entrance to the grounds of La Deserta it was still a long climb up the heights to the old convent. Little green lizards ran across our path, and in and out of the chinks of the wall, and little children started up like the lizards from odd corners, and offered us roses. At last we reached the convent door, and an old brown-robed monk, with a nose like an eagle's beak, bade us welcome, and led us to the house-top, which, indeed, seemed the summit of the Delectable Mountains, whence one could look forth on Paradise. On all sides stretched the glorious panorama, made up of near mountains rising ruggedly from the Bay, and distant ones like clouds on the horizon. Then there were little white villages at the feet of volcanoes, and everywhere oranges and olives and roses, and not a sound to break the waiting stillness save the occasional long call of some lonely bird, or the childish voices of the little black-haired children playing in the garden far below, — so far that their talk and their laughter seemed like the vague murmur of a hive of bees. Happy children they, in that lovely spot among the flowers, and with the kind old brown monks for guardians.

Our own especial monk was curious to know from whence we came. We asked if he had ever been in England. He smiled at the thought of such far wanderings, and shook his head.

"In England? no; in Florence? no; in Rome? no; but sometimes to Sorrento, and twice to Naples!"

What a life, — bounded by a short day's journey! But it held the vision of heaven. We parted with him, after all, with a vague envy, to go on our worldly way, down the long path again, startling the green lizards on our way, chaffering with the happy children; and then back to Sorrento, when the sun was low, for an evening of music and moonlight and memories, — a last Sorrento night, for the next morning was to see us on our way to Pompeii.

POMPEII, AMALFI, AND PAESTUM.

WE drove from Sorrento to Pompeii in all the glory of the sweet spring morning, and it was a strange contrast to go in, out of the gay, ever-young world, to the Museum of Pompeian Antiquities through which we passed on our way to the dead city of the dead.

In this terrible museum you find eight human bodies, killed in the eruption that overwhelmed the city in the year 79 of the Christian era. How many millions of the dead have mouldered into dust and been forgotten while these have remained in awful permanence, thus turned to stone!

Here, too, you find loaves of bread baked on that fatal August morning, more than eighteen hundred years ago, and grapes which were ripening in that morning's sunshine. Dogs and cats, buried with their masters in one dire moment, were here also. Ah me! it was a grewsome place, and one was glad to flee from it even into the streets of the dead city.

Pompeii was first mentioned in history three hundred and ten years before Christ, but certain of its monuments prove it to have been of much greater antiquity than this.

It is said to have been founded by the Oscans, and to have shared the civilization of the Greeks; but nearly a century before the Christian era it became subject to Rome, and was a favorite retreat for Romans of the wealthier classes, even including some of the emperors.

Sixty-three years after Christ a fearful earthquake assailed it, and completely destroyed a large portion of the city.

This was hardly likely to happen again, said Pompeii to itself, with some consoling superstition that lightning never strikes twice in the same place. So they built up the town more nobly than ever, and the next sixteen years were devoted to filling it with all such luxuries as Romans loved.

The walls were covered with beautiful frescos; temples were built, a theatre, an arena for gladiatorial combats, marble baths, deep wine-cellars, — all, in short, that belonged to a Roman holiday. And they sang and danced and made festival and lived on fearlessly, as if there were no danger nor sorrow in all the world, until suddenly, "like a strong man armed," destruction fell upon them.

In A. D. 79 came an eruption of Vesuvius, of which the first symptom was a dense shower of ashes that covered the town to the depth of three feet. Thus warned, many of the inhabitants had time to escape. Others were too paralyzed by fear to move, and still others, having once fled, returned to gather up their treasures; and then the final catastrophe came, and the whole number of those who perished in it is estimated at about two thousand.

For nearly fifteen centuries was the place given over, undisturbed, to its sad sepulture, and it is only in the present century that really important excavations have been made. Scarcely more than a third of the old city has even yet been exhumed, and it is computed that, at the rate the excavations are going on at present, it will be seventy years before they are completed, though there is no doubt that the world is already in possession of by far the most important part of the old town.

These ruins are almost our sole source of information as regards the details of ancient domestic life. It must have been a prosperous city; for, so far, not one indication has been found of that pauper race, with forever outstretched hand, so numerous in the Italy of to-day.

We form mistaken ideas of Pompeii from the novelists and the poets. I, at least, had expected its houses to be far more complete. The ground plans are perfectly distinct, but comparatively few of the walls are standing.

The streets are straight and narrow, and admirably paved with lava. In many of them are deep ruts worn by the chariot wheels of long ago, and at the street-corners you still find placards recommending for public office men dead for how many silent centuries. Your imagination fills the dumb streets with pictures. You see Pansa driving home to his stately house, or the Tragic Poet turning the next corner.

Sallust lived here, and Diomed, and here the people went and came, and loved and hated, and led their busy lives, until suddenly, into the midst of the music, the Eruption burst, and they had to stop living.

Here were their shops — here their temples. Here are their daintily frescoed bed-chambers, their marble baths, their dining-halls with scenes of hunting and feasting upon their walls, a statue here, a *bas-relief* there, a fresco elsewhere; though the most beautiful and valuable of their works of art have been transferred to the Naples Museum.

Here is a "Phallus" for averting the evil eye; and everywhere you find stone snakes, to symbolize the gods of the hearth and of the cross-ways.

From Pompeii we drove on to La Cava, and on our way a wild thunder-shower came up. Lightnings flashed and thunder pealed from height to height, and the stone-pines crashed with the mighty wind. In the very midst of it all we met a funeral, actually as gay as a Punch and Judy show.

It is a strange feature of life in Southern Italy that they sedulously divest funerals of all solemnity. This hearse might have been the show-wagon preceding a circus, for it was all gilt and tinsel, and the dead body inside was covered with a mound of bright-colored paper flowers.

After it followed a motley band of mourners, gayly clad, and protecting themselves from the rain with gaudy-hued umbrellas, and evidently more concerned about their own shelter than about the dead whom they were following.

" 'T is a mad world, my masters!"

La Cava is a good place to go from, — the best possible centre from which to make excursions. Salvator Rosa found it a good place, indeed, for a painter to abide in, and embodied many of the wild scenes around it in his best pictures.

We drove from there to Amalfi, — a drive of about three hours, by the most wonderful road, hewn in the very cliffs of the coast, and frequently supported by galleries and vast viaducts from one hundred to five hundred feet above the level of the sea.

On the heights above grow oranges and lemons and olives, and still above these orchards rise heights that seem to scale the blue Italian sky. I have no adjectives for this three hours' drive. I have used them up on scenes lovely indeed, but yet less fair; and for this supreme beauty I have no tribute but silence.

Amalfi itself, as George Eliot says in her Italian Journal, "surpasses all imagination of a romantic site for a city."

We climbed to the old monastery, which is now a hotel, at the very top of the height on which Amalfi is built, and there we sat in a reading-room, which was once the refectory of the old monks, and awaited the preparation of our luncheon. Meanwhile we looked over the visitors' book.

People had written there of going to Amalfi for a fortnight, and remaining for months, unable to tear themselves away; and one lady had gone for a week and stayed a year.

My only wonder was how, after a year of Amalfi, one could ever endure life elsewhere. Our own Longfellow was one of the visitors who had recorded in this well-filled book his joy in Amalfi, and afterwards, when a sharp New England snow-storm was keeping him in-doors, he saw the place again as in vision, and wrote about it his poem beginning : —

> "Sweet the memory is to me,
> Of a land beyond the sea,
> Where the waves and mountains meet,
> Where, amid her mulberry-trees,
> Sits Amalfi in the heat,
> Bathing ever her white feet
> In the tideless summer seas."

The next morning we went to Paestum through a waste country tenanted by wild horses, swine, forlorn-looking sheep watched by fierce dogs, and great herds of brown, shaggy buffaloes with evil eyes. The air was heavy with malaria. We seemed to be passing through the "Valley of the Shadow of Death," — fit route to dead temples, built in dead centuries, in honor of dead gods.

When history first took account of Paestum, it

was called Poseidonia, from Poseidon, the Greek name for Neptune. It is said to have been settled by a Greek colony from Sybaris as long ago as about six hundred years before Christ.

Some two hundred and seventy-three years before Christ it fell into the hands of the Romans; and from that time it steadily declined in importance, until, in the middle of the ninth century A. D., it was almost destroyed by the Saracens. Now its very roses, which the Roman poets used to praise, are dead.

But happily its walls are standing still, and its glorious temples remain, not yet wholly ruined, to give us the best idea it is possible to obtain, out of Athens, of pure Greek architecture.

They are three in number, — these temples which now are Paestum. The central and by far the most important one is that conjecturally called the Temple of Neptune, sixty-five yards in length and twenty-six yards in width. Like its two neighbors, it was built of gray travertine, but time has turned the stone to a warm brown.

It stands in the centre of a great waste plain, and on one side it looks toward the sea, over which the deity in whose honor it may have been built was ruler, and on the other toward the mountains.

To the perfection of its form and color is added the charm of the uttermost suitability of position. Wise indeed were the builders who chose this site more than two thousand years ago.

Standing before this temple, I received my first keen sense of what absolutely perfect architecture might be, and my heart thrilled at its beauty as at glorious music. The lesser temples, its neighbors, would have been wonders of beauty elsewhere; but here Neptune triumphed, and one forgot to worship at the shrine of the other gods.

Did some one get hungry, in spite of the beauty? We lunched at last under our umbrellas, and half-sheltered by the roofless Doric pillars of the great temple.

Then our German professor marched at the head of his feminine following, and made us wise about all sorts of technical details in the architecture of the three temples, and we gathered in this waste plain of ruins just such wild-flowers as we could have found in a New England meadow in June.

But the rain, that had coquetted with us all day, now began to pour down in desperate earnest, and we hurried back to the railway station and started with the out-going train for Naples.

IN AND ABOUT ROME.

ALL ROADS LEAD TO ROME.

IF you cross the Atlantic by the French line, you will be told that to get your ticket through to Paris, and have your trunks checked for that destination on the pier at New York, will be a great saving of trouble; and so, no doubt, it usually is. But it befell me otherwise. I was assured that I need concern myself no farther with my luggage until I came to the end of my journey. So when I reached Paris at noon of Tuesday, April 8, I looked about confidently for my three trunks. Two were there, but the third was missing. The representative of the Transatlantique company searched with me; the head man of the custom house lent a hand, or rather an eye; and we looked at every trunk in the place, but in vain. "What was your trunk like?" asked the agent of the steamer company. I described it with the realistic faithfulness of a Zola. He would telegraph to Havre, he said, at once. I should have the trunk that night; or, at least, I should have news of it. As soon as an answer came to his telegram, he would send me word, at Hotel Normandy.

At the hotel the concierge encouraged me. Just such a thing had happened, he said, to a lady who came there three weeks before; but she got her trunk the next day at noon. I had meant to start on Wednesday morning for Italy. All Tuesday afternoon I waited in vain for the expected message from the man at the station; but no message came. Wednesday morning,— still no news. I stayed in until noon. Then I betook myself to the general office of the Transatlantique company. I was told I must go to the Bureau of Reclamation, on another street. At the bureau I found a man in charge who spoke French-English, and who listened to my tale of woe with the most sympathetic courtesy.

"Mais, madame, it is sure that your trunk will arrive."

" But I wanted to start for Rome this morning."

"It must be another of mornings. I regret it, madame."

Ah me! we can bear the loss of other people's trunks with such calmness!

"But I must do something," I cried. "I cannot be kept here forever by that missing trunk."

"Very true, madame. I shall now at once go with you to the Gare St. Lazare. You will please make me the description of your trunk."

So once more I described the poor black box to a dot, and he wrote it all down. Then we started for the station. We found there the custom house man and the company's agent. The agent "had telegraphed to Havre — yes — but certainly — and had received no answer," and he shrugged his expressive shoulders.

"I will telegraph, and I shall be answered," said monsieur from the Bureau of Reclamation, and forthwith he sent a despatch a yard long. He also told me that I should have word at my hotel as soon as he got his answer. Late that afternoon the message came. The trunk was on its way from Havre. On Thursday I drove once more to the Gare, and there I reclaimed my trunk and drove back with it in triumph to Hotel Normandy. But it was Friday morning, instead of Wednesday, on which I finally started for Rome.

"Is there a moral?" Oh, I forgot that! I should get my trunks checked for Paris before I left New York all the same, if I were going again; but I would try and make acquaintance with them when they were landed on the dock at Havre.

"All roads lead to Rome," so they say; and at any rate the number of different routes suggested to you is quite bewildering. You may go by the most luxurious of expresses to Lyons, Marseilles, and along the Riviera, — but this is the longest route, though many prefer it; or you may go by Milan and Florence, which, if you are in no special hurry, is, I think, the pleasantest thing to do; but if you want the shortest route, you will go by way of Turin, Genoa, and Pisa. This is what I concluded to do. Cook's people urged me to start at 9 o'clock at night. The 9 P. M. train is certainly the best and quickest train to take, and I should take it if I had a friend to share my section in the sleeper. But if you are alone, you must either have some stranger in the same section, or you must not only buy the whole section (which one would gladly do), but also you must buy a second railway ticket, which makes your night's journey rather expensive. I preferred to go on by day, and stop over, for the night, at Aix-les-Bains; so I took the 8.50 train in the morning. I found in the compartment "for ladies only" two ladies from Chicago,— pretty and pleasant, and, oh, so wise! One was a medical student,— a fair girl graduate, who is to pass the summer in listening to medical lectures at the Medical University of Zurich. The other was a scientific student of evolution, who had pursued the human race backward farther than my fancy can follow her. But they were both delightful. I adore people with specialties. They save you so much trouble. The day wore away swiftly in such company, and the night came on. The evening seemed long to our fatigue. It was thirty-six minutes past ten o'clock when we stopped at last at Aix-les-Bains. I have passed a season there, and certainly I found it a gay place then, where every one went to the theatre at night, and then wicked people played baccarat till morning. I was not prepared to find, on reaching the station, a dark and terrible solitude. I had planned to stop there, feeling sure that omnibuses from all the hotels would await the train, and that eager hotel porters would be striving together for the pleasure of our company. Presto! One dingy looking man, coming from Heaven knows where, dragged the hand luggage from the train. Happily for me, the ladies from Chicago stopped there also. We demanded an omnibus,— there was none; a cab,— not one to be had. What should we do? The dingy man produced from somewhere a sort of truck, and heaped our hold-alls and our portmanteaus upon it. If we would follow him, he said, he would guide us to the nearest hotel; it was not more than five minutes off,— oh, no! Did I not thank Heaven then for the company of those ladies from Chicago? What if I had been there alone? There was scarcely light enough to make darkness visible, and how should I, singly, have dared to follow the dingy man out into the vague, dark world, wherever he chose to take me? Think what a plot for a Gaboriau novel! But there is courage in numbers, and the three of us went on our way. It had rained heavily in the day, and our feet sank in the mud as on we toiled for the longest five minutes I can remember. At last, however, we reached the lighted entrance of the Grand Hotel d'Aix, and two or three sleepy servants provided for our wants.

It was nearly midnight before we were in bed, and the night was short; for we were called again at 4.45, and at 6.30 we had dressed, breakfasted, and were on the train.

Turin was our next stopping-place, and there I

parted company with the wise women of Chicago. They were to "repose themselves" at Turin, while I sped on toward Rome. But I have not told you how lovely was the world we looked on from the windows of our railway carriage between Aix-les-Bains and Modane. Mountains rose all along the way, and all their tops were white with snow, which glistened in the morning sun with a dazzling lustre caught from heaven itself. On one of the lower heights was a forest of trees, that looked like serried ranks of marching men, and each tree-soldier was clad, for suit of mail, in glittering ice. You could easily fancy that one of the armies that marched on over these paths toward Rome long centuries ago was there reincarnated, and once more glad with the breath of life.

At Modane came the examination of the luggage, and then we entered the Mont Cenis tunnel. We were precisely one half-hour from the time we entered the tunnel till we came out of it; one half-hour without a ray of illumination save from the little eye of light in the roof of our railway carriage. The train moved on with a deep and awful reverberation like underground thunder. It seemed like a transit through the Inferno; and I should hardly have been surprised had King Pluto appeared to demand his tribute money. Just half-way of this transit through the kingdom of darkness came a wild, prolonged scream from the engine, which the stone walls of the tunnel caught and clamorously repeated. For an instant one's heart stood still with fear, — it sounded so like the trumpet of final doom; but the cry ceased at last, and only the low, awful reverberation went on, and we went on with it, and came out into the light at last, after this half-hour that had seemed interminable.

We had left France behind when we went into the tunnel. We came out of it into Italy; and already the character of the landscape had changed. Mountains rose still along our way, but on these heights no snow glistened. The sun rested on them soft and warm, as if it loved them, and a wonderful purple light bathed their sides, — a glory of color that suggested the untold splendors of Paradise, as the horrible darkness and mystery of the tunnel had suggested the Inferno. We reached Turin at two o'clock in the afternoon, and there, as I said, the travellers from Chicago remained, while I went by myself, on the road that leads to Rome. Fortunately I was quite alone, — mistress of an entire compartment, free to sit at whatever window I pleased, to bask in the sun or retire into the shadow at my own sweet will.

The aspect of the landscape had once more changed. Going from Turin down to Genoa you pass through a region chiefly level; at least there are no high mountains, and even the hills are few. As I looked out, I recalled Lady Verney's chapters on peasant holdings in Italy. People in this part of Italy must be very poor; there seemed to be so few houses that indicated even comfortable middle-class respectability. Almost all were cottages, scarcely better than hovels, in which pig and peasant were alike at home.

Finding no compelling attraction in the outside world, I devoted myself to re-reading Rudyard Kipling's "Plain Tales from the Hills," and was happy.

I used to despair of finding a Guy de Maupassant to tell short stories for the English-speaking world; but here he is. Scarcely De Maupassant himself could put so much story in so little space.

I turned from the book at last, when we had reached the shores of the Mediterranean, so blandly blue in the April sunshine,— so treacherous, I know, for I have sailed on it. It was 5.30 of the afternoon when we reached the "City of Palaces," — Genoa "the superb." I had meant to stop there for the night; but as I had my compartment to myself and could rest there comfortably enough, I determined to go on through the dark and be at Rome in the morning. The half-hour we waited at Genoa gave me time to take a nice little table d'hôte dinner in the very good restaurant attached to the station. I was strongly tempted to stop over and renew my impressions of Genoa. I recalled in my fond vision its marble palaces full of glorious pictures; its streets with no sidewalks, where you are jostled by the ever-present donkey; its sumptuous churches, fairly glittering with gold; and the monument to Columbus, to which we

Yankees have a personal right. But Rome was at the end of my journey, and Rome conquered, as she conquered the world long ago.

When we were approaching Genoa, she was fairly ablaze with the glory of sunset. Every window was aflame, and her marble palaces shone like the jewelled walls of the New Jerusalem. The sun had set and the night had fallen when we moved away again, and the city that had been as glad as hope was pensive now as memory. The sea looked cold and dark, though the stars were rising above it, and their reflections flashed like jewels here and there in its depths. As long as enough twilight lasted to reveal a glimpse of sea or shore, I looked from my window. Then I slept a fitful, unrestful slumber, waking with a sudden start every time the train paused at a station. At sunrise I was broad awake again, and still we were speeding on beside the sea, and sea and sky and earth were glorious with the great mysterious "rose of dawn." After a while we left the sea and turned inland toward Rome. I suppose the Italians must have some holidays; but here it was Sunday morning, and men, women, and donkeys were all toiling patiently in the fields. Oh the hard, hard life! oh the bitter bread, bitterly earned! I do not understand — I wish I did — why there should be people with millions on millions of money, great wastes of land "preserved" for hunting and shooting; pretty women, whose only task is to choose the fittest adornment for their loveliness; and then these others, Heaven's children also, but forsaken and forgotten of men, toiling, from sun to sun, for food a well-bred dog would scorn, and rags to wear that would affront a beggar. Oh the everlasting puzzle that it is! How one wishes Mr. Bellamy's golden dream were realized; but looking on the world as we see it now, does not such a future seem as impossible as the wildest wonder tales told in "Arabian Nights"?

Rome at last, — yes, Rome! What magic is in the word! When I reached this same station for the first time, — how long ago it seems now, — I remember there was a choking of my breath, a dimness in my eyes, that was like first love, perhaps. I could breathe freely this morning, I could see clearly; but, all the same, Rome is Rome, and there is no other place like it under the sun. I got to my hotel; I rang for my morning coffee; and if I had been brought hither in a dream, I should still have known that it was Rome, for here on my butter-pat were Romulus and Remus, and their foster-mother the wolf.

MOST ROMAN PART OF ROME.

HERE I am at the Hôtel de Londres, in the most Roman part of Rome, in the Piazza di Spagna, just at the foot of the Spanish Steps. At No. 25 Shelley lived, and at No. 26, Keats. I wonder if they loved to watch, as I do, the models that congregate on the Spanish Steps, — picturesque creatures in their gay peasant costumes! I wonder if the beggars swarmed round them at every step, as they swarm round me when I go out of my door! I am sure they must have loved this gay, bright, varied scene. The city government is doing its best to obliterate Roman Rome. An ugly iron bridge crosses the Roman Forum, and vandalism can hardly go farther than that. They are levelling here, and pulling down there, and blocks of commonplace houses are supplanting Roman ruins; but, Heaven be praised, the dear old Piazza di Spagna is not likely to be interfered with at present!

Do you remember the pretty story they tell of Ruskin when he was here? He used to come down the Spanish Steps morning after morning, and there was one beggar who always begged of him, and to whom he always gave a copper coin or two. One day the beggar, touched by this long-continued kindness, caught his hand and kissed it. The beggar's own hand was not over-clean, and involuntarily Ruskin shrank from his touch. Then the strong sense in him of human brotherhood triumphed, and he bent over and kissed the beggar's cheek. Next day the man came to the house where Ruskin lived, and brought him the most precious thing he had in the world, — a fragment of brown cloth which had once been part of the monkish robe of St. Francis of Assisi. They say that it was this incident which especially turned Ruskin's thoughts to the life of St. Francis, and to those frescos by Giotto of which he has written so eloquently.

What have I seen beside the beauties and the beggars of the Spanish Steps? Not so very much, as yet. Somehow one does not care to hurry at Rome, but there is always something to do. One day I drove to the Church of St. Onofrio to see the tomb of Tasso. We drove there by that superb new road along the Janiculum Hill, which commands a view of Rome worth going far to see.

The Janiculum Hill used to be consecrated, long ago, to Janus, the sun god. The first Sabine king of Rome, Numa Pompilius, was buried here with the sacred rites of the sun worshippers. Ancus Martius, the fourth Roman king, connected the Janiculum with the rest of the city by building the Pons Sublicius, the first bridge over the Tiber. From the crest of the Janiculum Hill, Lars Porsena, King of Etruria, looked upon Rome and retired in fear for his life, after he had seen such examples of Roman courage as Horatius, who kept the falling bridge, and Mutius, who burned his hand in the charcoal and waved the triumphant stump of it to the foe.

On this hill stands the Church of St. Onofrio, forever associated with the memory of Torquato Tasso. He came to Rome in 1594, on the invitation of Pope Clement VIII., that he might be crowned at the Capitol; but he arrived in the month of November, and the weather was then very bad. So it was decided to postpone the ceremony of crowning him until the spring. In his secret heart Tasso felt that he should now never be crowned at all, for the presentiment of death was upon him. Long before the time appointed for his crowning he went to the monks in the convent of St. Onofrio (which adjoins the church) and said to them, "Brethren, I have come to die among you;" and to a friend he wrote, "I am come to begin, in this holy place, the conversation of heaven."

During the fourteen days through which his illness lasted he was absorbed in the contemplation of heavenly mysteries, and on the last day of his life, having already received the papal absolution, he exclaimed, " I believe that the crown I looked for at the Capitol is to be changed for a crown in heaven." He was only fifty years of age when he died thus, gladly resigning earth in the sure hope of heaven. The room in which he died, three centuries ago, still contains his crucifix, and various other relics of his life, beside a mask which was taken from his face after death,— a poet's face, sad and thin, and with a look of aspiration and of yearning from which one turns away with dim eyes. I lingered in the Roman sunshine, under that old oak-tree beneath which Tasso used to sit through the long twilights, gazing toward Rome, and thinking,— was it of heaven, or of Leonora? Italy, always loyal to genius, does not forget her poets, and in the little amphitheatre near Tasso's oak the "Academia" still holds, on every 25th of April, a musical festa in honor of his memory, at which his bust is crowned with the laurels he did not live long enough to wear.

We drove through the Trastevere on our way from the Church of St. Onofrio to the Pincian Hill. The Trastevere always interests me. It is the "city across the Tiber," the part of Rome least altered from mediæval times, where the narrow streets are overlooked still by ancient towers and gothic windows and curious pieces of sculpture. The inhabitants of the Trastevere pride themselves on being different from the people on the other side of the Tiber, with whom they seldom inter-marry. They claim to be direct descendants of the ancient Romans, and they speak a dialect of their own. They are said to be stronger and more vigorous of body than other Romans, as well as more passionate and revengeful. There are more murders here than in any other part of Rome, — though murder is never so frequent in Italy as in England. They are handsome creatures, these Trasteverini, and, marrying among themselves, have kept their type unvitiated.

To go to the Pincian Hill of an April afternoon should have been included among Sir John Lubbock's "Pleasures of Life." The winding road that leads up the Pincio is the oldest and quite the most important public pleasure drive in Rome. The road along the Janiculum Hill, through the Corsini grounds, is out of easy reach, and too new to be so generally popular; while the beautiful park of the Villa Borghese is the private property of Prince Borghese, and is only free to the public on certain days. The dear Pincio is always open. You may climb there to watch the sunrise gild the dome of St. Peter's, or linger there on May evenings, while the nightingales break your heart with the passion of their singing; or you may drive there, with all the Roman world, on a bright afternoon, and listen to the military music, and, if you are fortunate, receive a smiling bow from the Queen, or a gracious salute from his Majesty the King. King Humberto is the only monarch who could reconcile me to monarchy. Since the days when, forsaking all the pleasures that invited him, he went to Naples and held the hands of those who were dying there of cholera, and said, in the house of the Black Death, "My place is here," he has seemed to me the one king who was truly the father of his people, and who had a father's right to rule. I never see him without longing to be one of his subjects.

But about the Pincian! It is not one of the traditional seven hills of Rome. It stood for many centuries outside the walls. The great Northern road — the Flaminian Way — ran at its foot, and along this road were stately sculptured sepultures, many of which were afterward destroyed when the Porta del Popolo was built. It was known of old as The Hill of Gardens, and it took its present designation from the Pincian family, who owned it toward the close of the Roman empire. Long — oh, how long — ago the villa of Lucullus was here. Afterward, Messalina coveted the place. It was a very simple thing with her to get what she wanted. She had only to murder the proprietor, which she did without scruple, and then took possession.

It was about A. D. 270 when the Emperor Aurelian inclosed the hill with the walls that still surround it. The wall farthest from the city is so very high that it is a favorite place for suicides; though I should think that, were one ever so determined on shuffling off this mortal coil, if once he looked down from here he would fall in love with life anew, and resolve to stay in this world as long as possible. For, beautiful as is the Pincio, yet more beautiful are the enchanting grounds of the Villa Borghese. They are kindly opened to the public on Tuesday, Thursday, Saturday, and Sunday afternoons; and, whenever there is nothing else that clamors to be done on one of these four afternoons, I drive out to the Borghese while the day is wearing late, and am happy.

Now and again I go earlier still, before the place is thronged with the beauty and fashion of Rome, as it is in the late afternoon. I like to be quiet there for a while, and dream my own dreams and think my own thoughts. I do not wonder that Miriam and Donatello could forget their fate in these enchanted glades, and dance as the sunbeams danced with the shadows. Sometimes I seem to see them where the sun sifts through the young green leaves, and her beauty — her human, deep-souled beauty — and his fantastic grace are the only things here that cannot change.

The walls will crumble, the busts of kings and heroes and poets lose a nose here and a chin there; the lovely Roman ladies who come and pass will grow old and fade, and vanish from sight and from memory; but still these two, hapless yet happy, will dance in these wild glades, immortally beyond the reach of the effacing years.

How sweet is the breath of the spring morning! My window is open. This April day in Rome is like the lavish June of New England. It is good to be alive, and alive among these dear Italians. They are the gentlest, kindest people the sun shines on, and the friendliest, also.

I heard such a pretty story yesterday of a certain doctor who just now occupies the Keats house here on the Piazza di Spagna. I think the doctor himself is Danish, though I am not quite sure. At any rate, he had lived long in Capri, whence he removed, six months ago, to Rome. On Easter Monday there was to be a sacred festa, on which faithful children of the church could be admitted to the presence of their father the Pope. On the Saturday before Easter Dr. Munthe went home and found, tranquilly sitting on his steps, six peasants, old neighbors from Capri. "How did you find me?" he asked, after he had exchanged salutations with them. "Oh, we knew that the doctor" (I believe there are several hundreds of doctors here) "was in Rome, and we got here this morning, and went all about asking for *il dottore*. And at last we came to the Spanish steps, and here every one knew, and then we waited." It was very simple, you see. "Ah, well," said Dr. Munthe, "now I will work a miracle. I have my dinner ordered for one. I shall make it enough for seven. Come in, all of you, and we will dine together." He was as good as his word. The dinner was enough for seven; and when they had well dined, the doctor went out with his old neighbors, and found them a friendly inn, where they could abide until Monday, and await the Pope's benediction. Somehow I don't think just this would have happened anywhere except in Italy.

I am sure that, as a clever English friend of mine remarked yesterday, there is no place in the world where so many people can afford to live without doing anything as live so here. There are more loungers, I believe, in Italy, than anywhere else on earth; and certainly there are more beggars than I have ever known anywhere else except in Spain. You step out of your door and a throng of them surround you. You can hardly see your way for the brown hands thrust in your face. Women hand round their babies as a church warden does the contribution plate. I never saw so many monstrosities in the way of deformity. This seems the native country of the halt, the maimed, and the blind. And as for ugly old women, — the vision of some of them haunts one like a nightmare.

They seem ill-tempered, too. You cannot give to a quarter of them, if you would; and when you chance to see something unusually pitiful in some face or attitude, and drop a few pence in an outstretched hand, the others fly at you like hornets. It was, I am sure, a good old thing, bent by many sorrows, to whom I gave a small *douceur* yesterday; but instantly her next neighbor cried : "She ought not to have it — she ought not! She is a bad old woman — she!!!" But as no one of them seems to be provided with a certificate of good character, we can only trust to our own impressions. I own that, as a rule, I give to the most hideous, as one gives to the grinder of a bad hand-organ, to get rid of him. These old beggars bring before me, a dozen times a day, one of the most pathetic statues I know, that of "Roma," by Miss

Anne Whitney, poet and sculptor, — "Roma," with her sad eyes and her outstretched hands, asking alms of the world.

But, beggars and all, Rome is an enchanting spot in which to linger. This is a pleasant hotel, too; and there is an atmosphere of neighborly kindness about it which makes one feel at home. It has the drollest little lift, with a red velvet-covered stool in each of the four corners. They send you up in it by yourself from below, having made some mysterious compact with its machinery by which it will stop at precisely the right inch. The manager of the hotel was taking me aloft in it to show me a room the day I came. He speaks English, and I enlarged a little on the roomlike "elevators" of the land of my birth. He listened almost incredulously. "Ah," he said at last, "I fear they must go by steamerage," and he shook his head very gravely. "Not for anything you could name would I trust my life to a lift that goes by steamerage."

AMONG STATUES AND PICTURES.

OH, how mockingly fast these golden weeks whirl by! I am haunted by a sentence from Richard Jeffries: "Never again the same thing in the same place!" Shall I ever be here again? Who knows? And if I come, will it be this I, or another? for surely I am not now the same person as when first I came here, so long ago. And she is dead who came with me then, — the "Sherwood Bonner" of several pleasant books — the Kate McDowell of my tender love. In many of our excursions we were joined by a brilliant young student who was just taking a Roman holiday after a winter of hard study at Athens. And he also is what we call dead. Yesterday I was walking through the beautiful Villa Wolkonsky, where the roses run riot in these days of May, and these two came out of the past and walked again, every inch of the way, beside me, as they did all those years ago. Their steps fell silently, and I think no one else saw them; but Kate's heavy golden hair shone as of old in the sunshine, and Kimber's eyes were frank and smiling as ever. They paused, when I did, to look at the far-off views, or hear the nightingale singing his soul out to the roses; but when I came out into the busy Roman street I left them behind me. They always loved the stillness of shadowy walks, and they lingered at the villa.

There are stately dwellers here in Rome whom time does not change. It is to these I make my first visits whenever I return. Some of them are in the mighty palace of the Vatican, others dwell in state at the Capitol. The beautiful Antinous still wears his crown of lotus in the Villa Albani, and the Juno whom Goethe worshipped reigns forever at the Ludovisi. I can never put into words the pleasure I find in the presence of these immortals. They are more real than any one else, — they are so used to living! If we ourselves could pass centuries on centuries in this world, might we not be educated at last to their grand calm, their serene self-possession? It almost seems so. But our little span of life is so mockingly short that we have to make the course at a gallop, and get to the end of it before we have learned to live.

To go to the Statuary Museum of the Vatican is to pass an hour in Olympus. Surely this is the most glorious collection of statues in the whole world! Here is that divine " Eros " of Praxiteles, — the first statue, it always seemed to me, to recognize the soul. We have in its neighbors the joy of living, — the Faun's roguish mirth, the pleasure of Bacchus in his wine, the might of the conquering hero; but he who wrought this " Eros " had caught a glimpse of the wayward, longing, baffled human soul, that can suffer as keenly as it can enjoy. Here are the "Narcissus," the "Mercury," and the "Apollo of the Belvedere;" the cruel "Laocoön," which Pliny describes as "superior to all other works of art;" the "Meleager," the "Young Augustus," "Antinous" the beautiful, and how many more! Here, too, you have the busts of the Roman emperors, and of some of the philosophers.

The Museum of Statuary at the Capitol is scarcely second in importance. The colossal statues of Castor and Pollux are at the head of the steps leading up to it, and in the square in front of it is the equestrian statue of Marcus Aurelius, — the most perfect piece of ancient bronze work in existence. At the fountain in the court opposite the entrance is the statue of the river god Marforio, who was the friend and fellow-gossip of Pasquin. Lively dialogues between them, satirizing the government and the times, used to be discovered in the early morning placarded on their respective pedestals. These pasquinades were often extremely uncomfortable for those in authority.

The statues of most importance in the Capitol Museum are the celebrated "Venus of the Capitol," the "Dying Gladiator," the "Antinous," and that "Faun" of Praxiteles which suggested to Hawthorne his immortal novel, "The Marble Faun." At the Capitol also are eighty-three busts of Roman emperors, their wives and their near relatives, — the most interesting portrait gallery in the world. It is curious to note how many of these ill-fated personages came to a violent death. Here is Agrippina, the wife of Germanicus, who was starved to death when Tiberius came to the throne. Claudius was poisoned; and he had himself put to death his third wife, Messalina. For sixth wife Claudius had Agrippina the younger, and she was the mother of Nero, and was murdered by her son. Nero ended his crimes by killing himself. Among the other murders he committed was that of his second wife, Poppæa, whom he killed by a single kick. Galba was murdered in the Forum, Otho killed himself, Vitellius was murdered, Titus was poisoned by Domitian, Domitian was murdered in the palace of the Cæsars, as was also Commodus; and so the appalling list goes on, with "murdered" after at least half of the names. What a world that old Roman one was to live in!

"The Hall of Illustrious Men," with its ninety-three busts of philosophers, statesmen, and poets, is less tragic in its suggestions. Socrates was so ugly, so phenomenally ugly, that in beholding him one can't help forgiving Xantippe for her temper.

Among the important new "finds" at the Capitol is a bust of Commodus, singularly beautiful, and of a polish and purity so exquisite as to seem almost transparent. Here in one of the ground-floor rooms is the skeleton of a girl. She was found with all her jewels perfectly preserved. Rings glitter on the bones that were her fingers, and a necklace sparkles on her skeleton neck.

She is thought to have been about sixteen, and yet her doll was buried with her! I suppose when girls had no novels to read they played with their dolls the longer. There is another full-length skeleton in another coffin-shaped case of glass; but I do not like looking at these reminders that life is brief. Give me rather the white immortality of my marble gods.

I have made the acquaintance during the past week of some artists whose work I had not before known. In Rome it is at studios, and not in the shops of the dealers, that one finds the best pictures. The other day we went to the marvellous studio of Villegas, one of the greatest of the great painters who are making the Spanish art of to-day illustrious. He has built for himself a wonderful villa outside the gates of Rome, in which he has copied the Moorish architecture of the Alhambra. This villa is full of fascinating things. The most exquisite stuffs from the far East, royal embroideries from Japan, vases, sculpture, — all, in short, which could be found of precious and beautiful. It is an enchanting place, and a fit shrine for the noble pictures we found there.

We did not penetrate to the inner studio where the great painter works. He received us in what I should call a studio for exhibition. The walls were completely covered with sketches, finished pictures, and pictures in different stages of completion. Of the many, I can only speak of two, — the "Dying Toreador," and the "Venetian Wedding." In the "Dying Toreador," besides its superb art, there is infinite pathos. The poor fellow has been mortally wounded in the midst of the bull-fight, and he lies there dying. A priest stands at his head; the woman he loves — wife or sweetheart — is bending over him, her eyes wild with the passion of loss and despair. His comrades are grouped at a little distance, and each of their strongly painted faces is clearly individualized and tells its own story.

The "Venetian Wedding" is an immense picture. It filled almost completely an end wall of the large room. It is a *tour de force* in color. The steps on which the bridal party meet are covered with red velvet. The dresses of the bride and her attendants are white, and with them contrast the sumptuous robes of the bridegroom (who is the just elected Doge) and his group of followers. The scheme of color is superb and audacious; and there is a wonderful open-air effect about the whole picture that was explained when one learned how it was painted. Villegas posed all his models under glass, and painted them in the full light of the Italian sun; but the task cost him the temporary loss of his eyesight. The dazzling colors, in the dazzling light, were too strong, even for his eagle vision; and before the picture was completed he was absolutely color-blind, and was obliged to suspend work entirely for some time.

Another Spaniard, whose paintings interested me

extremely, was Poveda. His studio was full of charming bits of Roman and Venetian scenery and architecture.

One of the pleasures of a Sunday afternoon in Rome is a visit to the studio of our own countryman, Elihu Vedder. Vedder's present studio was formerly occupied by J. Rollin Tilton. Vedder had long coveted this studio, and had often said to Tilton, "If ever you get ready to give up your lease, don't forget that I want it." An afternoon came at last when Tilton was engaged to dine with — I think — some Italian friends. They waited for him nearly an hour, and then dined without him, quite puzzled by his unexplained absence. And Tilton, meantime, had journeyed on, far beyond the recall of any earthly summons. He had gone home to dress, and suddenly that intermittent heart, of whose queer freaks he used to complain, stopped beating altogether, and the studio was free for the next comer.

That next comer was Elihu Vedder, perhaps the most imaginative and poetic artist America has yet given to the world. There is, it seems to me, something in his genius akin to Hawthorne, and yet more akin to William Blake. When did Blake die? I cannot remember, and I cannot, therefore, be sure whether the spirit of Blake could possibly have been reincarnated in the painter of "The Cup of Death." At any rate, a wonderful spiritual power is in this man, who has perceived so many strange things. I saw a picture in his studio the other day, "Waiting for Judgment," which no man could have painted who had not the spiritual vision. He has solved the enigma of "The Sphinx," — he has caught the poignant yet vague despair of "The Lost Mind." He has discovered "The Sea Serpent," — he has seen the "Sybil" with her wild eyes and her flying hair.

It occurs to one sometimes to feel a profound curiosity as to what will be the verdict of future centuries concerning the works of our own time, whether in art or in literature. I spent the morning, a day or two since, in the Borghese gallery. How noble was that art of the far past which looks from those walls to-day! The fair women and strong men who served as models are dead so long, so long ago! and the artists who painted them would be dead too, had they not painted themselves into immortality, and thus remained more alive than any of us. Oh to come back, some centuries from now, and see who of the men we know will be thus alive then!

Sometimes it strikes me curiously to think how different the ruins of New York or Boston, or even London, would be from those of Rome. In Rome you meet at every turn what Byron called

"Fragments of stone, reared by creatures of clay."

The eyes of some Greek god look into yours. A marble smile mocks you with its centuries-old sweetness. The dead, exhumed from the realm of death, have part in the mystery and the wonder.

When the New Zealander walks among the ruins of London, where will be these immortal guests? There will be acres of good solid brick and mortar and stone, fallen in shapeless heaps; but where the noble arches, the pillars round which the acanthus clusters, the faces of the gods?

AMONG THE MANY CHURCHES OF THE ETERNAL CITY.

I THINK there is no place where the days are quite so mockingly short as in Rome. There is so much one longs to be doing, all at once, — roses and ruins, ancient art and modern art, studios, churches, libraries, — it is always a question what thing to choose, among the tempting many, for that particular hour. One day of the past week we gave to churches, another to the pictures at the Vatican, another to a ramble among the ruins and relics of ancient Rome. Perhaps the most fascinating afternoon of all the week was one that began with an hour in W. W. Story's [1] studio, after which we drove to "St. Paul's Outside the Walls," and then to the Protestant Cemetery, and finally to the Pincian, with its gardens and its music, and the beauty and fashion of Rome passing to and fro in it, as one sees them in Hyde Park in a London June.

It was a pleasure to renew one's acquaintance with Mr. Story's "Cleopatra," — I mean with the second of his Cleopatras. The first was there also; but the second is infinitely more charming

[1] These pages were written before Mr. Story's death.

and seductive. She is the Cleopatra of Shakespeare, and she is the Cleopatra of Mr. Story's own poem. There was a beautiful "Alcestis," too, with the dream still in her eyes; and there was a most touching figure of the Christ, with invitation and promise in his face and in his outstretched hand, saying, "Come unto Me." I was looking at a noble statue of Saul, which recalled to me the Saul of Browning's poem, and led me to speak of the dead poet. And Mr. Story told me of his own last interview with Browning at Asolo. It was but a short time before the poet's death, and these two who had known each other so long and well had talked of all sorts of intimate things, as old friends use; and Mr. Story had got into his carriage to drive off. Suddenly Browning, who was moving away, turned back, and reached his hand once more into the carriage for a last word. Looking into Story's face with that deep, all-seeing gaze of his, "Friends for forty years," he said, — "forty years, and never a break! Good-bye." It was the last sentence Story was ever to hear from those long-loved lips.

And talking of American sculptors, I have been to one modern studio where I saw statues which have given me pleasure of the same kind that I derive from the masterpieces of the past. The "Circe" of Mr. Richard S. Greenough has been exhibited at the Boston Art Museum, and, though it was in a singularly bad light there, no one can have failed to perceive its enchanting loveliness.

I use the word "enchanting" advisedly. It is the veritable enchantress that we have here. I had never thought marble could wear a smile so seductive as curves her lips; and the cup she offers, — I would drink it from that hand though I knew I must dwell henceforth and forever in her pigsty. Look at that hunting leopard under her chair! He was once a man. He loved her, and he drank from her cup. But is his fate so hard who dwells forever in the sunshine of her beauty? Perhaps she puts out her hand and touches his head sometimes, when we are not there to see.

Mr. Greenough has been cruel to Cupid — no, it was the nymphs who were cruel to him, and the sculptor only made his portrait. The nymphs have clipped his wings and bound them with silken cords, and set him on the tortoise, slowest creature that moves at all; and here he is, with the half-pathetic, yet half-mischievous look upon his face, — as lovely a vision as sculptor ever summoned from the white depths of the marble.

And this Portia, — if you have never understood Portia before, you will know her when once you see this bust. A more beautiful face I have seldom beheld, — high-bred, gracious, graceful, "so innocent arch, so cunning simple," her look showing as plainly as words could show that he whom her heart has already chosen is choosing the right casket. And this "Nemesis," near by! I have always feared Nemesis; and I fear her more than ever now that I have looked into this pitiless face of stone. She would not care, though you broke your heart at her feet. It is given to few among the moderns (in these days of remorseless and lowering realism) to walk with the gods, and to create shapes worthy of a niche in Olympus. But, like many another, I have been beguiled by Circe, — it was of churches that I meant to write.

Glorious indeed is that noble church, St. Paul's Outside the Walls, built to commemorate the martyrdom of St. Paul. The first church on this spot was begun in the time of Constantine, and was enlarged into a Basilica in 386, A. D. It was restored by Pope Leo III. (795–816), and every succeeding century added to its magnificence, until on the 15th of July, 1823, the very night before the death of Pius VII., it was almost totally destroyed by fire. It was the church of the Pope's dearest love. He had lived there long, as a quiet and studious monk, in the days of his youth, and those who surrounded his dying bed were careful not to tell him that the church was burning. But suddenly, so runs the legend, he looked up and asked: "Why did you not tell me that St. Paul's was on fire? It is burned now; God's will be done!" And so he died.

Then contributions were levied on all the Catholic world for the rebuilding of the great Basilica. It was reopened in its present form by Pope Pius IX., and though it has not the attractions of the ancient church, rich with the accumulated treasures of centuries, it is full of objects of interest. Royal gifts have been made to it by heretic as well as Catholic sovereigns, among which the superb malachite altars, presented by the Emperor Nicholas of Russia, take a first rank. The cloisters of St. Paul, with their wonderfully wrought pillars, are the most exquisite in Rome.

From there we drove to the Protestant Cemetery, — the most touchingly beautiful cemetery, it seems to me, in the whole world. There is, near at hand, the old cemetery, in which no more graves will be made, where Keats lies at rest after his brief life, so full of sorrow. Shelley wrote of this old cemetery, in his preface to "Adonais," that "it might make one in love with death to think that one should be buried in so sweet a place." On the stone which marks the grave of Keats we read the sad inscription : —

"This grave contains all that was mortal of a young English poet, who, on his deathbed, in the bitterness of his heart at the malicious power of his enemies, desired these words to be engraven on his tombstone : 'Here lies one whose name was writ in water.' Feb. 24, 1821."

In the spring of 1882 the remains of Keats's most faithful friend, Joseph Severn, were placed in a grave beside the poet's. They are neighbors now, underground, these two who loved each other so well in life.

If Shelley thought that the beauty of Keats's

burial place should make one in love with death, he should be content indeed with his own tomb in the new cemetery, surrounded with its dark and solemn cypress-trees. It was opened — this "new" burial place — in 1825, and it stretches along the slope of the hill under the old Aurelian wall. It is carpeted with violets, and there I heard the other afternoon the first nightingale of this year. The place was so shadowed with its cypress-trees that he had fancied the day was done; and so he began, even before the sunset, to sing his vespers. Shelley's grave contains his heart only; the rest of him was burned upon the shore of the Mediterranean, where it was thrown landward by the sea. Leigh Hunt wrote his epitaph, with his name and the date of his birth and death, and to this Trelawney added, from Ariel's song, these lines which Shelley had loved:

> "Nothing of him that doth fade,
> But doth suffer a sea change
> Into something rich and strange."

Another noticeable tomb is that of Gibson the sculptor, and there is a monument to the memory of the beloved wife of that other sculptor, Richard S. Greenough, — whose loss, he said, was like that of the "keystone of an arch." This monument is surmounted by Mr. Greenough's beautiful statue of "Psyche divesting Herself of Mortality," — a statue of which Mrs. Greenough had been especially fond. One other tomb impressed me profoundly, — that of a young Russian girl who died at eighteen. Her beautifully sculptured statue is there. The eyes have a look of wonder and interrogation. It is as if she had come out of her grave to survey her silent neighbors, and to question the meaning of this strange stillness. I read on these Roman tombstones names from Boston, names from New York, names from London, and my fancy pieced out names and dates with the life-stories that had ended here. And then I turned once more to the grave of Shelley, and gathered a white rose from the sod above the poet's heart, and went on my way into the living world, and saw the sunset from the cheerful Pincio, where the gay people of Rome were *en promenade.*

Inevitably one spends much of one's time here in churches; and, of course, one always begins with the most marvellous and imposing of them all, St. Peter's. Do you realize by how much this is the largest church in the whole world? I believe that St. Paul's in London is next in size; and St. Paul's is $520\frac{1}{2}$ feet in length, while $613\frac{1}{2}$ feet is the length of St. Peter's. The entire area of St. Peter's is two hundred and forty thousand square feet; and it is said that fifty thousand visitors at a time have often been gathered together in it. When you stand at one end of this vast church, the people at the other end look scarcely larger than walking dolls. St. Peter's tomb is under the high altar; and in the shrine above it a circle — countless, it seems — of lamps is always kept burning.

There are so many separate chapels — each one large enough for a country church — that numerous services could be conducted here at the same time without in the least interfering with each other. No catalogue of its statues and tombs and mosaics could give the least idea of the artistic wealth of this mighty church. One returns to it again and again, finding always some new discovery among its prodigal treasures. Surely, it is not only the largest, but the most magnificent church in the world; yet, despite its splendor, it never seemed to me a church to pray in. Your sentiment there is wonder, profound and ever-increasing wonder, at its vastness, at the riches of its ornamentation, at all the unequalled grandeur of this temple to the "Son of man," who had not "where to lay his head." It is in some smaller, humbler church that one seems to come nigh to the Father of Pity, and is moved to kneel in its dark corners, and cry, out of the depths of human sin and sorrow, to Him who alone can heal and save.

At the side of St. Peter's you enter the Vatican, and it seems to me it must be miles of stairs that you climb before you reach the lofty gallery where hang, so near to heaven, the works of the immortals. One room contains "The Last Communion of St. Jerome," by Domenichino; "The Transfiguration," by Raphael; and "The Madonna di Foligno," also by Raphael. Hare pronounces "The Transfiguration" the "grandest picture in the whole world."

It is audacious, no doubt, to disagree with this verdict, but I own that I am not so impressed by "The Transfiguration." It seems to me not only very far from being the greatest picture in the world, but very, very far from being the greatest work by Raphael. I would rather have the "Sistine Madonna" than a million of "The Transfiguration;" and I would even rather have the "Madonna di Foligno," in this very room. To my mind, "The Last Communion of St. Jerome" is the most impressive of the pictures of the Vatican. But "The Transfiguration" derives a pathetic interest from the fact that it was the last picture that Raphael ever painted. He had not wholly finished it when he died. All the upper part — all the ethereal vision — he had completed; but the lower part of it was still unfinished, and in this state it was hung above his bier when all Rome came to look on him for the last time, and, as one who was present wrote, "every heart seemed like to break with grief." Giulio Romano finished it afterward. It was Giulio Romano's mission to finish things.

But I was talking about churches; and I should say that there are more churches in Rome than in any other city of its size in the world. One of the most interesting is Santa Maria Maggiore. It was founded A. D. 352. The Virgin appeared in a vision to a faithful Roman named John, to say that on the spot where snow should fall on the 15th of August a church must be built in her honor. The 15th of August came, and with it the snow, on this one spot only in all the sun-bathed city. John had previously communicated the vision to Pope Tiberius, and after having seen the snowfall these two laid the foundations of the church. This legend is still commemorated every 15th of August by the feast of the Madonna of the Snows, when, during a solemn High Mass, showers of white rose leaves are constantly let down through openings in the ceiling, till they lie like a soft snowfall between priests and worshippers.

The roof of Santa Maria Maggiore is gilt with virgin gold — the first gold ever brought from America — given to the church by Ferdinand and Isabella. In front of the high altar, but below it, Pope Pius IX. prepared a monument for himself by constructing a splendid chamber, to which you descend by marble staircases, and which is lined with the most precious alabaster and marbles; but, when death approached him, the Pope's wishes changed. His heart turned from all this pre-arranged splendor, and he desired to be buried "with the poor" at San Lorenzo. His wishes were carried out, but a noble statue of him has been placed in this marble chamber, looking toward the high altar.

What a good and blessed man he seems to my memory! I was in Rome, for the first time, two years before his death, and how well I remember the benign serenity of his presence when, with a few friends, I was so fortunate as to be admitted to a private audience. It seemed to me that the very peace of heaven was in the face of the aged Pope as he turned back, when he was leaving the audience chamber, for a last blessing. "Of what use is it," he said, "that I bless those of you who do not believe? But I ask God to bless you, to bless also those who are dear to you and who are afar, and to show to them and to you the true light."

In 1839 an Englishwoman, who before her marriage was Lady Gwendoline Talbot, and who married the Prince Borghese of that time, was buried at Santa Maria Maggiore, with all Rome following her to her grave. The car which bore her body was drawn by forty young Romans, and behind it trooped all the poor of Rome, the procession gathering mass, like a rising flood, in every street it passed through, while flowers were showered on it from the overhanging windows. An old usage connected with the funeral ceremony of great personages at Rome was observed in the obsequies of this beloved Princess Borghese. When the body is lowered into the grave a chamberlain comes out to the church door and tells the coachman, who is waiting there with the family carriage, that his master or mistress has no longer any need of his services, and the coachman thereupon breaks his staff of office and drives solemnly away. When this announcement was made at the funeral of the princess, the whole of the vast crowd outside broke into tears and sobs, and kneeling, as by one common impulse, they prayed aloud for the soul of their benefactress. There has been a strange story told of late concerning the reappearance of the princess, — coming back as the saints are wont to do, in vision, — and the people listen to it eagerly, for they already regard her as one of the saints.

By the way, faith in the supernatural is not dead in Italy, whatever rationalism may have effected toward its extinction elsewhere. Still pious pilgrims go, on their knees, up and down the holy stair (supposed to have been the stair in the house of Pilate) which no foot must touch, and an Englishman who resides here in Rome told me that he had just returned from a pilgrimage to a far-away little church at Genazzano, where is a wonder-working Madonna, and all the pilgrims, he said, came into the church and went up from the door to the altar upon their knees. It sounds difficult; but he assured me that they seemed to find it easy enough. This Madonna at Genazzano heals the pilgrims who seek her of all sorts of ills. She lived in a church some otherwhere at first, — at Scutari, I think it was, — but the people in that neighborhood did not please her: I believe they were too wicked; so, frame and all, she quietly went out of the church door, as a winged bird might, and on through the air for many a mile, until she found a home with which she was content, in the church at Genazzano.

You think this wonderful, perhaps, but it is nothing at all to the transit of the Holy House at Loreto. The Holy House is the chamber of stone where Mary Virgin sat when the angel announced to her that she should be the mother of our Lord. I don't know just how long ago it was that this Holy House came, all by itself, and quite without mortal aid, across land and sea, to settle in Italy. It went somewhere else first, — I think it was to Dalmatia, — but it presently moved on and established itself at Loreto. Dean Stanley wrote a book to prove that this transit of the Holy House never took place; but he was answered by a Catholic writer, who gave the strongest possible proofs of the genuineness of the wonderful miracle. The stone of the Holy House is the stone of Syria, and is not known in Italy, and the chamber is so built that it would precisely fit on to the house in Syria from which it is believed to have taken flight.

To look at the votive offerings by which the Madonna in the Church of St. Agostino is surrounded is to have a fresh evidence of the triumph of faith. The legend of this Madonna is that long, long ago a poor woman knelt at its sacred feet and prayed for help, and suddenly the Madonna answered, "If I only had something, I could help thee; but I myself am so poor!" This story was told far and wide, and then throngs of believers came to dower the Madonna with their treasures. She shines now with diamonds and pearls and all sorts of precious stones. Princes give her their jewels, and humble peasants lay their silver hearts and strings of beads at her feet. Even bandits, I am told, have striven to consecrate their evil gains by paying tribute at this holy shrine; but it is not for such as they that the Madonna will open her long-silent lips.

Last Sunday we went to hear the nuns sing vespers at the Trinità de' Monti, at the top of the Spanish Steps. It was an hour not to be forgotten, — that in which one sat in the dim church, with the countless lights burning on the high altar, and heard these sweet, fresh voices soar to heaven. Wonderful is the power of the Roman Catholic Church over the imagination. Breathing the incense with which the air was heavy, listening to the entrancing music, I could almost fancy that heaven's gates were open, and that angels came and went upon the incense-burdened air, listening also. "Glory! Glory! Glory!" how the sweet strains soared upward! Surely they found their goal!

SOME ROMAN VILLAS.

ONE of the chief pleasures Rome offers to a pilgrim is the lavish hospitality of its villas. But for this, indeed, one's drives would be confined to the stony, clamorous streets, or the Appian Way with its tombs and its memories. As it is, there is no day in the week in which you may not go to some lovely villa, blithe with blossoms and bird-songs, rich in treasures of art and of nature.

Every day, an' it please you, you may seek the Pincian Hill. The view of Rome is outspread at your feet, and beyond stretches the far-reaching Campagna. The grounds of the Pincio are small as compared with those of the Villa Borghese below it; but they are most skilfully laid out. The flowers of all climates spring from the soft, thick grass; the busts of poets and philosophers and statesmen look out from among the trees; fountains murmur here and there; and always you can see picturesque groups of young priests, some in purple, some in scarlet, and some in black. Here, on Sunday and Thursday afternoons, comes Italy's fair Queen, with all fashionable Rome in her train, to see the sunset kindle the spires of the great city at their feet, and to hear the music of the military band.

In old imperial times the present site of the Pincio Garden was occupied by the Villa of Lucullus, who used to give here his celebrated feasts, merely saying, by way of command, to the slave who was his major-domo, that he should sup that night in the Hall of Apollo. Ah, they have supped since then for many a century in the Hall of Pluto, both host and guests!

A terraced road leads from the Garden of the Pincio to the Villa Medici, and from the Garden Terrace of the Medici you look down on the Villa Borghese, which you can enter by a gate just outside the Porto del Popolo. Hawthorne devoted to this villa some of the most fascinating chapters in " The Marble Faun." There Donatello wanders amid such scenery "as arrays itself in the imagination when we read the beautiful old myths, and fancy a brighter sky, a softer turf, a more picturesque arrangement of venerable trees than we find in the rude and untrained landscapes of the Western world."

Here indeed are still the "venerable" ilex-trees, here are avenues of cypress, and here the stone-pines lift up from their slender trunks their umbrella-shaped tops, so remotely high that they seem almost "like green islands in the air." Cascades tumble from rock to rock; shy flowers crop up among the grass.

The Casino, at the farther end of the villa, contains a collection of sculpture which is opened to the public on Saturday afternoons. Quite the most amazing thing here is the statue of the Princess Pauline Borghese (sister to the Great Napoleon), taken as "Venus Victrix." She conquers still, this Venus, the attention of all beholders. Canova himself considered this statue one of his best works; but this is not the Venus of the poets, or of Olympus. She is perky and pretty and French; and she is naked, or nearly so, and not ashamed. "How disagreeable it must have been to pose like this!" a friend once said to Princess Pauline. "Oh, not at all," she answered, "the room was very well warmed."

But when once the statue was completed, the modesty of Prince Borghese took alarm, and not even Canova was ever allowed to look at it again. As long as the prince lived, it was zealously locked from sight, in a room to which he alone possessed the key.

Another villa where one finds important works of art is the Ludovisi, where there is a collection of sculpture of great interest. Here is the superb head of Juno, known as the "Ludovisi Juno," which I think one may safely pronounce the most noble single head in the whole world. Goethe was so enchanted with this colossal head that he had the best possible copy made of it, and he used to say that he said his prayers to it every night and morning.

The statue of Mars, with Cupid at his feet, and

the beautiful group of "Arria and Paetus" are also among the gems of this collection. In a casino at the end of the garden are Guercino's famous frescos; but Guercino's "Aurora" is far inferior to that of Guido Reni in the Rospigliosi.

The grounds of the Ludovisi are solemn with great groves of sacred ilex-trees; and in one shadow-haunted nook is a deserted fountain, over which a broken-armed nymph patiently watches. Immemorial silence seems to have fallen on the Ludovisi. It is not suited to be the meeting-place of a gay throng, such as you encounter in the Borghese, or on the Pincian Hill. Stately ghosts from a stately past walk under these trees. Why should I fear them? Would they not welcome to their ranks a fellow-worshipper of the Silence and the Calm?

Not far away from the Ludovisi is the Villa Albani, built by Cardinal Alessandro Albani, but at present the property of Prince Torlonia. This villa contains an interesting collection of pictures; but it is still more rich in its statuary. Here is the "Apollo Sauroctonos," which Winckelmann believes to be the veritable statue by Praxiteles of which Pliny wrote, and which many critics have pronounced the masterpiece among the bronze statues of the world. But for me the gem of the whole collection is the relievo of Antinous, crowned with lotus, — the beautiful, proud, melancholy face, with the sad eyes, that look into the eyes of Fate, forewarned but unafraid.

I am half inclined to think that the wildest, sweetest, loveliest of the lovely villas of Rome is the Villa Pamphile Doria. It crowns the summit of the Janiculum Hill, where once, they say, was the villa of Galba. Peacocks spread their tails proudly as they marched on the terrace. Swans were at home in the placid lake, and flowers were springing everywhere. We picked orchids from among the wild grasses. The roses lavished their fragrance as, according to Tom Moore, they did in Persia, — though travellers tell us now that far the larger part of Persia is given over to barren sands.

From the gate three separate roads lead through dense ilex groves. Narrow paths penetrate depths of solitude, and now and then you climb some hill whence you see a prospect of far-stretching campagna or distant mountains. From the terraces above the house itself, you have an unrivalled view of Rome with the great stately dome of St. Peter's, of Mount Soracte, of the Sabine Hills, and, farther on, of Albano and Frascati. Two afternoons in a week these grounds are thrown open to carriages, and you may drive or walk through them, and enjoy them almost as if they were your own, — not quite, for what could fully match the pleasure of daily intimacy with such a place, of knowing by heart its deepest depths, of living among its wood-nymphs, and listening to the secretest murmurs of its fountains?

A very different place is the Villa Wolkonsky, which seems to me the sunniest, brightest, gayest spot in all Rome. To be sure, the broken arches of the Aqua Claudia intersect it, and summon up memories of a mighty past; and here and there are hoary cypress-trees, which might have been standing when Great Cæsar fell, they look so old; and here are crumbling urns, and pathetic fragments of broken gods whom no man worships more, and here in one corner is "The Path of Tombs;" and yet, despite all that is solemn and memory-haunted, I still must claim for Villa Wolkonsky that when the sun of an April morning shines on it, it is the gayest spot in Rome. I should like to know how many millions of roses I saw running riot there on one such morning. They made hedges along the walks, they climbed the solemn old trees and thrust their bright heads out of the gray gloom, they swung in festoons from tree to tree, they sprang up everywhere. They were of every kind and degree, — moss roses, jacqueminots, Queen This, and Duchesse That; I should need a florist's catalogue to give you half their stately names. All night long the nightingales had been singing to them, and had not yet finished the song, though it was ten of the clock and the sun was high. It was the very concert-room of the birds, as it was the chosen parade-ground of the flowers. There were great beds of lovely Irises and lilies, and from the lush grass sprang Roman violets, and over them all fluttered wavering white butterflies, as if Psyche and all her following were breathing the morning air.

Purple figs hung from the fig-trees, and dates were ripe on the palms, and oranges and lemons were ready for gathering. And yet this Enchanted Garden was so near the outside world that from some points you could hear the chatter of passers-by in the streets below, or the martial music from an open square in front of some near barracks.

It was strange to find among all this brightness, this glowing life, what I have called "The Path of Tombs." At the entrance of it was an inscription setting forth that it was dedicated by the Princess Wolkonsky to "Filial Piety, Gratitude, and Friendship." The inscription on the father's tombstone seemed to me one of the noblest tributes ever paid to the dead. "I have seen" — so the faithful daughter recorded — "I have seen under his roof the unhappy comforted; artists, poets, and philosophers fêted and favored; strangers received as brothers; servants protected and happy. His words were eloquent, his acts pure and generous. Happy the family who called him father!"

There was a tablet to an old nurse; to a Governess, "from her grateful pupils"; to a Patriot. One touching inscription was on the tomb of a young girl: "She tried the loves of the Earth, but they were not pure enough for an angel."

These inscriptions I have quoted — these and various others — were to persons connected with the Wolkonsky family; but there were tablets, also, in memory of various authors and artists, — among them Sir Walter Scott, Goethe, and Byron.

In a corner by itself was a little stone inscribed, "To Topsy," suggesting that Princess Wolkonsky was familiar with "Uncle Tom's Cabin," and had chosen from it a name for some favorite cat or dog.

As we turned away from The Path of Tombs, a white horse came up and looked at us over a paling; he might have been the White Horse of Death, only he looked so gallant and so gay that I preferred to fancy him a steed from fairy-land: for indeed fairy-land seemed all about us, and an enchanted steed was but native to this place, with its blithe birds singing their unknown songs, its rose-gardens, its statues of old, forsaken gods, its soft turf starred with daisies and king-cups and violets.

Ah, how one's homesick heart pines, sometimes, for Rome, — for the City of the Seven Hills, which enshrines all the glory of Ancient Art, all the associations of Ancient History, the passion and pathos of the immemorial years, and yet is glad with the fresh beauty of every newborn spring that entwines the ruins of the Long Ago with the roses of To-Day; that is at once as sad as Destiny and as blithe as Hope.

1890.

FLORENCE THE FAIR.

FLORENCE THE FAIR.

HOW is one ever to get the strength of mind deliberately to go away from Florence? The past ten days have been full of interest, and I can see things enough that I want to do, places enough that I want to visit, to keep me here indefinitely. Out of town I have been to Certosa and to "sober, pleasant Fiesole," as Browning calls it; and speaking of Browning reminds me that I passed all this happy morning in the Pitti Palace: and I looked long at the portraits of Andrea del Sarto painted by himself. In one of them he was young, daring, brilliant, hopeful, — all that he was before he knew Lucrezia, at the time when Michael Angelo said to Raphael, "There is a little man in Florence who, if he were employed on such great works as you are, would bring the sweat into your brow." One believed this, looking at the young, bright, hopeful portrait; and then one went into another room, and there hung that later portrait, of Andrea and Lucrezia together; and in that the glory and the vision seemed gone from Andrea's face. He looked — oh, how very wrong it seems to say it of a dead great man, but he did look — henpecked.

Was Lucrezia beautiful? Yes, I think so; but not beautiful enough to account for the thraldom in which she held her lord. I am a dear lover of Andrea at his best; and, as Swinburne has said in his " Essays and Studies," only at Florence can one tell how great and how various a painter Andrea really was. I caught a glimpse to-day from the opposite side of the room of his picture called " A Dispute about the Trinity;" and before I was near enough to see the name, or those details by which I should have known its authorship, I was so profoundly impressed by the nobility of the conception, the stately grace of the figures, the sober richness of the coloring, that I said to my companion, " Could there possibly be a better illustration than that picture gives us of the qualities in which ancient art differs from and excels that of our own time?" "Paint what you see" is the art motto of to-day; but there be those who choose to see barmaids, and there be those who prefer to see saints in conclave.

What an exhaustless pleasure are the Pitti and the Uffizi galleries ! To-day my thoughts are with the Pitti, from whence I have just returned. I think I should like to make a bonfire of all its Carlo Dolcis, and then how happy could I be with what was left! The loveliest examples of Perugino are there. There are glorious Titians: the "Bella Donna," of whom I fear Titian was a good deal too fond; the "Holy Family, including St. Catherine;" some of his superb portraits;

his beautiful, unrepentant "Magdalen," who certainly had not fasted, however she may have prayed. Was Titian the greatest of portrait painters? One might think so, certainly, if one had not seen the work of Velasquez in Madrid; and if one had not seen the portraits by Raphael in this same Pitti Palace, — the "Pope Julian," the "Leo X.," the "Angelo Doni and his wife." Raphael's "Madonna della Seggiola" is here; and the beautiful "Holy Family" he painted for that handsome, art-loving young Florentine, Bindo Altoviti. Oh, how alive they all were, — and they have been dead so long! It makes one shudder and turn cold to think of it.

"The Three Fates" is the most interesting picture by Michael Angelo that I know, though at least half the critics say he did not paint it. There are so many noble and beautiful pictures in the Pitti that if I spoke of them all I should want a whole book for the purpose. Are there still more in the Uffizi? I almost think so. To climb to the Uffizi is like climbing to the picture gallery of the Vatican; but, Heaven be thanked, there is now a lift, — but such a lift! The man who sends it up takes your franc, and then looks at you to see how much ballast you require to make you mount at precisely the right pace, to precisely the right height; then he puts in blocks of iron accordingly. I think he miscalculated my weight and put in too much iron, for the thing moved upward so slowly that I had time for all sorts of forebodings. I recalled Howells's farce of "The Elevator." It amused me very much when I read it, but it did not amuse me at all to remember it when I was on my upward way at the Uffizi.

It was no joke to fancy myself hanging between heaven and earth, for who knew how long. The lift moved more and more slowly the higher it climbed. What if the cord should break, and I should make a wild plunge to the far-off earth? What if the thing should stop short, in mid-career, and I could never reach my destination? It really was a wretched business, but I got to the top at last, and had my reward.

I had been to the Uffizi often and often, in other visits to Florence, but somehow it seemed to me that I had never quite seen it till now.

I want to come to Italy and live. What is the use, since life is short, of passing it in a country where there are no stately palaces, no picture galleries worth mentioning, no marble gods, no history going back for almost immemorial years? If ever I am again in Florence, I mean to come as near to making my home in the picture galleries as the governmental regulations will permit. What banal creatures the men and women of to-day seem in contrast to the stately figures on these walls, and the long-dead masters who painted them!

One goes first to the Tribune, where are collected the masterpieces of the masters. You have an opportunity here to adore the "Venus de'

Medici," — an opportunity of which, perhaps, I do not avail myself so "much as is reason." I do not like the way she holds her arms and her hands. It seems to me unnatural and artificial. I must tell the truth, — I, who am a countrywoman of George Washington, — and, wrong though it may be, I do love better the "Venus of the Capitol" at Rome. Yet she, too, is very lovely, this Florentine in marble, and of a truly ethereal grace. Behind her is Titian's painted "Venus," — and what a contrast! The "Venus de' Medici" needs no clothing for her white symmetry, — she is clothed upon in purity; but one feels like starting a subscription to buy some royal robes for the "Venus" of Titian. They must really be royal, though, for she is a regal creature. Yet one can well imagine her a queen of the demi-monde, and leading the dance at the Jardin Mabille. Her proportions are superb, she is drawn perfectly, and her flesh-tints are a dream of beauty. All the same, she is of this lower world, and could have no passport into Olympus.

Five works in sculpture have been chosen for this select collection of masterpieces, — the Tribune of the Uffizi. Besides the "Venus," there are the "Wrestlers," "The Slave whetting His Knife," the "Young Apollo," and "The Dancing Faun." But it is its pictures which are the glory of the Tribune. There is an Andrea Mantegna here which alone would rank Mantegna among the immortals. There is a lovely "Holy Family," by Orazio Alfani, so beautiful that it makes me wonder why one so seldom hears his name mentioned. Titian, Vandyke, Correggio, Andrea del Sarto, Perugino, Lucas Van Leyden, and many another; and all are represented at their point of highest achievement. If, as I think, you must visit the "Sistine Madonna," at Dresden, to see Raphael at his very best, yet his Madonnas here in the Tribune are of a loveliness that leaves nothing to be desired; and the "Fornarina" of the Tribune is the only picture of the baker's handsome wife that offers the slightest excuse for Raphael's infatuation about her.

I do not recall any picture in the Tribune by Sandro Botticelli, who certainly much better deserves to be represented there than does Guido Reni, who has a place of honor. But in a neighboring room devoted to the Tuscan school there are some Botticellis of a grace and beauty truly divine. Among them the "Madonna of the Magnificat" lingers in my memory as a work fit to hang in some picture gallery of the New Jerusalem. But I will not give you a catalogue. Let me rather stir in you a fine discontent which shall send you hither for yourselves. I must, however, say just one word more apropos of Titian's superb "Magdalen" in the Uffizi. She is a beautiful impenitent, with glorious hair that makes you think of Browning's

"Dear dead women, with such hair, too —
What's become of all the gold
Used to hang and brush their bosoms —
I feel chilly, and grown old."

Why, I wonder, does no one ever paint the Magdalen as a penitent? Had she been truly sorry for her sins, would she not have veiled those seductive contours so lavishly exposed? Would she not have cut off that glorious hair, or at least have twisted it up tidily?

How different is the spirit of Fra Angelico's art from that of Titian! I went the other day to the convent of San Marco, where, perhaps, one sees the angelical painter at his very best, lovely as are his pictures in the Uffizi. No black-and-white monks guard now the entrance to San Marco. It is the property of the government; and chapter house, refectory, and library, all are open to visitors. This was the convent both of Fra Angelico and of Savonarola, — could any one enter its doors without a thrill at his heart? It was here that Savonarola preached to vast crowds of eager listeners; it was here, at last, that Florence, gone mad, besieged him, athirst for his life. Here is his cell, and here are preserved his hair shirt, his rosary, his chair, and a fragment from the pile on which his body was burnt, after he had been put to death by hanging. His portrait is also here, painted by Fra Bartolommeo, who was his ardent disciple.

How divine is the beauty of the work of Fra Angelico in this convent I should vainly try to tell you. His pictures were born of the very atmosphere of heaven, and they brought to the painter no earthly honors or rewards. He always began his work with an appeal to God, solemnly kneeling. Vasari tells us that, when he was painting a crucifix, he was so penetrated by the thought of the divine suffering that the tears ran down his cheeks. He painted his heavenly visions on the walls of his own convent; what celestial witnesses assisted at his holy task who shall say? Pope Eugenius proposed to him to become a bishop and accept the see of Florence. But the angelical painter had no longing for a loftier station, no desire to govern monks and men. Painter and monk he was; painter and monk he preferred to remain. He did not refuse, however, to go to Rome to paint there some sacred subjects; and it was in Rome that he died, at the age of sixty-eight, having retained all his powers, with no apparent failure, unto the very end.

Speaking of the age at which Fra Angelico died reminds me that I was looking yesterday over some of the lives of the painters to see how many of them lived on to old age. Titian lived longest of them all. One year more, and he would have been one hundred. It really seemed a pity that he should have been cut off at ninety-nine. He had not been a saint or an ascetic, and his longevity was certainly not the reward of self-denial. Michael Angelo's stormy, strenuous, active life held out until eighty-nine, but Titian got the better of him by ten years. Andrea Mantegna lived to be seventy-five, which seems rather an early death when one thinks of Titian. Paul Veronese died at sixty and Sandro Botticelli at fifty-three; Andrea del Sarto — was it the fault of Lucrezia? — made an end of it at forty-four. Correggio died at forty, and Raphael at only thirty-seven. It was something to have won, in thirty-seven years, an earthly immortality; and Raphael's work, however it may go out of fashion, is not likely to be ignored or forgotten while "Pope Julius" hangs on the walls of the Pitti Palace and the "Sistine Madonna" abides at Dresden.

There are noble pictures also at the Academia and at the Corsini and at various other places besides; but I must not linger with them. I cannot leave the works of Luca della Robbia at the Bargello without a word. Luca was apprenticed to a goldsmith in his youth, and thus he learned the secret of delicate and careful work; but as soon as he had acquired a mastery of the goldsmith's craft he gave it up, and turned his attention to sculpture. Not even there did he find himself entirely at home. He wanted a medium of his own, and he discovered it, and began, while yet under twenty, to make the lovely groups in porcelain — the white visions of beauty — that will forever be associated with his name. They look softer and sweeter than marble can, — these round-limbed cherubs, these gentle angels, these sympathetic Madonnas. Hung in some sombre nook, they seem to brighten it with a sweet radiance all their own.

I never return to Florence without driving to Certosa to see how many of the white-robed monks are still to be found there. When the Italian government suppressed the convents, they allowed the Carthusian monks at Certosa to remain in their monastery, though they were prohibited from receiving any new-comers. Who will live in the place, I wonder, when the last of these dear old monks has joined his silent brethren? There is something that always touches me profoundly in this home of graves. What a sad, colorless life that of the monks here seems to the onlookers. They are never allowed to talk to each other. They eat at the same table only on Sunday; but even then they do not chat together like happier mortals. A religious lesson — a sort of sermon — is read to them while they eat. On all other days than Sunday each one takes his slight repast in his own little cell. They eat no meat. They are not even allowed eggs, except when seriously ill. They are locked into their cells during the forty days of Lent, and not permitted to walk, as they may at other times, in the lonely, sunlit garden. One would do a good deal to save one's soul, but to lead one to be a monk at Certosa, faith and fear must alike be strong. Yet they make things there that the gay world loves, — delicious scents, choice soaps, and the red, green, and yellow Chartreuse, best beloved and most beguiling of cordials.

I never cross the old Ponte Vecchio, or Jeweller's Bridge, in Florence, without thinking of Longfellow's noble sonnet, and quoting to myself : —

"Taddeo Gaddi built me, — I am old."

Nor could I ever approach the superb equestrian statue of the Grand Duke Ferdinand without thinking of Browning's "The Statue and the Bust." "The passionate pale lady's face," wrought by Luca della Robbia, no longer "watches it from the square,"

> "leaning out of a bright blue space
> As a ghost might lean from a chink of sky."

But still the statue is all that the grand duke dreamed when he cried:—

> "John of Douay shall work my plan,—
> Mould me on horseback here aloft,
> Alive, as the crafty sculptor can,
> In the very square I have crossed so oft;
> That men may admire when future suns
> Shall touch the eyes to a purpose soft,
> While the mouth and the brow stay brave in bronze—
> Admire and say, 'When he was alive,
> How he would take his pleasure once!'
> And it shall go hard but I contrive
> To listen the while, and laugh in my tomb
> At indolence which aspires to strive."

I have no space to write of half the scenes that poets and painters have touched with ideal light. How can one ever be content elsewhere who has once breathed the air of this happy land? I do not wonder that our artists who come to Italy — like Story and Greenough and Vedder — for a brief sojourn, linger on, year after year, until a quarter or a half-century has gone by; and before they know it, they are too old ever to make a home elsewhere. There is plenty of gayety and fashion here, too. Drive in the Cascine of Florence, especially on a Sunday afternoon, and you will see as varied and brilliant a display as you are likely to find anywhere, It differs from Hyde Park in its democracy. The convenient little one-horse victorias of the street are admitted here just as freely as the stateliest equipages of prince or marquis; while in London, if you would join the fashionable throng, you must at least get from a stable a turn-out that plays as being a private one. But not even in London will you see finer horses, or handsomer carriages, or more imposing liveries than in Florence. And I should not know where to look for prettier girls than some I have seen here.

The costumes that are worn here are much gayer than in Paris or London; or perhaps it is that the costumes of this present year are gayer than those of the past, and I am first introduced to them here. How odd are these crownless bonnets, which are only a wreath of flowers around the soft hair, or a tiara of jet, or perchance a feather! And how startling are these frocks of vivid red! It is not scarlet, and it is not crimson; it seems redder than either, and might have been dyed in melted rubies. Florence is the city of flowers, as all the world knows, and the heaps of flowers one sees in the Cascine are a striking feature of the show. A bouquet is the tribute a cavalier pays to a lady, and they are often as numerous as the bouquets ♠

New York girl receives at her coming-out party. As a pretty girl drives along you will see actual mounds of bouquets piled in the back of her carriage. To be sure it is a cheap attention. For ten cents I have purchased on Thursday — the day of the flower market — fifty-four superb roses. The flower girls are as numerous here as the beggars are in Rome, and for half a lira you can get your two hands full of roses or carnations at any street corner. I end as I began, — how is one to go away from this city of the loveliest art and the loveliest nature, this beautiful, fascinating Firenza ! And yet I must pack my pilgrim's scrip and be off to-morrow.

FROM FLORENCE TO PARIS.

I HAVE been told that we pass through sixty-nine tunnels in the not quite three hours' railway journey between Florence and Bologna. I meant to count them, but they got the better of either my energy or my arithmetic, and I gave up the task somewhere in the thirties. At any rate, I believe it is true that in no railway journey of the same length do you go under ground anything like so many times. You are either in purgatory or in paradise. One moment the darkness of the Inferno; the next moment a veritable glimpse of Heaven, with the soft purple lights upon the hills, the serene blue sky, the deep ravines through which gay little streams rush singing, the near hills sombre with their wealth of green foliage — you just begin to think how entrancingly lovely it is, and the next tunnel shuts it from your sight.

I had taken the three o'clock train from Florence to Milan, and all the way I had my railway carriage to myself. I liked this isolation very much at first, but after a while I began to want some one to share my pleasure ; and I thought of the Frenchman who said, "Ah, yes, I always like solitude, if only there is some one with me to whom I can say how pleasant solitude is!". I think solitude à deux is quite the most perfect kind of solitude; only "the other one" must be the right one, and not the wrong.

After Bologna the scene changed. Heights and tunnels were alike less frequent, and while the daylight lasted I was glad to take refuge from loneliness in a book. It was one of Jules Case's novels, "Bonnet-Rouge," with which I beguiled my way as the *rapide* bore me on toward Milan. It is a strong and clever book, certainly; but I wonder, are such men as Olivier, the hero, often to be found in France; and, if so, I wonder whether they are native to that country only! He reminds me, in some regards, of Guy de Maupassant's "Bel-Ami." There is nothing of similarity in the two stories, but the men have something the same traits. "Bel-Ami" is the more masterful, and the more successful, but I fancy Olivier would have liked to be Bel-Ami, if he could.

I was fortunate in my day at Milan, for it chanced to be Ascension Day. My hotel — the Europa — was but a few rods from the Cathedral. I went to one of the Masses in the morning and heard the divine music. I had never realized before how beautiful the Cathedral is. I had imagined that I liked better the Duomo at Florence, but I found that I was mistaken.

The Milan Cathedral attracts me incomparably more than that of Florence. I cannot tell you how glorious it was on this day of days. The sun shone remorselessly out-of-doors, as if it would set the world on fire, but the Cathedral was cool and dark. Through its stained-glass windows the softened light fell, resting upon the great crucifix like a crown of gold, touching with azure the robe of the Madonna, resting in purple gloom on some of the sculptured saints. The archbishop who officiated was clothed in splendor; assisting priests were gorgeous and numerous; the music, ah, how lovely it was! how it soared like the cry of a tortured heart toward heaven, and then how it sobbed its penitence and its despair, until there came an answering note of pardon and of hope, and then arose the glad, free, exultant cry of faith and of triumph.

The audience? Oh, what an audience it was! Noble ladies were there whose footmen brought their sumptuous Prayer Books. Men with swords at their sides came to worship in the temple of the Prince of Peace; and besides, and mingled with these, were the crowd of shopkeepers, workingmen in blouses, women-servants in caps and aprons, and peasants gay in their holiday finery, with strings of beads, and silver armlets, and all sorts of fantastic ornaments. And one and all knelt together to pray, and rose together to praise; and the incense was heavy on the air, and the music soared and sobbed and died, until one's very heart seemed borne upon it toward a presence mysterious and unknowable. The tension was so keen that I was almost glad to get out into the open day, when the bells began to ring for noon.

I drove in a little Milan cab to the Church of St. Ambrozio, and then to the Brera gallery, where my visit was all too brief. It is open only from noon till three P. M., on Sundays and feast days, and I looked at it only long enough to perceive that it was full of treasures, and that I wanted to look much longer. Then I sped away to Biffi's, the best-known restaurant of Milan, where I had promised to meet a friend for luncheon. You have a little table out of doors at Biffi's, and you lunch both well and reasonably. The waiters are complaisant, and you can linger on as long as you please, and see the gay Milanese go by. They are the handsomest Italians that I know, — these men and women of Milan. I suppose people toil there, and weep and starve, perhaps, and die at last, like the rest of us; but to the transient observer it seems as if they were keeping perpetual holiday. And the gay clamor of their life goes on all night long; at least, I heard it under my window till long after midnight, and then went to sleep in the midst of it, and at five o'clock in the morning the church bells were pealing like mad, and there was no more sleep for anybody.

Talking of church bells, I went twice more in that one day to the Cathedral, — once between services, when no one was there but a stray traveller or two; and then later, to hear the divine music of the vesper services. It seemed to me I could never have enough of it. One dines well and pleasantly at the Hotel Europa, where I stayed; and as for me, though there were theatres and concerts and operas and all sorts of gay temptations outside, I resisted them all, in memory of the "early to bed and early to rise" lessons of my childhood, — for at least the early rising would be a matter of necessity. An evening in Milan, in the early summer, is delightful. You can get your little street carriage for a few pence, and drive to and fro. You can stop in front of a fashionable confectioner's, and have the daintiest ices and the coolest drinks, without once leaving your cab; and there is always something to see in this city so full of life and of movement.

I was off on the morning train for Basle, by the St. Gothard route. I believe it is the most fascinating day's journey by rail that one can take in the wide, wide world. The friends I had travelled with in Italy chose to make this transit by night, to their infinite loss, as it seemed to me; but I shared my railway carriage with a young Frenchman and his newly wedded bride. I think I have never seen two people so much in love or so happy. Their joy overflowed on everything and everybody. It was like the affluent May sunshine. They had sous and smiles to spare for the beggars along the route. They had such superabundant happiness that they shed some of it even on me, and my day was gay with it. Their delight in the glorious scenery through which we passed was a divine rapture; for the magnifying glasses through which Love looks see double. But, indeed, no such glasses were needed to enhance the charm of that journey. Words are wasted in trying to describe it. It mocks at one's poor attempts. What can you say that has not been said of other places? Snow-crowned summits, that seem to pierce the blue sky; wild, deep gorges; the lovely lakes of lovely Italy along the first part of the way, and later on those of Switzerland. All that reads tamely enough; but there was a breathless excitement in catching one new revelation of beauty after another; in discovering in how glorious and wonderful a world we creatures of a day are allowed to disport ourselves. I could no more see such a world and believe it the result of chance, and not the purposeful creation of an All-wise God, than I could see the noblest pictures of Titian or Velasquez, and imagine that the pigments had chanced thus to arrange themselves on the canvas, and that there was no creating hand and brain of the artist behind them.

Two or three hours before we reached Basle, my two French lovers left the train. We parted with mutual good wishes. They stopped to enjoy their dual solitude in the quiet of a little Swiss town on the Lake of Lucerne. " Love is enough," wrote

William Morris. These two were in the stage when that sentence is the heart's gospel. They were glad, I fancy, to get to their honeymoon retreat and shut out the world; but the day seemed colder after their smiles had ceased to warm it. Do newly married American or English lovers feel just the same enthusiasm of joy as did these French lovers? It may be so; but I think they never show it in quite the same frank way. Despite such men as Guy de Maupassant depicts in "Bel-Ami" or Jules Case in "Bonnet-Rouge," there is certainly a Frenchman of another type, who loves frankly and entirely, — perhaps it were not too much to say dotingly, — and the families of the French *bourgeoisie* are, more often than not, the most domestic and the happiest I know of anywhere.

The sun had just set when the train reached Basle. All the mountain tops were pink with the afterglow. There was a faint young moon half-way up the sky, and one or two stars were looking out shyly, as if to see when it would be their cue to appear on the scene. What a cordiality of welcome awaits one in Switzerland! Who was it said that the modern Greeks encouraged bandits, because they did not want the traveller to carry anything away with him out of the country, but that the Swiss "went the Greeks one better," and found that hotel-keepers answered the same purpose more effectually? Whoever said it, it is slander. It seems to me there is no place where you get more comfort and more cleanliness for your money than at the majority of Swiss hotels. I simply crossed the street from the station, and found myself at home in the Hotel Victoria; and when I left in the eight-thirty train, next morning, for Paris, the porter walked across with me, and got my luggage registered, and saw to all my small needs as sedulously as if he had been my own courier.

The journey from Basle to Paris is, on the whole, commonplace and uninteresting. I was glad to divert myself with a book. The ten hours of travel seemed interminably long; and so did the waiting at the customs, before the men in authority found time to ask me whether I was wickedly smuggling into Paris any spirits or tobacco, — the chief things about which they concern themselves. But at last it was over. A porter, not much bigger than Tom Thumb, took my great trunk, in some marvellous way, upon his little head, and got it on top of a four-wheeled cab, and then wanted ten cents extra "because the trunk was so big." I gave it to him with a silent thanksgiving that his little back had not broken under the burden. The driver cracked his whip, and we were off. I think Paris is the noisiest place on earth. The drivers are by no means cruel to their horses; this cracking of the whips in the air seems to be a harmless diversion, and the horses, perhaps, would resent its omission. Any way, crack, crack, we whirled on through the familiar streets, and here I am at rest in the heart of Paris, on the Avenue de l'Opera, within three or four rods of the grand boulevards, in the midst of the shops, theatres, cafés, — all that makes the Paris in which the traveller delights.

PARIS AND PICTURES.

PARIS AND PICTURES.

I HAVE a confession to make,—I have been falling in love with Paris. In the depths of my heart I well know that I prefer London; but Paris in May,—ah, well, one must be a stoic indeed to resist its charm! It is no wonder that the true Parisian always feels that to be compelled to live elsewhere is to be exiled from paradise. Paris is a sincere enough city, I believe, to its own children. The native can live here delightfully, at small cost; but it is another thing for the foreigner, for whom its delights are expensive.

The shops beguile you with promises in their windows of English spoken and of Spanish spoken; but as regards the smaller shops the English-speaking person has an unfortunate habit of being gone to breakfast, or if he be, by some happy accident, *en evidence*, his English is usually that of the phrase-book, and equal only to inquiring if you have the glove of your brother.

"You my flowers buy?" said to me the dirtiest little *gamin* on the Rue de Rivoli, stretching up a grimy little hand holding some violets and a bunch of mignonette. He had learned his two or three words of English painfully, but he had a touching faith in them; for when I shook my head at him, he said, "You me give a penny,— poor leetle Eenglish boy!" He amused me, and I confess with shame that I rewarded his barefaced attempt to pass himself off as a compatriot with the sous it pleased him to call pennies.

It is odd how little English is known in Paris. Well-educated Russians speak English as a rule; Germans, Swedes, and Norwegians speak English; but Frenchmen seem to cultivate a profound indifference to the language of the dear little island across the Channel. When I passed a winter in Paris, I was offered by a London poet — who was himself half a Frenchman in his knowledge of and love for French life and language and literature — letters to a large group of the French poets and novelists of the day.

"But," said my friend, "only one of them speaks English; somehow they never seem to think it worth their while to learn. Monsieur M., you will find, speaks very well. In fact, he is professor of English in a French college."

Monsieur M. was a great comfort and pleasure to me that winter, and his English was such, at least, as I could readily understand; but he always made three syllables of "themselves,"— "them-sel-ves," he called it,— and he used to say "lov-ed" and "wish-ed." He talked of things as "unuseful" instead of "useless," and he usually put his objects before his verbs instead of after them. And *he* spoke better English than I have heard from any other Frenchman above the rank of a valet or a courier.

The very streets of Paris are full of interest, — the interest of a life as unlike as possible to that of America or England. In England you meet a funeral *cortège*, and the external trappings of its woe are overwhelming. From the corners of the big, cumbrous hearse nod lofty sable plumes. The horses look as if they had come out of some strange world of night and of darkness. They are great creatures " of the blackest black our eyes endure," without a white hair anywhere; and they move with preternatural gravity, as horses should whose daily work it is to make

> " Funeral marches to the grave."

The drivers, and the men sitting beside them, are clad in the deepest mourning. Their hats are swathed round with bombazine, which falls down their backs like a woman's mourning veil. But here their solemnity ends: they wear a cheerful air, as if rejoicing that business is prosperous; and I have seen them joke and laugh with each other, as if they might have been telling good stories of the dead they were carrying to his long home. As to the English crowd through which this gloomy-looking procession passes, not a hat is lifted; no notice is taken of it whatever.

You meet the simplest French funeral, and a band of mourners follows it, on foot, and bareheaded, however cold the weather. As the procession passes, every man in the street lifts his hat and waits, uncovered and reverently, until it has gone by. I have just met on the street a funeral procession fairly melodramatic in the intensity of its gloom. The great hearse was literally covered with flowers, and to the flowers was attached a huge scarf of purple satin, wrought in silver, with the motto, "A Notre Grandpère." Men clad in the deepest mourning, with immense "weepers" of black crape, followed it with lugubrious faces and slow and melancholy steps. I wondered how much of this grief was paid for by the hour. I do not know whether hired mourners are as common here now as of old, but a friend of mine who lived here twenty-five years ago tells me that no funeral of any pretensions at that time lacked its band of them. Two of them used to precede the hearse, leading the solemn way, — the rest used to follow. The chief mourner, the most noted of them all, was Clodoche, the celebrated clown, who combined the two very opposite avocations of mourning at funerals by day, and dancing the *cancan* at night.

My friend once saw him dance madly at an opera ball the very evening after he had seen him mourn dolefully at a grand funeral in the morning. M. —— sought an introduction to him, and asked him how he could possibly contrive to do two things so opposite, and to do each so well. Clodoche said he did the one as a relief from the other. "If I mourn for the dead," he said simply, "I must earn my money. I must put myself in harmony with the occasion. I must bring the tears to my eyes by thinking of the hearth which is lonely, and of the grave which is dark and deep. Monsieur, my heart grows cold with fear and sorrow. Then in the evening I dance; I feel under me my limbs which are strong. I grow gay with the music. I dance — I dance — I live; if I did not dance, I should die of the sorrow." But mourning got the better of mirth at last, and Clodoche dances no more. He has been followed to his grave, — he who made so many funeral marches! How fares he in the dark country?

There is another imposing vehicle which dominates the French streets besides the hearse. I refer to the omnibus, which attracts the attention of fear and dismay, rather than of sympathy. French omnibuses are drawn by three strong horses, usually white, all harnessed abreast, and they tear through the streets at an incredible pace, like an army bent on destruction and charging at double quick. I do not think a French omnibus ever yet halted on its fatal course for man, woman, or child. All you can do is to get out of its way, and that you must do very hurriedly. I never see one without fancying that it is the European revival of the car of Juggernaut.

But the French people seem, in spite of the omnibuses, to live and prosper and grow fat, — oh, how fat they *do* grow when they pass middle life, especially the women! They are a light-hearted people as a whole, though in the faces of some of the men there is a solemn gloom, as if they were longing for the red days of the Revolution to return. But this very sullenness is unlike the brutal, hopeless sullenness of the English lowest class, — those hideous, bleared, sodden wretches who stand leaning up against the walls of the big-windowed "publics." These English have no hope, — save for more gin, — no intention to struggle, no longing to rise, no vestige of self-respect. The sullenest French boor respects himself, even unduly, and believes that he is worthy to adorn a palace. These men in blouses crowd before the windows of picture shops when any good thing is on exhibition with as eager an interest as you feel yourself. They appreciate art, these French *roturiers*, as the Germans do music. They have one supreme love, however, and that is Paris.

And after a while you begin to understand this passion. You walk through the garden of the Tuileries, populous with Coustou's statues; you hear the gay out-of-door music; you see the sunset on the Seine; the evening lights flash out in arches and in clusters on the Champs Elysées, and the little bird begins to sing in your brain that sings forever and forever, "How beautiful is Paris!" and, however far away you go, his song will lure you back, and each time your pretty, perilous Paris will hold you in her toils more firmly than before.

Many hours of my happy May days have been passed in the two salons, and I have had an equal pleasure in making the acquaintance of pictures not to be seen in either of them.

It was M. Stéphane Mallarmé, the poet, — one of the best art critics I know, — who took me to see the impressionist pictures at the gallery of Boussod, Valadon, & Co., on the Boulevard Montmartre, and at both the gallery and the house of M. Durand-Ruel, who is said to have the finest private collection of impressionist pictures owned by any one man. M. Mallarmé wrote me a list of the living impressionist masters in, approximately, the order of their importance. It reads thus: Claude Monet, Renoir, Degas, Sisley, Pissarro, Mme. Berthe Manet, and Raffaelli. Having handed me this list, he took it back again, and added the name of an American lady, Miss Mary Cassatt, who was of too much consequence, so he said, to be ignored in selecting his chosen few.

Besides these impressionists, I have to speak of another artist, quite as original as any of them, and perhaps, for my own taste, quite as fascinating, — Adilon Redin. The impressionists say that they paint what they see; Redin says he paints what he sees — in his dreams. He has for me an intense and quite unique attraction. I saw eight or ten strange pictures by this strange man, — a silent man, I am told, who paints his visions, but does not talk about them. There was a landscape born of night and gloom, with misshapen trees that you could fancy had been contorted by human pain. There was "A Nightmare,"

— the vision of an armed man who rode desperately into the dark, on a skeleton white horse, the horse of death. There was one picture called "A Fallen Glory," the head of a marble god lying low among the weeds; and there was the most enchanting of them all, "The Goddess of Dreams," the very incarnation of slumber, with the white lily of her pure thoughts just taking shape beside her in the darkness. These, indeed, are the pictures of a poet. Like Blake, it seems to me that Redin might paint with brush or pen, whichever came most readily to his hand. His work is doubtless what one must call literary art; but for me it is enchanting. I saw at both galleries superb pictures by Monet. Claude Monet is by no means unknown, even to untravelled Americans, since pictures by him have been frequently shown in New York and Boston. He is a sort of modern Turner. He too "paints what he sees," as is the impressionist's formula; but then he sees what no one else sees. In one of the pictures I looked at the other day was a tree whose rich leafage almost suggested a peacock's plumage by its wonderful gradations of bluish-green, clothed upon with sunlight. I myself have never seen such a tree; but should I say so to Monet, his lip, I have no doubt, would curve with the same fine scorn which Turner's wore when a Philistine once said to him, "I never saw such a sunset as that," and Turner looked him over from head to foot, and answered, "And I don't think you ever will."

But if I never saw in nature Monet's peacock-plumaged tree, I believe that he has seen it, and I gratefully accept his transferred vision. I must confess, too, that many of Monet's wonderful landscapes appeal to my own memory. So have I seen the great sea roll, reflecting the sunset sky. So have I beheld the young green on those trees under which lovers walk. So for me, even for me, have the distant hills seemed to soar into the very heavens, and search out the secrets of the skies.

The very noblest and loveliest Monets of all that I have seen were in the private gallery in the house of M. Durand-Ruel. In that same gallery, too, I made my first acquaintance with the work of Pissarro, — work so lovely and so ideal, as well as so true, that I do not understand why the great picture-buying world was so long in finding him out. A few amateurs, genuine art lovers, discovered him and bought some of his pictures; but he worked on long with comparatively little encouragement. He is old now, old and poor; but his art and his heart are as young and alive as ever, and he has never painted more exquisitely than to-day. Such enchanting landscapes as he discovers, with the soft mist on them, and the dear peasant people in their midst!

I saw Degas, too, at his very best, in the private gallery of M. Durand-Ruel. I had seen in the Boussod-Valadon gallery plenty of his well-painted girls getting out of bath-tubs and wiping their feet after a bath. They were clever, undoubtedly, very, very clever, though they did not charm me; but Degas has his own reason for them. "In point of fact," said he to a friend, "the only occasion on which people of modern times are nude is when they take a bath." This idea may not appeal to your imagination, but it certainly will to your common sense. Here, in this collection which a great picture dealer has made for himself, I saw work by Degas which did attract me profoundly. I liked best of all a gentle landscape, "wherein it seemed always afternoon," with, for living things, two horses standing tranquilly, the head of one thrown over the neck of the other. Less lovely, but more wonderful, were the numerous dancing girls. No one, surely, has ever painted the dance as has Degas. The wind born of the dancing motion blows through these airy skirts. The poise of foot and head, the swirl of draperies, all are caught as by instantaneous photography, and yet with a grace and charm that photography never knew. And the colors are fairly dazzling, though they never give you the least sense of exaggeration. I do not wonder that Degas is the talk of artistic Paris. Buy him or not, as you please, he has a fortune of his own; and gaunt Famine, who is always sending in her card to some of his neighbors, will never knock at the door of Degas.

Renoir, on the other hand, is poor. His work is absolutely adorable. I stand before his landscapes dumb with pleasure. Then I see his figures, and I say, "No, he is first of all a figure painter;" and then a landscape beguiles me back again to my first love. He is best of all, perhaps, when he unites his gifts, and gives us figures in the midst of landscape. I always loved Jules Breton's work; but Renoir touches the same kind of scenes with a tenderer grace. Some of his pictures of young girls and of little children are so sweet and so perfect in their simplicity that it almost seems as if no one had ever known how to paint them before, and Renoir had discovered the secret for himself.

There were also in this private gallery some of the pictures of John Lewis Brown; fancy a Frenchman, born at Bordeaux, named John Lewis Brown! I had seen and admired Brown's work in the salon of the Champ de Mars. He is the fashion in Paris. Parisian Vanderbilts and Astors buy his gay, spirited hunting scenes. He is the friend and comrade of the impressionists, though his work suggests a student of Meissonier rather than of Manet or Monet. There was one lovely picture by Mme. Berthe Manet, the sister-in-law of Manet, (the first impressionist of distinction), who died a few years ago. This one picture is the only one I have seen by Mme. Berthe Manet. She does not exhibit; and as she is at present out of town, I cannot visit her studio.

The landscapes of Sisley, which I saw for the first time at this private gallery, were almost as charming as Monet's, but infinitely less powerful. There were also beautiful marines by Boudin, and various other works by other artists whose memory reproaches me for my omission to mention them.

I must say one word about Raffaelli, whose works I saw at the Boussod-Valadon gallery, where there are, just now, two rooms full of them on exhibition. Raffaelli deals with Paris and its neighborhood. He paints the types one meets in these Paris streets, — the blue-bloused peasant, the pretty grisette, the French *grande dame* on her way from the races, the hungry little orphan, the really domestic and managing mother.

His pictures are bright, open-air creations. An apple orchard is breaking into bloom, and those fair French demoiselles have stopped for a moment to catch the breath of its fragrance. These children are at play, and their young mother calls them. This old man has sat down to rest under one of the trees that border the Champs Elysées. A glance at any of them, and Raffaelli has his subject ready for his hand.

He makes wonderful bronzes, too, like no others I have ever seen. They are like silhouettes in bronze, — a sort of bas-relief, with the open air between the work and its background. They are full of life and spirit, — a line suffices for a likeness, — and they are absolutely unique. I went twice to see the pictures at the New Salon of the Champ de Mars before going at all to the Old Salon of the Champs Elysées ; for the impressionists reign at the New Salon, and they have for me a weird but inescapable fascination.

Could anything be more absolutely mad than the "Vision de Femme," by Paul Albert Besnard, who is the god of the younger impressionists? They swear by him, and, indeed, he has wonderful qualities of color; but this picture! — I don't know what Besnard means by it: I rather wonder if he knows himself. It seems to me like a leaf torn from the "Inferno." It is pervaded by just the blue flame that you see flash along a wall when you have drawn a lucifer match across it. The woman seems to have just reached Sheol. She has taken one plunge, perhaps, in the lake of fire and brimstone; for the robe that clings to the lower part of her body seems drenched with sulphurous flame. And round her naked bust and arms lines of that strange blue light, which suggested to me the lucifer match, seem to writhe like serpents. There is nothing human in her face; no hope, no love, no joy; not even suffering or despair. Perhaps the look is of sheer wonder. It is the most amazing conception I ever saw, this "Vision of Woman!" What woman? I might think that Besnard had gone mad but that he has surrounded this picture by a group of comparatively sane paintings. One of them, "Une Famille," — his own family, I am told, — is quite charming in its simplicity and naturalness. There is, too, a picture both beautiful and striking, called "Une Salvationiste," of a woman of the Salvation Army, clothed in black, and with a wonderful light upon her face, by which the whole picture seems to be illuminated.

Another quite impossible, but really most fascinating picture, is by Paul Hoecker of Munich, — "La Religieuse," — in which the meekest and loveliest of nuns is sitting at one side of a double avenue of trees, between which leads a grassy path. A light that literally never was on sea or land pervades this picture. It turns the white cape of the nun to a strange but lovely green. It bathes the tree-trunks near her with soft purple, and all the grassy path between the two rows of trees is dappled with spots of opaline light, — rose, green, violet; the colors seem actually to change as you look at them. All these hues could only be rationally accounted for on the supposition that the sky was a huge dome of stained glass, through which shone the transfiguring sun. But then, why should one be rational, when it is yet more delightful to be charming?

One very striking picture here is certainly not charming, but there is scarcely anything more weirdly powerful in the whole Salon than "Dans les Dunes," by Liebermann of Berlin. It is the picture of a wild, desolate moor, — such an one as Thomas Hardy drew in his "Return of the Native," — a gray landscape, over which some strange blight rests, and a hideous human creature, blighted also, toils up a wind-blown, sandy slope, painfully leading two wretched goats. The hag, the goats, the arid, cruel landscape, — there is nothing in it all but misery. Yes, there is something else, — that strange, compelling power which is art, and it drew me back to the picture again and again. I defy any one with an atom of imagination, having once seen it, ever to forget it.

There is a commanding group of portraits by Carolus-Duran. I do not like them all, — I mean I do not like all the faces; and I especially dislike the face of the woman who wears a dress of the superbest red, with a fur-trimmed cloak falling back from her shoulders. But the red of that robe, — how magnificent it is! and that fur, — who else could have painted it!

Talking of portraits, here is the "Ellen Terry as Lady Macbeth," by Sargent, which was the sensation of "The New Gallery" in London last summer. It provoked much discussion then. It holds its own gloriously among the French masters. You may like or dislike it as you please, from the point of view of its Shakespearian fitness; but it would be scarcely possible to praise too strongly its splendid power and the artist's subjection of every detail to the commanding whole.

Another "Lady Macbeth" in this Salon of the Champ de Mars is by Alfred Stevens. He has chosen the moment when Lady Macbeth studies her hand in the strong lamplight and sees that all the perfume of Araby will never make it pure again. Her eyes seem fairly wild with terror. I can scarcely recall in any picture I know such an expression of mad, despairing horror. Stevens has an "Ophelia" also, and a taking picture which he calls "La Jeune Veuve," which, with its background of yellow green, the widow's gown of a deeper green, and the black velvet of her jacket, is a veritable harmony.

I could say the same of William T. Dannat's "Portrait de Mme. C. C.," the only full length in Mr. Dannat's group of five superb portraits. It is a harmony in white and gold and rose, this portrait, and it has all those qualities of truth and power and brilliancy which make Mr. Dannat the noble painter he certainly is. Mme. C. C. ought to be happy by virtue of this picture. We shall die, and worms will eat us; but to have bequeathed a vision of immortal loveliness to future centuries, — surely a woman thus painted can resign herself to the effacing touch of time more placidly than *les autres!* A fine portrait of Mr. Theodore Child, and the charming girlish head of "Mlle. H." are also among Mr. Dannat's contributions to the exposition.

I must not forget the landscapes of Alexander Harrison. With Sargent and Dannat holding their own so triumphantly among the French figure painters, and Harrison rivalling their landscape artists, we of the United States have a right to believe that we are not quite barbarians in art.

I have not neglected to visit the Salon of the Champs Elysées, with its miles on miles of pictures. Figure to yourself thirty-seven different halls, and each one of them crowded, and then fancy what it is to walk through them. Here also was good work by certain Americans, — the noble and beautiful portrait of Mrs. F. P. Vinton, by her husband, for instance; and two of James Macneil Whistler's fascinating "Nocturnes" — but one never knows whether Mr. Whistler prefers to be called English, or American. Sometimes he exhibits in one section, and sometimes in the other, and always he is *sui generis*.

I think I have never seen quite so many nude figures as in this year's Old Salon,— people walking, reading, engaged in the ordinary avocations of life, and with no possible reason for taking off their clothes except total depravity. And scarcely one of them has even the excuse of beauty.

I have left till the last the mention of one artist who will paint no more, but whose hold on the memory of those who read her story must needs be long-enduring. I have passed two afternoons in the studio of Marie Bashkirtseff, who, dying at scarcely twenty-four, left behind her several hundred pictures and sketches (of which two hundred and twenty-four are in this studio), and various pieces of sculpture, of which the studio contains five.

In 1883, the year after Marie's death, an illustrated catalogue of her work was published, and of this catalogue I was so fortunate as to procure one of the few remaining copies. To this memorial of Marie's work François Coppée, the poet, contributed a preface, in which he describes Marie as she appeared to him on his one interview with her, a short time before her death. "I saw her," he writes, "only one time, — I saw her for only one hour; but I shall never forget her." She looked to him younger than her twenty-three years. He describes her little figure, her face so exquisitely modelled, her fair, soft hair, her sombre eyes, with the slumbering fire in them burning with the desire to see and know, the mouth firm, yet sweet and dreamy, the nostrils quivering with every emotion, like those of a wild horse of her own Russian steppes.

One saw in her will veiled in sweetness, energy expressing itself through grace. In this adorable girl everything betrayed a superior mind. Under the feminine charm you felt an iron force more than virile.

Coppée describes his visit to Marie's studio, where, in one corner, he saw her favorite books, — the very masterpieces of the human mind. There they were, each in the original, — the greatest works of the French, English, Italian, German, and even the Greek and Latin classics, all of which came within the wide range of this girl's eager, intellectual curiosity. Her piano was there too; and there was the music of the masters, which she rendered with singular power. Madame Bashkirtseff, with maternal pride, called the poet's attention to these evidences of her daughter's varied gifts; but Marie seemed to shrink from such allusions, and laughed off all attempts at eulogy.

It was only a month after this that the black-bordered card announcing the young artist's death reached Coppée. It scarcely surprised him. While he stood in her very presence, and looked into her proud, sweet face, a presentiment had seized on him that this creature, who had lived so much more vitally and swiftly than others, was near the end of it all.

One portion of this interesting catalogue is devoted to the "*Hommages*" which followed the death of this wonderful girl. We have poems to her memory by various poets, notices of the press, and M. Saint-Amant writes briefly concerning her funeral, which he says was more poetic and more touching than any obsequies at which he had ever assisted. The house where Marie had lived and died was hung with black and filled with flowers. From this house of death was borne the casket of black velvet in which lay all that was left of her who had suffered and enjoyed so keenly. She was put in a hearse hung with flowers and drawn by six white horses, and this hearse the poor mother had the courage to follow, on foot, to the Russian church where the funeral ceremonies took place, and then on to the cemetery at Passy, where a monument has been erected to Marie's memory.

But I began to speak of the works of this girl, who died eleven days before what would have been her twenty-fourth birthday. "Would they be wonderful in themselves, these works," a friend asked me, "if there were no more romantic interest attaching to them than to the pictures, for instance, that hang in the New Salon?" Yes, I think I may safely say that they would be valuable and interesting in themselves, even if they were the work of some artist likely to paint for a half-century to come; but of course one's interest in them is intensely emphasized by the thought that this girl, so much more keenly alive than the rest of us, died almost before she had learned the secret of life, and can paint for us no more. Here, within these four walls, is the legacy to the world of her brief, brilliant, tortured life, her burning, restless heart. And a remarkable legacy it is.

Her portraits of her cousin, now Comtesse de Toulouse, are admirable, full of character, and bear the unmistakable stamp of close study from the life. Her pictures of Paris *gamins* are delightful. "The Meeting," in the Luxembourg, represents half a dozen of these *gamins* occupied in the discussion of the use to which a piece of string they have found shall be applied, with as much excitement as a group of congressmen might show in discussing the silver bill, or a group of authors in arguing concerning the results of international copyright. She gave to each face its own individuality, and the figures of this group, snatched from the street, stand out strongly from the sombre background.

I liked even better "Jean and Jacques" (exhibited at the Salon of 1883), which I saw in the studio at 63 Rue Prony. Two boys, victims of compulsory education, are trudging reluctantly to school. The elder brother, Jean, leads the unwilling little one by the hand. Jean has a make-believe paper cigarette between his lips, and he has the responsible business-like air one sees so often in the children of the poor who have been accustomed to take care of their baby brothers and sisters from the time they could stand on their feet. Another striking painting is "The Umbrella," in which a girl of about twelve stands in the midst of a driving rain, wrapping her old shawl round her, and holding over her head a great shabby umbrella. Then there is a vigorous picture of Julian's studio, — that scene of Marie's own toil and hopes and fears and her heartburning jealousy of Breslau.

There are some adorable landscapes in this studio; one, "An Avenue in Autumn," which has a tender melancholy, a poetic suggestiveness, it would be hardly possible to praise too strongly. There are visions of spring, — such as Marie painted in words in her wonderful "Journal," — where she describes the fresh green of the young leaves, the blue of the rain-washed April sky, the colors that affect you as do the tones of a flute heard across an inland lake.

But others besides Marie Bashkirtseff have painted strong and faithful portraits; others have given us the *gamin* of the street (though perhaps few have painted him with so intimate and clearsighted sympathy as did Marie); others have painted the melancholy of the autumn, the young gladness of the spring; and I should do Marie's art injustice did I mention these things only, and omit to speak of its fantastic and entirely original phases. Strong and fine as was her work in the directions in which it ran parallel with that of others, one gets a yet subtler perception of her character from its vagaries. Here, for instance, is a child nursing at a breast. You see of the woman only this fair young breast to which the baby's lips are pressed. All the rest of her is veiled in impenetrable shadow. Here are two hands; one rests on a sheet of paper, the other holds a pen and is writing, — who knows what? A palmist would construct the whole woman and her fate from these nervous, impatient fingers. Again, here are two feet, with the slender limbs to which they are attached cut off just above the knees. Here is a single hand which holds an apple. Is it the hand of Eve, plucking the future misery of her race from the fatal tree of knowledge? Here is a girl, quite nude, but rich in all the loveliness of life, looking into the eyes of a skeleton, who seems to have come upon her unaware. Does she hear a murmur from the fleshless lips, — "What I am thou shalt be?" Here is a man with murder and mystery in his look, a convict whom she painted in Spain, — such a man as would make one shiver and grow cold if one met him upon a lonely path.

Ugh! let us turn from him to this jolly little peasant child, trotting along with a bottle in one hand and a tin pail in the other; or this burst of honest sunshine through the pink blossoms of the orchard.

Ah, what years were those last two or three of Marie's life; those years in which she coquetted with grim death while she read Homer, and Livy, and Dante; improvised music, painted pictures, and modelled in wet clay! And, indeed, her few pieces of sculpture were scarcely less wonderful than her pictures. There was one — a bronze statue of "The Grief of Nausicaa" — which impressed me profoundly. The head was bowed upon the arms, — you do not see the face at all; but I can think of no more perfect expression of hopeless and absolute despair.

Marie herself wrote that, from the point of view of an artist, there was nothing wanting in her environment. She had an entire story of the house appropriated to herself. The spacious studio had a glorious light, and on one side was a gallery to which one mounted by a short stair. Her library and her sleeping-room were on the same floor. In this library one still finds the best editions of the Greek and Roman classics beside the chief authors of Italy, France, Germany, England, and Russia. Opposite the writing-table is a striking photograph of Zola, of whose lurid power Marie was an ardent admirer.

In the bed-chamber one came strangely near

to the real Marie. She was more than usually fastidious about her appearance, and more than usually eager for admiration. Her dainty hands were scarcely more a source of pride to her than were her Cinderella-like feet; and in her sleeping-room is a cupboard with (so I am told by some one who took the trouble to count them) forty-five pairs of foot-gear, — shoes, slippers, boots, etc. One almost fancies the leather or the satin warm still with the pressure of those little feet. I think no one ever lived so fast as did this marvellous girl. She herself wrote in her "Journal," "No one, it seems to me, loves everything so much as I do." In the last year or two of her life her sensations almost overwhelmed her. Time seemed so mockingly short that she longed to do everything at once. She learned to know Bastien Lepage then; and surely she came, in that knowledge, nearer to love than in any other experience of her life. Her admiration for Bastien's art was unbounded; and I think her feeling for him was the sweetest, tenderest, most unselfish of her life. It was that life's impassioned sunset. He told her no other woman had ever achieved such noble work in art at so early an age; and she was wildly happy at such high praise from the painter of "Jeanne d'Arc" and "Le Soir au Village." Then they were both ill together. He, too, was looking into the awful eyes of death, as was the girl in Marie's symbolic picture.

During the summer before Marie's death these

two met almost daily. The same goat whose milk Marie drank served also for Bastien. One almost feels that she would have dreaded his recovery, since then he could not have gone with her into the valley of the awful shadow. That summer , she began a picture, to be called "La Rue," which , hangs now half-finished in her studio, — an infinitely pathetic reminder of those last sad weeks and the courage that endured to the very end, when strength failed her to hold brush or pen. The picture is of a seat on the Boulevard des Batignolles, with its usual occupants. She had had a photograph taken of that corner of the street; she had made her preliminary sketch, and she said pathetically: "All is ready. It is only I who am missing." But she began the picture, and worked on it till her strength gave way. It hangs there now, half-done; and one can see how strong and fine it would have been had death been less clamorously impatient.

One of her last works was a portrait of herself, with her palette in her hand. I can scarcely recall any pictured face by which I have been so moved. She was so young and so lovely; those passionate deep eyes of hers were so full of the longing for life and joy! She makes me think, somehow, of Amy Levy; but she never would have done what, at the last, Amy did. It was not in Marie to invite the approach of unwelcome death. And yet, in the sombre, brooding eyes of these two there seems to me some strange kinship.

How happy Marie should be if the dead people are aware of what goes on in this world they have forsaken! She wrote once, — in a moment of mad revolt against her fate, — "To die, great God, to die! without leaving anything behind me! To die like a dog, — like a hundred thousand women whose names are scarcely engraved even upon their tombstones!" If she can know that the French government has enshrined two of her pictures among the art treasures of the Luxembourg, that her "Journal" is read wherever the French or the English language is spoken, that her studio is a shrine for art lovers from far-off lands, — must not that restless, longing soul of hers, with its desperate thirst for fame, be appeased and happy?

1890.

RAMBLES IN SWITZERLAND.

IN SWITZERLAND: AT LUCERNE.

TO leave London at ten o'clock one morning, and arrive in Lucerne at half-past two in the afternoon of the next day, not having stopped longer than twenty minutes upon the way, is to be too tired to be roused to appreciation by anything short of a miracle, and that a miracle of loveliness, as Lucerne is.

As you stand on the quay, the lake stretches out before you in its wonderful beauty. At the right, Mount Pilatus rises rugged and dark; and at the left the Rigi rears its proud height to catch the sun on its summit. These mountain kings, crowned with clouds as with a diadem, hold their high court forever above the placid lake and busy town lying below; and to turn one's eyes toward them is to catch, among the small tumults of earth, a glimpse of the peace and the splendors of heaven.

I drove out of town quite by myself, the first day I passed in Lucerne, and came back through the falling dusk. What a region of soft enchantments Lucerne seemed, wrapt about with the magic and the mystery of twilight! One would not have been surprised to meet Fay Vivien upon the shore, or to know that the Happy Islands of Avalon lay off there in the vague blue distance.

The Swiss are certainly a commercial people. They have something to sell you at every turn; but you need not buy unless you choose. I must own that you usually do choose, and that you are usually sorry afterwards.

The shops are full of wood carvings and of ivory carvings, of lapis lazuli and amethysts and Rhine stones. Usually you buy during the first week you are there a rather large assortment of cuckoo clocks, and Swiss cottages carved in wood, and various other rather bulky articles; and then you pass the rest of your time in wishing you had never seen them, and contriving how to get them into your over-full trunk.

One thing amused me greatly in these Swiss shop-keepers. When they had pressed upon you in vain some bit of carving, or some Alpine painting, and you had shown yourself obstinate and obdurate, they were wont to inform you, as a last persuasion: —

"Madame, it is the work of my family."

Really there was something almost touching in the household sentiment which took it for granted that the wares on sale were in some sort enriched and adorned by this link with domesticity.

There is one carving only in Lucerne which is not for sale, and which must endure as long as the town itself endures. I refer to the celebrated Lion of Lucerne, modelled in clay by Thorwaldsen, and sculptured in the living rock of dark gray sandstone by Lucas Athorn.

Carlyle has written some glowing words about this Lion of Thorwaldsen's, which one of our own countrymen calls "the most moving piece of sculpture in the whole world."

An artificial cavern has been hollowed in the rock, and within this cavern lies, stretched in the agonies of death, the lion, a broken lance piercing his side, while his paw rests on the Bourbon coat-of-arms, in token that even in death he will not forsake his trust. A pool of clear water sleeps at the base of the rock, and over it arch oaks and maples. The murmur of streams trickling down from the heights above falls pleasantly on the ear; you can almost fancy that the sylvan peace about him is soothing the lion in his immortal pain.

This noble piece of sculpture is a monument to the valor of the soldiers and officers of the Swiss Guard who laid down their lives, to the number of about eight hundred, at the Tuileries in Paris, in defence of King Louis XVI., in 1792. Above the lion, carved in the rock, is the inscription, *Helvetiorum fidei ac virtuti* (To the faith and valor of Switzerland), and beneath are engraved the names of the slain officers.

From Lucerne almost every one makes the ascent of the Rigi. We went up in the afternoon, that we might see the sun set, and stayed there all night, that we might behold the splendid pageant of his rising. Early in the afternoon three ladies might have been seen, as G. P. R. James would have said, making their way to the steamer landing at Lucerne, where they embarked for Vitznau, a sail of an hour's duration.

At Vitznau we took the Rigi Railway for the Rigi Kulm, or summit. This railway is seven thousand seven hundred and fifty-five yards in length. It reminds one of the railway up Mount Washington, but the cars were better arranged for seeing. They were open all round, though roofed, and one could get a good view from every seat. The locomotive, whether in going up or coming down, is always at the lower end of the train. It pushes it, in the one case, and holds it back in the other. The views, as one winds slowly along, are beautiful beyond any power of words to describe.

The Rigi Kulm is six thousand feet high. It is clothed with grass to its summit, and I gathered familiar wild-flowers of New England from its very top. It commands a sweeping and magnificent prospect of blue lakes, green valleys, and snowy mountains, — a picture some three hundred miles in circumference. We reached the top about two hours before sunset, and spent the intervening time in studying the details of the superb panorama, — the Bernese Alps with their crowns of perpetual snow; the lovely lakes, — Lucerne and Zug and Sunpach; the valleys crossed by shining streams; the mountains that seem so perpendicular you would scarcely think any but a winged creature could climb them, and yet which are dotted here and there by tiny little cottages in which some one lives, at the imminent risk, as Mark Twain would say, of falling out of his front yard.

At sunset a strange glory flushes all this wide landscape. No pomp of dawning can compare with the enchanting loveliness of the day's decline. A rosy mist seems to bathe the whole scene, and the charm of vagueness, of suggestion, of infinite possibility, takes hold on the soul like the most wonderful music, the divinest poetry. It seemed almost a sacrilege to go in from this scene of enchantment to the prosaic refreshment of a well-served dinner in the spacious dining-room of the Rigi Kulm Hotel.

With the prospect of sunrise before us we went to bed early. Our rooms were comfortable and pleasant, but in each one was a printed placard forbidding the visitor to wrap himself in his bedblanket to go out to see the sun rise. The idea would not have occurred to us but for this warning, upon reading which we began to reflect how nice the scarlet blankets would have been by way of wraps, and to feel it an actual hardship that we were prohibited from their use.

We slept the sleep of the weary, which I think must be even deeper than that of the just. Never was night so cruelly short. We seemed but just to have got to sleep when the Alpine horn began to sound its reveille through the halls. Not one mild summons, but a wild clash and clang, which one almost fancied would awaken the dead. Surely never people dressed in such mad haste before. In an incredibly short space of time we had joined the shivering multitude outside, who were awaiting in motley garb the rising of the kindly king of day, so gracious or so great as not to be particular about the toilets of those who assisted at his levee. How cold everybody looked! How they all huddled together and drew their wraps about them! I even saw three or four rash men making themselves comfortable in the prohibited bed-blankets.

We had been out there for a good half-hour before his majesty arose, — but then one is used to wait in the courts of kings. Rose-clad heralds appeared first in the east; then cloud-shapes touched with flaming gold; and then, suddenly, a whole wide burst of splendor, and you knew the sun was there, but you were forced to turn away your eyes from the brightness of his glory. It was a magnificent spectacle certainly; but, of the two, I would rather behold the sun's decline than the too dazzling pomp of his up-rising.

We went in willingly to a warm breakfast; and in an hour or two more we were again on our way, by rail, to Vitznau. From Vitznau we sailed to Fluelen, and from Fluelen back to Lucerne, the whole lovely length of Lake Lucerne, which is twenty-seven miles. This most beautiful of the Swiss lakes is nowhere more than three miles in breadth, and it so winds in and out among its circling hills that it often seems as if you were sailing straight against the solid, impassable rock; and it is only as you draw near that your watery way opens before you. The water of the lake is the loveliest blue-green, — a peculiar color that I have found nowhere else, — and the scenery along its banks is such as no one who has not seen Switzerland can possibly imagine for beauty.

It seemed to me that it had never been so softly beguiling as when I drove about it that night after my return from the Rigi, and knew that I was saying farewell, and must go away from it all on the morrow.

TO, AND IN, GENEVA.

THE single day's journey from Lucerne to Interlaken over the Brünig Pass gives the traveller a sufficient feast of beauty to reward him for his pilgrimage to Switzerland, if he went no farther. You start at seven in the morning by boat from Lucerne, and cross the lake to Alpnacht, — a sail of somewhat more than an hour. This sail takes you under the very shadow of Mount Pilatus.

Pilatus is an out-post of the great Alpine chain, so lofty that its top is almost always shrouded in mist. It takes its name from a wild legend that Pontius Pilate, after he was banished from Galilee, fled thither, and dwelt for a time among the jagged rocks which form the top of this mountain, and from thence — when he could no longer bear the burden of his loneliness and his remorse — flung himself down into the lake below.

At Alpnacht you take the diligence for Brienz, — or rather, if you are wise, you *don't* take it, for a diligence is not half so agreeable as a carriage; and the laggards, for whom there is no room in the diligence, are put into supplementary carriages.

The drive, some seven hours long, was a constant succession of delights. One very quickly exhausts one's adjectives in Switzerland. There is nothing for it but to say, "Oh, *how* beautiful it is!" and then again, "Oh, how beautiful it *is!*"

Early on the way we passed the place where St. Nicholas, or St. Klaus, the children's friend, was born. The first Christian church in the neighborhood of Sarnen was named for him, and they say his bones are resting in it to this day.

He had a family of ten children, so he certainly had domestic experience enough to know what children want. At the age of fifty he is said to have left this family and betaken himself to a hermitage; and the legend is that he subsisted for the first twenty years of his seclusion solely upon the sacramental bread and wine, of which he partook once a month.

After his death he was canonized as a saint, and his memory is held in the greatest reverence by the peasantry in the valley of the Melchthal, where almost every cottager possesses what passes for his likeness.

What shall one say of the heights we passed that day, dotted with little châlets here and there, and with white, feathery mountain cascades leaping and tumbling down them, spanned by rainbows!

It was a perfect day, until just before we reached Brienz, when a sullen, unaccommodating rain began to fall. We took a steamer at Brienz and crossed Lake Brienz to Interlaken, or rather to Darlingen, some ten minutes from Interlaken by rail.

On the way we stopped at Giesbach, and saw the beautiful waterfall, in a state of nature then, but destined to be turned into a show that and every other evening of the tourist season, and illuminated bravely with Bengal lights, bathing it in sudden floods of brilliance, changing swiftly from red to green or white, and back again.

You pay thirty cents to look at this show from a good place, and it has countless spectators in the course of the season; so that altogether the people of Giesbach make good money by it.

It was between five and six in the afternoon when we drove into the busy main street of Interlaken, and halted at last before one of the numerous green-embowered hotels.

Interlaken is shut in between two ranges of hills. All the hotels front the range, behind and above which towers the Jungfrau, white as a bride and shy as a maiden. Most of the time she wears her misty veil upon her head, but early in the morning she lifts it to greet the dawn, and reveals the cold, pale beauty of her stately shape. Morning after morning I rose early to see the splendor of her unveiling, until I quite felt that I had made her intimate acquaintance.

The Höheweg of Interlaken, a double avenue of walnut-trees, is the chief resort of visitors. Besides the hotels, it is flanked with tempting shops, where all the accustomed Swiss commodities repeat themselves, and where I saw more beautiful specimens of the Swiss precious stones than anywhere else.

Walking along that path one day I beheld a sight painful enough to my American eyes, — a woman to whom a small cart of refuse was attached, which she was drawing as patiently as if she had been a horse, and with a man beside her who was probably her husband, and who appeared to be driving her.

All through that part of Switzerland where the German language and German customs prevail you will see women working in the fields. This may be equally true of French Switzerland, but I did not happen to notice it so much.

Interlaken offers the pilgrim the most charming walks and drives. One pleasant ramble is to the ruined Castle of Unspunnen, which legend says is the veritable Castle of Bluebeard. We climbed to it on a summer afternoon, and saw, or fancied that we saw, the turret from which Sister Anne looked forth to see if her knightly brothers were on their way, while the sad-fated wife was saying her prayers.

There is a *Kürsaal* in Interlaken, for the use of which your hotel charges you, whether you make use of it or not. There you go, if you like, to read and chat; there you can hear very good music from three to five in the afternoon, and from eight to ten in the evening.

While you sit at little round tables in the open air listening to the music, girls move to and fro among the people, bringing trays of ices or glasses of mild beer. They are picturesque creatures in their peasant costume, with black velvet bodice and stiff white sleeves, and numerous silver chains and ornaments.

We lingered at Interlaken for a week, and then went to Berne, taking steamer first over the lovely lake of Thun to Thun itself, and then from there proceeding to Berne by rail.

Scarcely had we washed from our faces the dust of travel before we set out to "interview" the famous bears of Berne. There is a great bear-den in the heart of the town, — a sort of enormous circular hole walled round with stone and divided by a stone wall through the centre.

On one side were the younger bears, and, on the other, two large, venerable, and gigantic creatures, who looked almost as if they might have been coeval with the city. To these latter we paid our loyal tribute of bread, which they caught cleverly, sitting up in a very human kind of way and holding out their expectant fore-paws.

Everywhere in Berne you see the bear, the heraldic emblem of the town. Bears appear in the pediments of monuments; they keep guard at the entrances of stately buildings; they surround the fountains; and a whole troop of them, moved by some skilful mechanism, march round a seated figure on the clock-tower whenever the hour strikes.

In the shops you find bears upholding drinking-cups; bears ornamenting clocks; fiddling-bears, dancing-bears; bears adapted to every conceivable use under the sun.

Berne has preserved its ancient characteristic features more faithfully than has any other town in Switzerland. In the old part the houses are built over stone arcades, underneath which the foot-passenger finds his way. The site of the city is perhaps more beautiful than that of any other Swiss town. It is built on a peninsula of sandstone rock formed by the windings of the river Clare, which flows a hundred feet below, and down to which lead grass-grown terraces.

Its one unrivalled attraction is the superb view it commands of the snow-clad Alps of the Bernese Oberland. From every coign of vantage you can see these distant, surpassingly lovely heights, contrasting with the shining river near at hand, the happy, verdant fields, and the great trees with their boughs waving softly in the summer air.

Interlaken was too shut in to seem to me a pleasant place for a long-continued stay; but Berne was so bright and breezy, and with such a magnificent outlook, that I felt as if one could linger there forever with ever fresh delight.

In spite, however, of all its temptations, we gave ourselves only a day and a night there, and then hurried on by rail to Geneva, — another paradise.

People are always passing through Geneva to

go somewhere else; and very few of them seem to find out what a really charming place it is for a protracted sojourn. It has the commonplace merit of being the richest and most populous town in Switzerland. It is full of good shops and good hotels, and is the headquarters of Swiss watchmaking, so that the class of travellers whose chief object is to spend their money could find here plenty of opportunities. It is an excellent place, too, to improve one's mind.

Here are a fine conservatoire of music, a good university, an extensive public library, museums of pictures and sculpture; museums, too, of archeology and of natural history; a botanical garden, with over five thousand different plants; in short "apples of wisdom" are to be gathered in every possible direction.

If you are worshipfully inclined, you can go to church at every corner. The old church of the Madeleine dates from the ninth century, and is the first one in which the Reformation was preached; and there are churches of all ages, from this venerable Madeleine to that youngest Protestant church whose corner stone was laid by our American General Grant in 1878.

Then, again, Geneva has antiquity enough to delight a fossil. It was an important place in the time of the Roman empire, and Julius Cæsar writes in his "Commentaries" of stopping to throw up some fortifications here. In the fifth century the town embraced Christianity, and in the sixteenth century it was one of the most prominent centres of the Protestant reformation.

On yonder hill, near the town, Calvin had that good Unitarian, Servetus, burned for his heresies, and for many years Calvin practically ruled Geneva. He not only told the Genevese what they must believe, but how many courses they might have for dinner. I should think they would have been glad when they buried him at last. They can't show you his grave, for by his directions no stone was placed over him, and no one knows just where he lies.

The most exacting lover of the beautiful would be content with the site of Geneva, on the shore of its own fair lake, with the sleepy Rhone, arched by six bridges, running through the town and cutting it in twain; and with the range of the Juras on one side and the Saléves and Mont Blanc on the other. Midway between two of the bridges, the Pont du Mont Blanc and the Pont des Bergues, is a pretty little island called Rousseau's Island, and consecrated to the memory of this later Genevese celebrity, who was perhaps the greatest contrast to the austere reformer, Calvin, that one can well imagine. Rousseau was a thorough Frenchman, though he was born at Geneva in 1712, and passed a good deal of his life here. On his "island" is his bronze statue by Pradier, — a beautiful work of art. The self-torturing sophist — the too frank confessor of sins he had not moral sense enough to blush for — the man who preached human kindness and sent his own children to foundling hospitals that he might not have the trouble of taking care of them, — looks down with an enigmatical smile on the people who come to study his lineaments thus immortalized in bronze.

This statue of Rousseau is the only good out-of-door monument in all Geneva. Most of them are ugly, and the most hideous of all is the huge, costly one to the Duke of Brunswick in the Place des Alpes. A droll old reprobate was the duke, but he deserved a monument from the Genevese, for he bequeathed to their town a nice little present, — no less than $5,000,000. He was an extremely eccentric old gentleman, and had almost as many wigs as Queen Elizabeth had dresses. As a lady of fashion arranges with her maid what gown she shall put on for any occasion, so this old duke used to discuss with his valet what color and style of wig he should assume each day. He had martial-looking wigs; wigs of sentiment, in which to go wooing; wigs of a certain *chic* suggestiveness; blond wigs, brown wigs, curly wigs, straight wigs; and he had a room full of barbers' blocks, on which these wigs were carefully dressed and set forth, and from this various assortment the old fellow chose each morning, according to his mood. He had also the largest collection of jewels in the possession of any private individual, and various grand residences in one place and another, among them a costly and curious palace in Paris, a haunt for

Sybarites, and celebrated for orgies not unworthy the maddest of the Roman emperors. I wonder where his wicked old soul is now! At any rate, his big, ugly monument is here in Geneva, and the Genevese are grateful for his money, and would pray, no doubt, for his unquiet spirit's repose, only that they are such strong Protestants they dare not.

Near Geneva is the Maison Diodati, where Byron and Shelley lived for a time together; where Mrs. Shelley wrote the strange, grewsome tale of "Frankenstein," and read it, evening by evening, to the two poets; where our "sad, bad, mad brother" Byron, as Swinburne would call him, made fatal love to Mrs. Shelley's half-sister, who had the dishonor of being the mother of Byron's daughter Allegra.

A short and most charming drive from Geneva takes you to Ferney-Voltaire, the last residence of Voltaire, the French philosopher, playwright, novelist, man of affairs, historian, etc., whose influence on the mind of the eighteenth century was hardly second to that of any other. You drive out from Geneva, with the grand Alps rising on one hand and the mist-shrouded Juras on the other, and of course you quote Byron. Ferney is the place founded by Voltaire, to which he retired in 1756, to remain until his death in 1778. One of the first things you notice in approaching it is the Protestant church which Voltaire built for his humbler neighbors, and which bears the haughty inscription : "Deo Erexit Voltaire" (erected by Voltaire to God). I have no doubt the arrogant philosopher thought that if there should happen to be any God he would be greatly flattered by this attention. At the gate of Voltaire's grounds is a lodge, in which there is an interesting room hung with numberless portraits of the great man, — Voltaire young, Voltaire old, Voltaire crowned by the French Academy, Voltaire in all sorts of attitudes and costumes, but always with the same cynical, self-pleased face.

The grounds in which the house stands command a delightful view, with fountains making murmurous music and great old trees overshadowing tempting seats. Going indoors you are shown Voltaire's sitting-room and his bed-chamber, and they are full of mementos of himself. In the salon is the mausoleum which was constructed to hold his heart, and bears the inscription, "His spirit is everywhere, but his heart is here." This record is no longer true, however, since his heart has been carried away and placed in the Bibliothèque Nationale in Paris.

The chair-covers in the salon were embroidered by Voltaire's nieces. On the table is his inkstand, in which you dip your pen to record your name in the visitors' book. Paintings by Titian, Boucher, and Watteau, of the philosopher's own choosing, are on the walls of the salon, and pictures of more personal interest are in the adjoining bed-chamber. Here is the stiff little bed where the wily Frenchman used to sleep, and on the walls of this bed-chamber hang the portraits of those whom he most loved or most honored.

I was especially interested in that of Madame du Châtelet, who loved him, not wisely indeed, but so long and well that one is moved to forgive her unwisdom. Ah! how fair she is, in her blue velvet robe, with the soft laces around her soft neck, with her powdered hair framing her charming face, holding in her hand a mystic rose of silence, looking forever toward the bed where her lover dreamed and died, and smiling a strange, inscrutable smile, which lights her beguiling eyes and curves her fresh and tender lips.

Here, too, hangs the grand, full-length portrait of Catherine the Great of Russia, presented by herself to Voltaire; and, near by, his portrait, embroidered by her imperial hands. What a woman she was! Looking on this picture you cannot help believing her capable of all the cruel wickedness which history ascribes to her; and yet she has a stately presence. A royal devil she!

Near a fine portrait of Frederick the Great hangs a picture of Voltaire's pretty little washerwoman. Can she, possibly, have been the rival of Mme. du Châtelet? One never knows of what a man, and a Frenchman, may not have been capable.

Besides these portraits of especial and personal

interest, the remaining space is covered by likenesses, chiefly engravings, of the men whom Voltaire delighted to honor, — Milton, Helvetius, Franklin, Washington, and many another; so that the old Frenchman and his sweethearts are in good company.

Coppet is another pleasant excursion from Geneva, — Coppet, where for some time Mme. de Staël resided; and not far away from Geneva was that quiet home where the fat historian Gibbon went wooing Mme. de Staël's mother, Suzanne Curchod. There is a funny story about Gibbon's thinking it the proper thing to kneel before this lady, and, once having got upon his knees, being too fat to get up again without asistance.

There are plenty of distinguished dead people in Geneva. In the same churchyard with Calvin lies Sir Humphry Davy; and all about the town there is an odor of dead eminence. For my part, these memories of the past are the most interesting associations with the spot. They fitly haunt its beautiful streets and suburbs, and I like well that place where I move in the good society of gentle ghosts; yet sometimes their company oppresses you, and you turn willingly to the world of to-day, — to see the peasant washerwomen washing the city's linen in the Rhone, or the gay little pleasure-boats, with bright awnings, waiting for passengers, as the gondolas wait in Venice.

CHAMOUNY AND THE MER DE GLACE.

THE easiest and pleasantest way of reaching Chamouny is by diligence from Geneva; and we paid our five dollars apiece, two or three days in advance, and chose our seats on the front bench of the *banquette*, — the best seats for seeing that a diligence has to offer.

The diligences on this route are well arranged. The seats are so high that you mount to them by a ladder, and as they are only roofed, and the affair is quite open at the sides, they afford an excellent view of the lovely land through which one journeys.

There were, I should think, nearly thirty people in this one diligence. It was drawn by six horses, three abreast, and these horses were changed at the end of each hour and a half. Sometimes, where the road was very hard, a seventh horse was fastened on, though I could not see how he could possibly do any good from his position, far on the right side.

With each change of horses came a change of drivers, and the first time this took place I was intensely thankful. Our first driver continually heartened up his horses with a strange guttural sort of cry, a kind of "Hoo-oo-oo!" which inspired me with a wild desire to imitate it.

I sat behind the man, and I did not think he would notice my feeble effort. I was mistaken; he turned his head round over his shoulder and — *looked* at me. That was all he did, but what a look it was!

A while afterwards, just to try him, I asked him the name of some mountain we were passing. He answered not, but once more he turned and looked at me. Then fear entered into my heart. Would he accidentally put out my eye with that convenient whip he brandished so freely? Would he, by chance, drive us all over a precipice, just to punish me?

I was glad when he got down from his perch and was replaced by a brisk young man with a flower in his hat. You may be sure I let him "Hoo-oo-oo!" to his heart's content (for they all did it), and made no further attempt to learn his language.

The journey from Geneva to Chamouny occupies about eight hours, including a halt at St. Gervais-les-Bains for luncheon. The distance is forty-nine and a half miles, and after the first fifteen miles the scenery becomes constantly more and more enchanting.

It is well to have plenty of small coins in your pocket, for at every stopping-place children surround you, reaching up fruit for your inspection. They have a sort of pole, like the trunk of a slender tree, from which spring metal branches, each one terminating in a hook, and from each hook hangs a graceful little basket full of plums, or pears, or grapes, or peaches.

If the fruit were not a sufficient temptation in itself, you could not resist the winning smiles and the bright eyes of the youngsters who offer it to you.

Then there are other youngsters who *jodel* along beside you, and expect all your pennies as a tribute. I cannot say that the Swiss *jodel* is delightful as music, but it belongs to the mountains, and you would feel defrauded if you did not hear it.

About twenty miles, by the winding carriage-road, from Chamouny, the dazzling height of Mont Blanc suddenly becomes visible. It is twelve miles or more away from you, as the crow flies, but its gigantic shape conquers the distance, and you feel it to be your near and awful neighbor.

At a little past three o'clock, if you leave Geneva as we did at seven in the morning, you drive into Chamouny, a little village which seems all shops and hotels. There is plenty of time before sunset to explore the town. It is full of travellers. Everywhere you meet ladies on mules, or see groups of people waiting their turn to look at Mont Blanc through the telescopes, — with one of which each hotel is provided, — or bargaining in the little shops for drinking-cups, or wood-carvings, or strings of beads.

We went to the Hôtel des Alpes, endeared to my

memory by its hospitable and genial landlady. It has a charming little garden, where the people group round the accustomed telescope.

My room was at the back of the house, confronting Mont Blanc; and almost underneath my window was a mountain torrent, with a loud and constant roar, which some guests complained of as giving them a headache, but which lulled me to sleep like a cradle-song. I knew nothing more until just before sunrise the next morning. Did some watching spirit of the hills awake me just at the right time?

I only know that about twenty minutes before the sun rose I stood at my window watching and waiting for the coming glory. Of course I thought of Coleridge's "Hymn before Sunrise in the Vale of Chamouny," as every English-speaking traveller is bound to think. I chanted to myself:—

> "Hast thou a charm to stay the morning star
> In his steep course? So long he seems to pause
> On thy bald, awful head, O sovran Blanc!"

Just then the morning star faded in the greater radiance of coming dawn; then a ray of gold crowned first one snow-capped height and then another, until all the kings were crowned, and the day was come. It was very different from the sudden burst of sunrise splendor which blinded us as we looked down from the summit of the Rigi into the valley below. This sunrise at Chamouny was not dazzling. There was something unutterably solemn in it, as if each cold, pale, chaste height were consecrated with its own especial glory.

That was our sole day in Chamouny, and we devoted it to an excursion to and across the Mer de Glace. Four of us set out, triumphantly, at eight o'clock of the brilliant morning, — three ladies and one man, — each one on a mule, and each with a guide. The ascent to the Montanvert — two hours of mountain-climbing — is toilsome, but not dangerous. At the Montanvert we gave our mules into the charge of a boy, who was to take them round to await us at the edge of the forest below the Chapeau.

We lunched at the Montanvert, and bought the inevitable paper-knives and sleeve-buttons, and then we started for the Mer de Glace. As you look at it from Montanvert, it has the aspect of a sea whose rough and rapidly in-coming tide has been caught and frozen in mid-career.

Farther on it is like a sea frozen in the midst of a frightful storm, with great billows and gulfs of ice. We struggled down to it over the Moraine, a collection of rough bowlders of all sizes, and not the pleasantest walking in the world. To traverse the Mer de Glace itself was by no means so toilsome; but it gave you a shiver to look into the deep, blue crevasses of ice, and think how easy a single false step would send you to make part of their mystery.

The descent from the Mer de Glace to the Chapeau on the other side is infinitely more fatiguing, and the portion of it called the Mauvais Pas, or Evil Road, is enough to daunt the timid. I remember a description of it in one of Frederika Bremer's books which curdled my blood when I was a little girl.

A precipice of jagged rocks, I will not say how deep, is below you. Your only foothold is a series of small steps cut into the perpendicular rock, and your only hope of safety is in clinging desperately to an iron hand-railing secured to the rock. It takes you about half an hour to traverse this wicked bit of road, and you are rather apt to be seized with a trembling fit when you reach the Chapeau and feel that it is all over.

From the Chapeau you climb down, if such a contradiction in terms is allowable, to the edge of the forest, where your mules await you. I confess that the farther descent upon mule-back was the crowning misery of my day. I was very tired, and no doubt fatigue had demoralized me. When I first mounted, the mule mildly objected to the descent which awaited her. She intimated her desire to back round on a path about six inches wide and overhanging a frightful precipice. It took the utmost strength of the guide to restrain her from carrying out this cheerful intention. I asked desperately, —

"Is she vicious?"

"No, madam," the guide answered, reassuringly, "only reluctant."

Wherewith I began plunging down the mountain on a reluctant mule. I certainly never expected to get down alive. I gave the survivors instructions how to telegraph to my friends. I concluded that I dreaded death and loved life. I am afraid I shrieked a wild entreaty or two to be taken off the back of that unwilling mule; and I know my heart rejoiced when at last we reached the farther edge of the forest and came out into daylight and a level road.

We reached Chamouny about five o'clock, and joined some people who were watching, through the telescope, a party making the ascent of Mont Blanc, having left Chamouny that morning.

These people who were struggling up the great mountain did not excite my envy. I concluded I would rather ascend Mont Blanc by telescope than in any other way.

That night it looked like rain, and we debated the chances of driving next day to Martigny by way of the Tête Noire. We would not go if it rained, — on that we decided as firmly as mortals may; and then we took a last look at the lowering sky, and went to sleep with the wild, hoarse song of the mountain torrent in our ears.

OVER THE TÊTE NOIRE, TO CHILLON.

WE woke in the morning and it was raining; not a quiet, friendly, August rain, but such a rain as they have in the mountains, — sullen, heavy, a great deal wetter than other rains, and possessed, as it seemed, with a dogged intention of going on forever.

At eight o'clock the driver, whom we had engaged the night before with the solemn and distinct understanding that we would NOT go if it rained, appeared with his carriage and pair before our door.

We mildly remarked that it rained. He condescended to assent; but he said that if it kept on raining, the roads might be quite impassable on the morrow, and *if* we were going, it would be well to start at once.

Just then a sudden rift in the blackness of the sky revealed a faint line of blue, to which the guide pointed triumphantly. He assured us that it would clear in an hour or two, and we said that we would start if it stopped raining any time before eleven o'clock, and with that understanding the man went away.

Then evil tales began to be told us of fatal accidents in crossing this same Tête Noire. Only one week before, a party of three had attempted to drive across it, and a storm had come on. The guide had vainly tried to persuade his passengers to take refuge in a mountain hut, but they had insisted on going forward.

At last they came to a place — a sort of bridge — which the guide fancied might be dangerous, and here again he counselled them to walk, but they refused.

He himself dismounted and went to the head of his horses. He had just stepped across the dangerous place when there came a sudden crash, a wild, wild shriek of horror, and horses, carriage, and three human souls were all struggling together in the mountain torrent far below.

Two of the bodies were recovered and one wheel of the carriage; but no trace had been found of the other body or of the horses.

To hear of this terrible and so recent calamity was not a pleasant preparation for our own journey; but a benevolent Englishman, who seemed to know Switzerland well, assured us that just after an accident an unusual amount of care was always exercised; and told us that within the last week the road had been thoroughly inspected and repaired, under the care of the efficient Swiss Road Commissioners. He added that a day of rain might, however, make it unsafe again, and that it would be far better for us to make the trip that day if possible.

Just before eleven the clouds lifted and the rain

ceased. Promptly our charioteer appeared upon the scene. Some one looked out at him and told us that he was the very guide who drove the unfortunate people the week before. I supposed, according to our English consoler, that would only make him more careful; but one had a sort of grewsome feeling in setting off with him all the same. However, we started.

For half an hour all went merry as a marriage-bell; then the whole sky darkened again, and it began to rain as if a second deluge were impending. Still we all voted against turning back. The road would be worse to-morrow; the day might clear by-and-by; anyhow, we had started, and on we went.

It was a woeful day. The shining, distant splendors of the snow-crowned mountain-kings which should have rewarded us for our peril were for the most part hidden from us by the rain; but near at hand we saw the precipices whose very verge we were skirting.

Much of the way the road was so narrow that it seemed as if, should the horse swerve six inches to one side, we should never see again "the cheerful light o' the sun."

We had made up our minds beforehand that at least we would not lose our lives by refusing to walk when we were told to do so; and it seemed to me that the driver had divined our resolution, for the amount of walking he invited us to do was prodigious. Whenever we came to a pull hard for the horses he would tell us gravely that it was a dangerous place, and he thought we should do well to get out.

I will not hazard a guess at the number of toilsome miles we walked that morning, plashing through soft mud, ankle-deep, and soaked through and through by the persistent, untiring rain.

Midway in the journey we stopped for luncheon, and then proceeded with another carriage and horses, and a fresh driver,—a funny little old man whom we called "grandpa." For perhaps two hours we were climbing steadily.

Grandpa walked all the time, and the rain seemed to chill him seriously; so that, as a matter of protection against the cold no doubt, he quaffed at the doors of various little shanties the red wine of the country. At length it seemed not only to have warmed but to have inspired him. He mounted his box. He said, "We climb no more; we descend always now." And descend we did. We actually rushed down to Martigny.

The day before, on the back of my "reluctant" mule, I had arranged for having my decease telegraphed to those whom it might concern; now, in this carriage, whirling down the mountain at the rate of countless miles an hour, and turning corners with two wheels in the air, I began to make my will.

I assured my companions very solemnly of my belief that we should never reach the level ground alive. I even ventured a slight expostulation with "grandpa"; but he only smiled, and tore along as madly as ever. I could hardly believe my eyes when the lights of Martigny came in sight, and we drove quietly into town through the rain and the mist.

The next day it rained still. There was no pleasure to be had at Martigny in the rain, and we went on by train to Chillon, where we passed part of the long wet afternoon in writing letters to our friends, and the rest of it in reading aloud Byron's "Prisoner of Chillon."

The morrow's morn rose with a superb brilliance of sunlight. The sky was a deep blue lustrous vault, — as clear as if no cloud had ever darkened it since the world began.

Of course we made our way at once to the castle. A portion of it is still used as a prison, but the rest was open to our inspection. Externally it is a vision of beautiful architecture. Its shape, its color, and its location all lend themselves to enhance the ideal charm which Byron has bequeathed to it by his poem.

The origin of this castle is buried in darkness. It is a Gothic building, with massive and irregular walls, flanked by six towers and surmounted by turrets. The square tower in the centre is a lofty structure, whence you can see the whole lake and its borders; and it still contains the alarm bell which of old used to summon the inhabitants of the surrounding country to the defence of the castle.

In the other towers are the deep, dark dungeons where captives lingered out their painful and hopeless days; the chamber of the Question, where every conceivable instrument of torture was used to bring the prisoners to confession; and the beams from which the doomed men were hanged at last. The fair blue lake used to be their convenient sepulchre. The last and largest of the dungeons is the one to which Byron refers in his poem, where he makes his prisoner say: —

> "There are seven pillars of Gothic mould
> In Chillon's dungeons deep and old;
> Seven columns, mossy and gray,
> Dim, with a dull, imprisoned ray,
> A sunbeam which hath lost its way,
> And through the crevice and the cleft
> Of the thick wall is fallen and left
> Creeping o'er the floor so damp.
> And in each pillar there is a ring,
> And in each ring there is a chain;
> That iron is a cankering thing,
> For in these limbs its teeth remain."

This dungeon was occupied for four years by Bonnivard. He was confined for six years in Chillon Castle, but the first two were passed in a more comfortable apartment. Here, in the dungeon of the seven columns, his weary steps, passing so constantly over the pavement, have worn a little path in the rock.

He was a martyr to his love for Switzerland and for liberty. In 1530 his confinement began, and in 1536 the combined forces of Berne and of

Geneva effected the conquest of the castle, then held by the cruel Duke of Savoy, and the release of Bonnivard.

He was found chained to a pillar; and his first question when his chain was broken was whether his beloved Geneva had also regained her freedom. The Genevese from that time heaped upon him all the rewards it was in their power to bestow, and he died at last in 1571, full of years and of honors.

It has been supposed by some that Byron's poem was written in commemoration of the sufferings of Bonnivard; but Byron has distinctly stated that when he wrote the poem he had never heard the story.

No picture could render all the aspects of the place more faithfully than Byron has done. There are the old columns, looking as if they would stand forever; and there the long, narrow opening on high, through which the feeble daylight struggles, and at which Byron imagined the lovely blue-winged bird came to sing; and there the footing in the wall by which the prisoner strove to gain the narrow outlook from which he could see a glimpse of sky. Among the thousands of names inscribed upon those old pillars we found that of Byron himself, and that of Victor Hugo.

In the afternoon we bade farewell to Chillon, and took the steamer for a five hours' sail back to Geneva. I have no words of praise left for the blue waters of Lake Leman, — the bluest waters in all Switzerland, — or for the shining heights which are constantly coming into view as one sails over those fair waters.

After four weeks in Switzerland one becomes bankrupt in expression; but one has learned to love the place as one loves no other. Surely its haunting beauty must draw every traveller back, again and again. And to have seen it once is to be forever after as homesick as a Switzer for its hills and its lakes.

A POSTSCRIPT: AT RAGATZ.

I HAVE now been at Ragatz for two weeks, and my compassion is at the service of any one who does not know this paradise.

It would be a very small Swiss village but for the stranger within its gates, and the preparations made to receive him. Left to itself, it has scarcely two thousand inhabitants; but the number of guests during a single season, including passing travellers, often amounts to fifty thousand. The private houses are few, and mostly unpretending; but the hotels are various and agreeable.

The best are the Quellen-Hof and the Hof-Ragatz, both belonging to Herr Simon, the rich man of the town, and both connected with the Neubad, or new bath-house. In the same enclosure are the Kurhaus and its beautiful gardens. Besides these two grand hotels there are various others of lesser importance and less agreeably situated.

Quite as many people come to Ragatz for the beauty of the scenery as to avail themselves of the " cure ; " but it first came into public notice through the building of Pfæfers's Road from the Gorge of Pfæfers, two and a half or three miles distant, and the construction of the conduit of the same length to convey the waters from the Pfæfers hot springs for the use of bathers in Ragatz.

The little town is in the valley of the swift-flowing, mad little Tamina, and — as the local guide-book amusingly informs you — near the railway station beyond the village " the Tamina pours its sparkling waters into *the youthful Rhine.*"

Many a time, standing on the bridge that spans the Rhine near Ragatz, I have followed in my thoughts the long journey of this river, which, at this place, it almost seems as if one could wade across, and which flows from hence on and on, away from Switzerland, through Germany, into Holland, and loses itself at last in the North Sea.

In Ragatz you have none of the shut-in feeling which depresses you at Interlaken; yet the heights are near, — some of them tree-crowned bowers of beauty, others rough and rocky, and with the snow glistening white upon their summits.

On one height stand the picturesque ruins of the Wartenstein, and on another the equally picturesque ruins of the once mighty Freudenberg. The Guschenkopf is another near height, the path to which leads through an enchanted wood. Any one of these is an easy ramble for a summer afternoon.

Another walk is up the valley to the Gorge of Pfæfers, and every step of the way is from beauty to beauty, from grandeur to grandeur. All the time beside your path the Tamina is foaming down to Ragatz. At every turn some new aspect of the heights confronts you. Silvery waterfalls pour into the ravine from almost over your head, and the rocks so nearly meet that there seems, as you look forward, to be no passage between them.

Fir-trees spring from the bare crags above you, and sweet *Alpenrosen* start up almost from under your feet. I have traversed this path again and again, and always a fresh sense of its beauty takes me by surprise; for it is a beauty so changeful that you could never learn it by heart, or lose the haunting desire to see it again.

At last you get to the end of the ravine, and come upon the great stone building — half bathhouse and half hotel — through which you must enter the gorge. You procure your ticket, and start on your expedition to the hot springs, whence the water in which you are to bathe in the village below starts on its journey.

The guide leads you by a narrow, sombre passage, into the very heart of the mountains, where you half expect to be compelled to dispute your right of way with the elves. You pass along a narrow wooden footpath, five hundred yards in length, under which the Tamina froths and foams, and over which the jagged limestone rocks so lean together that scarcely a ray of light can find you out, and you need an umbrella to protect you from the water that drips from them.

In a niche of the rocks near the end of this passage is the little Chapel of St. Mary Magdalen, where in other days the "cure" patients used to stop and pray for their healing. A little farther on you are shown the place from which, long ago, the sick used to be let down by ropes, and not drawn up again until they were supposed to be cured.

At the end of your wooden pathway between the rocks you take off your wraps and leave them outside, while you enter a dark tunnel, ten yards in length, and with a temperature like that of a vapor bath. The tiny light carried by your guide only serves to make darkness "visible," and you feel a strange sense of awe and helplessness as you stumble along to the place where the hot spring bubbles up, and drink the accustomed draught from the subterranean tea-kettle.

You come out drenched with vapor and perspiration, and are glad to hasten back through the grand and sombre gorge, and out into the cheerful light of common day.

Down to the town you go hurrying along by the side of the hurrying Tamina, and reach the Quellen-Hof just as the band is closing the afternoon with music. You walk about in the sunset through the pleasant gardens, where the fountains toss their spray high into the air, and the roses and oleanders and heliotrope fill the gloaming with their penetrating fragrance; and then the soft dusk steals down from the hills, and closes in round you, and you go in to your excellent dinner, and finish the evening in the drawing-room, where you may be sure there will be such good company that it is a real sacrifice to go to bed early,— but you do it, all the same.

The next morning at half-past six you are awakened by the music under your window, to begin the quiet pleasures of a Ragatz day. First among these I should reckon the morning bath. In Ragatz there are four hydropathic establishments, eighty-one ordinary baths, and a large swimming bath.

Staying in the Quellen-Hof, you go to the Neubad by way of a long corridor, without leaving the house, and you find a luxurious bath awaiting you. It is octagonal in shape, fashioned of white tiles which look like white marble, and nearly full of the clearest, softest water by which tired limbs were ever caressed.

The temperature is ninety-seven degrees Fahrenheit, and this degree of warmth does not change, for it is the natural heat of the springs, and it is fresh every moment, since it is constantly flowing in through one pipe and out at another.

It is so transparently pure that it fairly glorifies the bather, and you understand the secret of that beauty which belongs to the water nymphs.

In connection with each bath is its own little dressing-room, and the attendant brings you soft, hot linen, in which you luxuriously wrap yourself dry. Then you go back to bed for half an hour of rest, and then comes the dainty Swiss breakfast of snowy rolls, fresh butter, new-laid eggs, excellent coffee, and honey in which, bee-like, you seem to taste the flowers.

And then you pass your busy, idle day: write your letters, read your books, chat with your neighbors, listen to the music, and, above all, climb the mountain paths, and so fill your very soul with the rapture of their beauty that it will rise before you, like a splendid vision, in days to come, when you are far away.

Besides the excursions I have mentioned as within the compass of an easy ramble, there are many longer ones, for which good guides are easily procured.

Moreover, the place is on the way to the Engadine, to Italy, to everywhere, and only three hours from Zurich, whither I must soon betake myself, leaving this sweet seclusion with something of the same regret with which Eve must have looked back into the forsaken loveliness of her Eden.

CERTAIN FRENCH CURES.

AT AIX-LES-BAINS.

WE drove away from our hotel in Paris at 8 A.M., and that gave us barely time to catch the 8.55 morning express from Paris to Aix-les-Bains, at the distant Gare de Lyons. The French are a very economical nation, and their system of railway travel is by far the least comfortable of that in any country with which I happen to be acquainted. I should think at least three times as many railway carriages, in proportion to the traffic, must be employed in England as in France. In Great Britain, by the judicious expenditure of a few shillings, even a party of two or three can almost always secure an entire compartment; but in France the directors have a sterner eye to profits, and put on so few carriages that each one is crowded. There were seven people in the compartment into which the Dark Ladye and myself were hurried on that August morning when we left Paris. Two corners were occupied by a Frenchman, who wore the red ribbon of the Legion of Honor, and his portly wife. The two other corners had been appropriated by the typical travelling Englishman and his pretty daughter. Next to the young Englishwoman sat her French courier maid; and the Dark Ladye and I meekly seated ourselves where we could.

We did not lose very much, however, by not being next the window, for one can hardly imagine scenery more monotonously uninteresting than that along this route, until the train reaches Culoz, some time in the late afternoon. After Culoz there is a change. Nature seems to have awakened from her long nap, and determined to see what she can do. She gives us mountains and ravines, and still deep lakes, and gay little streams that frolic from rock to rock, and great trees that laugh at the wind's will.

And then, as we sped along, came the splendid pageantry of sunset.

A man crowded in to fill the vacant six inches in the carriage. He looked aggressive rather than penitent, but I suppose he could not help himself. We might have been vexed at him but for the magic of the sunset, which diverted our minds from corpulent and intrusive Frenchmen. A low wind sighed its vesper hymn through the tree-boughs. Strange fires were kindled on the mountain-tops. Gates were opened into the very heavens; and suddenly one felt that a few inches more or less of space on that flying train mattered little when our eyes could roam at will through the spaces of earth and sky. And then, before the sun had fairly set, the moon — fair empress of a dead world — arose, and looked down on us royally.

It was nearly 7.30 when we reached Aix-les-Bains, and lo! on the platform I saw the faces — familiar and beloved — of two waiting friends, and instantly I was at home. Shall we feel thus " at home," I wonder, if beyond the sea of death, when the grim ferryman moors his bark and lands us on the far-off, long dreaded shore, we meet the gaze of eyes that our own have held dear in this lower world? I hope so, for who could bear the utter and horrible solitude of a strange land, peopled only by strangers? I was soon " at home " in another way also, for we came to the Hôtel Venat et Bristol, my abode when I was here in 1885. The intervening years seemed to me scarcely to have changed the place at all. We slept in front rooms on the night of our arrival; or perhaps it would be more in accordance with facts to say we tried to sleep and failed, for it seemed that there was not one half-hour, even in the dead waste and middle of the night, when wheels were not clamoring over the stony pavement underneath our windows. Next day, however, we came in for a stroke of good fortune, and moved to pleasant chambers on the garden side of the house. We look out into a soft labyrinth of trees and shrubs. White marguerites are in bloom down there, and blue corn-flowers, and red geraniums, and something yellow, I don't know what; and the grass is lush and green, and the tree-boughs droop toward it tenderly. And all is as peaceful as if we were in the wilderness, and there were no town here at all, and no stony streets or grinding wheels anywhere.

Far away, over the housetops, we can see the beautiful range of the Lower Alps. How I love to watch the sunset light on them, or the pale rose of the dawn! Sometimes a wild tempest of thunder and lightning springs to fierce life among these hills, and the very earth seems to tremble before it. No one knows what a thunder storm can be who has not encountered it in a region of mountains.

Of course we saw our doctor on the first day after our arrival; and the second morning we began the "cure." When I hear the bearers stamp along the hall and set down their sedan chair outside my door, I always think of the men that will bring the hearse, some day, for my coffin. It is a grim association; but I cannot escape from it. They are careful and kindly burden-bearers, these Savoyards. My pretty and sweet-voiced maid, Lucie, swathes me in flannels, and tucks me in as if I were a baby, and then the men take up the chair and carry me down two flights of stairs into the street; and at that hour, — seven of the morning clock, — lo! the whole street seems alive with these striped sedan chairs, and all Aix seems on its way to the Établissement.

My prescription sounds rather formidable; for it begins with eight minutes in the "boiling room." It rather suggests the Inferno; but I go in bravely, and it proves to be the hottest of hot vapor baths, where for eight minutes I am left alone to boil at my ease. Then I go into the next cabinet for my douches; and here are two good-natured peasant women who pass their lives in these hot rooms. They douche me, they knead me, they pat me in amiable approval because I take my doom patiently; and, meantime, I am wondering what the life must be like that is passed from morning till nightfall in tasks like these. I am foolish, no doubt; but I feel very sorry for these women. Perhaps they are far happier than I am myself, and would be amazed at my pity if they were aware of it; but I should not like to be in their hot places.

"At what time in the morning must you get up?" I said to them to-day.

"Oh, at half-past two in the summer, and get to the Hospice at three to douche the poor. Now it is later, and we don't get up till three."

"Till three!" Ye gods! Fancy getting up every morning, Sundays and all, not later than three o'clock! What would life be worth under those conditions?

I inquired about the Hospice. It is a free *établissement* for the treatment of the poor; and suffering wretches come to it from all the country round, — from Geneva, from Lucerne, from far-off Paris. And because all the comfortable and convenient hours of the day must be reserved for paying patients, these sad-fated recipients of charity must be boiled and douched, and the rest of it, between three and five in the morning, and the women of the baths must be up and ready to attend to them.

"It is hard," I said, when they had told me all about it.

"It is life," they answered philosophically.

It is always well to begin one's treatment here at an early hour, so as to have time for something else later on. I reach the Établissement at seven; I take my "boiling" and my douching, and am back again in my bed at eight o'clock. I am ordered to lie here for an hour; but at nine I may rise and dress, and then I have the rest of the long day to myself.

One might do much worse than to come to Aix for pleasure, for it is a charming place; but of the thousands — some twenty-five thousand per year — who come here it would be safe to say that nineteen-twentieths have come either in pursuit of health for themselves, or as the companions of health-seeking friends. An Englishman I met the other day was an exception. I had lost my way, and I asked him, in my best French, if he could tell me where was the house of Dr. Blanc.

"I am English, and I am well," was the somewhat startling reply; and, having astonished me by this statement, he proceeded to add that, being well, he had had no occasion to know where doctors lived. I have seen no other such specimen of proud independence; for it is as a "cure," technically so-called, that Aix is chiefly known, though Rousseau loved and lauded its beauty in his time. The regular inhabitants of Aix scarcely number five thousand; and it seems to me that most of them are either physicians, doucheurs, or keepers of hotels. I do not mention shopkeepers, for they are chiefly summer butterflies, — no, let me say, rather, keen-scented and industrious bees, — who come here from winter resorts like Cannes and Nice, and sell goods to the unwary at prices far higher than one would pay in Paris. Of course the great centres of attraction are the thermal establishment for health, and the Casino for amusement. Everybody wants to go to the Établissement des Bains in the forenoon, so as to have the afternoon free for pleasure; but also, of course, not every one can be so fortunate as to secure the early hours. The Établissement is an imposing building, and contains swimming-baths and douches of every possible variety, vapor baths, rooms for inhalation, steam baths for hands and feet,— patience would fail were I to try to enumerate them all. The doucheurs and doucheuses of Aix-les-Bains are said to be the best in the world.

If the early bird catches the worm, worms must have a short life of it in Aix-les-Bains, for the birds are very early indeed. I hear them singing in the garden under my window when the morning is only two or three hours old; and by 4.30 A. M. all Aix-les-Bains is astir, as well as the birds. The bath establishment opens at 4.30, and if you go into the streets at that hour you find them well filled with porters bearing invalids to their douches in sedan chairs. These chairs are like the old-fashioned square-bottomed chairs of a country farm-house. They are fastened to long poles, and each is borne by two men. Their occupants are curtained from the intrusive gazer with a sort of coarse linen, striped in pink and gray. The bearers jog on with them at a steady pace, which soon brings any one in this small town to the establishment of baths.

This little town, with its wonderful waters of healing, is situated in one of the most picturesque valleys of the Alps, bordering upon the Lake of Bourget, and not far from that of Annécy. It is three hours distant by train from Geneva and twelve hours from Paris. Its climate is deliciously mild, and the air is so pure and the water so good that nothing like an epidemic has been known here within the memory of man.

It is a lovely view which one has looking off from the terrace of the Hôtel Splendide, over the little village and the blue lake, to the beautiful mountain range of the Dent du Chat. I have seen this view when the mountains were clothed in storm clouds on the left, and the rays of the setting sun kindled the sky on the right to a golden glory which, contrasting with the grim darkness of the confronting storm, seemed almost too bright for the eye to endure.

If you want to be in Aix when the English and

Americans are here, and the streets are vocal with your mother tongue, you must choose May, June, or September for your visit. In July and August the place is pretty well given up to the French. By the first of July Monaco and the Riviera have sent hither their faded *habituées* and the streets swarm with the world of the Paris boulevards.

For these gay comers the "Villa des Fleurs" and the Casino — called "The Cercle" — provide unfailing amusement, as indeed they do for the more sober guests of the earlier season. The Casino is the centre of the social life of Aix. It has an admirable theatre, a large and perfectly appointed ball-room, a music-room, coffee-room, billiard-room, an extremely well supplied reading-room, several small sitting-rooms, besides the grand central hall; and, in a quiet corner, a room for baccarat, where the devotees of high play can lose their tempers and their fortunes as comfortably as at Monte Carlo or Monaco.

The grounds of The Cercle are beautifully laid out, and on warm nights, when the whole place is illuminated with colored lights, and the band plays in the little kiosque in the garden, it is as pleasant a spot in which to while away an evening as one need ask for. Sometimes there is comic opera, sometimes a French play, a concert in the music-room, a dance in the ball-room. And always there is the unholy fascination that lures one to the baccarat tables. I do not know the game, and I have never even sat down at the tables; but sometimes I linger near and watch the players. Here are brought together all sorts and conditions of men. Men of rank and title sit side by side with Jewish pawn-brokers; and ladies thorough-bred to the finger-tips, are elbowed by *cocottes* well-known to the Bois de Boulogne. What a tragedy I read in one woman's face! She looked as if she had come out of one of Ouida's maddest novels. She was well-dressed. You saw that she had once been handsome, though now her face made you think of a bird of prey. It was masked with pearl powder and rouge; but nothing could disguise the expression of ferocious greed, the look of the cormorant. I could read the whole progress of the game as I watched her. Now an evil light came into her eyes, like the flame the wreckers kindle to lure a ship to some fatal coast; again she wore an expression of baffled desire and unholy rage. A pretty, innocent-looking girl sat near her, and modelled her play on that of the elder sinner. The freshness of life's pure dawning was in the girl's blue and tranquil eyes and on her smiling lips; but how long can innocence play at baccarat, and be innocent still?

One reads of awful tragedies as the outcome of these evenings at baccarat; but you hear from the players nothing more than a murmured "Sacre!" and the man on whose dead face to-morrow's sun will shine is as self-controlled to-night as is the one at his elbow who is winning everything.

Aix is, above all, the chosen refuge for people afflicted with neuralgia, rheumatism, gout, and that disease we are wont to call rheumatic gout, though Dr. Garrod — the great London physician, who is its godfather — has given it a more stately-sounding name, which I am sorry to have forgotten.

"I might almost claim to have discovered rheumatic gout," said Dr. Garrod, in an interview I had with him in London. I silently wished that he had not made this discovery. "I mean," said he, perhaps by way of self-justification "that I differentiated the disease and classified it, as no one had ever done before. Twenty-seven years ago I gave it a name and wrote a book about it."

"You are then, in a way, its proprietor," I suggested humbly.

"I might almost say so. I have hundreds of patients with it in a single week. They come from every quarter of the world, — India, Australia, New Zealand, North and South America; and they are of all ages, too."

"Literally?"

"Well, pretty nearly. The youngest patient I ever had with it was a child of three years old, with every pronounced symptom, chalk deposits and all, and the eldest was an old man of eighty-seven, who had never had a touch of the disease till he reached that age."

I think he loves rheumatic gout, this Dr. Garrod, as an astronomer loves his telescope, or a chemist his bottles. And he believes in Aix-les-Bains devoutly. If you want to come here, you have only to go to Dr. Garrod's office, and he will send you.

Almost everybody here is ill, — not desperately ill, but suffering. "Who is your doctor?" "Are you here for rheumatism" "Are your pains less severe this morning?" These are the questions which form the staple of conversation. You discuss douches over your dinner, and pity your neighbors' aches as you walk about between the acts at the theatre. At any hour of the day, from half past four A. M. to five P. M., when the establishment closes, you meet the pink-curtained sedan chairs on their winding way. The "cure" is emphatically a water cure; but the chief reliance is placed on the baths and the massage, though you are usually required to sip a little malodorous, sulphur-impregnated water from time to time.

The very monotony of the days makes them pass quickly. You seem to have done nothing, and yet it is night. Scarcely have you gone to sleep before the birds tell you that it is morning. Then more douches, doses, drives, and dreams; and so the month of your stay has worn away before you know it. I have seen some honeymoon couples here. I don't know whether they came because they had twinges in their joints, or because they feared they might have, some day; but here they were, billing and cooing with the other love-birds in the garden, or standing with interlaced arms in balconies, or watching each

other, instead of the stage, at the theatre ; and the
sober rest of us laughed at them and envied them.
What a good thing it is to be young and foolish ;
and who would be old and wise if he could
help it!

I see the other extreme here, too: old, old
couples come, — so old that time seems to have forgotten them, and they are interesting, in all the
world, only to each other. And they too smile,
toothless smiles, in each other's faces, as they totter along side by side, — smiles, perhaps, over
memories of old days, when they were young.
Even they — ah, who knows how soon they may
be young again in some other world! God bless
them!

. . . .

It was Achard, I think, who said of Savoie : " It
is Normandy, with the horizon of Switzerland and
the sky of Italy."

I realized the truth of this sentence of description a few days since, when the Dark Ladye and I
spent four or five hours of the afternoon in a drive
among the loveliest of the points of view which
make the environs of Aix a perpetual delight.

We drove along the shores of beautiful Lake
Bourget, and saw mirrored in its placid waters
high mountains, low-growing trees, rocks, clouds,
— all the overhanging world. We skirted heights
too lofty for our stout pair of bays to climb; we
drove through avenues dense with leafage; we

smelt the new-mown hay that blue-bloused peasants were binding into bundles; and, best of all, we came home along the lake, when the whole world was aglow with sunset and the superb pageant on high repeated itself in the deep bosom of the waters.

Do you know that Mont Blanc, which we are wont to speak of as in Switzerland, really belongs to Savoie? Why Switzerland ever got the reputation of owning it I cannot see, for the property of Savoie it has always been, and Aix-les-Bains is on the direct road to it, though the ascent of it is oftenest made by travellers who are sojourning in Switzerland.

Of all the watering places with which I am familiar Aix has the most accommodating climate. It is never too cold for endurance, and it is never so hot that — to quote Sydney Smith — you want to take off your flesh and sit in your bones. Its bathing season, therefore, begins with April, and does not close until the very end of October. It is only since 1860 that Savoie has been annexed to France. King Victor Emmanuel of Italy was the hereditary Duke of the House of Savoie, and it was he who bartered this fair inheritance to France in a kind of commercial treaty. The character of the Savoyards seems to me both more sincere and more amiable than that of Parisians of the same class. I think one could not dwell among these people, even for a brief space, without loving them; and surely one could not come here at all and not love the natural beauties of the place. It is full of literary associations, too. Lamartine's " Raphael " might serve as an excellent guide-book for this fair neighborhood. He makes his hero, Raphael, choose Aix for his residence, because it combines the charms of valley and plain with the majesty of the on-looking mountains. Rousseau is yet more closely identified with Annécy and Chambéry, the neighbors of Aix; for while "Raphael" was a romance, the real life of Rousseau, in its most interesting years, was passed in Annécy, where he first met Madame de Warens, and in Chambéry, where he lived in the days of his golden prime.

Chambéry was the birthplace and capital of the House of Savoie. The old residence of this princely house was almost entirely destroyed in 1793, though three towers and the chapel remain.

But I fancy more people think of Chambéry in connection with Jean Jacques Rousseau than even in connection with the House of Savoie. Near Chambéry is the little place called "Les Charmettes," which was the home of Rousseau and Madame de Warens; and it is quite unchanged since they lived there. It is possible to make an excursion from Aix to La Grand Chartreuse and return in a single day, but it is much easier and pleasanter to take two days for the trip. The men of your party will be allowed to pass the night in the monastery which shelters the holy monks, but the ladies must seek humbler refuge outside the gates, in a little inn kept by some lay sisters. Another charming excursion is by railway to Annécy. There is a lake which flows up to the town, and the soft loveliness of the spot equals that of Como. But to find beauty and interest enough one need not go so far afield. A drive of twenty minutes brings you to the entrance of the Gorge of Gresy, and then a little steamer takes you through the Gorge. Your boat glides on silently. Trees meet over your head and seem to close impenetrably before you. Not a sound save the wind's low whisper breaks the stillness. You are veritably in some realm of Faery. Pan has taken refuge there, perhaps; and the wood-nymphs and the water-sprites meet on these banks. You hold your breath for very rapture, and glide through the charmed silence, too happy to break it by a word.

How glorious is this September weather in Savoie; and what a beautiful world this is when the sun shines on it! I think people grow lovely, too, when they dwell in the light. I wonder, sometimes, whether trouble, and privation from all the heart longs for, can possibly be good for any one. I am greatly inclined to doubt it. What plant thrives on which the sun never shines? What bird sings a blithe song in the gloom of November? If one is very unhappy one's self, what compassion has one to spare for other people? "Yes," we say, when we hear some tale of misfortune, "yes, it is hard; but then everybody has something to bear. Why should any one expect to be exempt from the common lot?"

No; it is when we are glad, when the world smiles for us, that we are grieved to see other people suffer, and feel moved to do somewhat to comfort them. What troubles one most of all is the inequality of human destiny. Why, for instance, should there be, here at Aix, fair ladies, clad in purple and fine linen, and with all the good things of the world at their command, and others who rise at three o'clock in the morning to begin a weary task that ends only with the night? Why, as Carlyle said, are one-half the world born saddled and bridled for service, and the other half booted and spurred, ready to ride them? Who knows?

BRIDES-LES-BAINS.

"ANYWHERE, anywhere, out of the world!" So might the pilgrim sing who sets forth on his way from Aix to Brides-les-Bains. At all events, one finds out what it is to travel by diligence in Savoie. The traditional " slow coach " is nothing to it, for the slow coach was supposed to keep moving. From Aix-les-Bains you go by train to Albertville, and there you will find the diligence with its five strong horses and its blue-bloused driver. The sun is bright, the air is clear, and the mountains are a joy forever. And on you go, or rather you don't go. Presently the diligence stops. The driver gets down and leaves his five horses to their own sweet will. You wait and wait, until finally you get tired of waiting.

" Why don't we go on ? " you ask.

" Pardon, madame; the driver he drinks," answers your French neighbor.

" But he can't drink forever ! "

You are answered by a shrug of the shoulders, which intimates that even that would be very possible. However, Jehu comes back at last, and the diligence jogs on a bit farther, and then comes another stop. What is it this time? Oh, this is a post station. The driver leaves one mail bag here, and picks up another. He might be writing the letters from the time it takes him. Then you go on for another space. Then he drinks again. Then another post-office. Then a change of horses. During the three hours it takes to go from Albertville to Moutiers you are tranquilly waiting the driver's pleasure for at least one hour. At Moutiers you part company with the diligence, and you wait another hour for the omnibus which is to take you on to Brides-les-Bains. You get into it at last, and on you drive, through scenery so lovely that you hardly dare mock it with an attempt at description.

You reach Brides-les-Bains at last, — droll little place in the hollow of the mountains, with its half-dozen houses and an almost equal number of hotels, the porters of which rush out and surround you as flies do a pot of honey, and deafen you with invitations to their several lairs. You are fortunate if you know beforehand, as I did, where you are going. I soon found myself at the Hôtel des Thermes, in the grounds of which is "The Source," as it is called, where you drink from the spring of healing. The bath establishment is in connection with this hotel, and so is The Cercle, or Casino, with its great salons, where the music plays, and where is one table for baccarat and another for some game of which I am not learned enough in gambling to give the name.

For what does one come here? For various things, I believe. The waters are something of the same nature as those of Carlsbad, and are celebrated for their beneficial effects on the liver, and as a general tonic. Also, a few years ago one of the doctors here discovered, and proclaimed far and wide, that they were a cure for too much flesh. This last I think it was that really made the popularity of the place. I have seldom seen so many fat people gathered together even at a "cure." Here are fat women, fat men, fat boys, fat girls; the Ohio fat girl of American fame would have seemed a sylph compared to some of them.

In this hotel there are, besides myself, only four persons who speak the blessed English language, — an American physician, with his wife and daughter, and an English spinster, so old she must have forgotten that she was ever young. She is very thin, and she looks with holy horror on the troops of the fat who arrive daily.

"*There* is another!" she will say tragically. "Look at her! *Look!* Just *see* the size of her dress-improver, — as if *she* were not big enough!"

I glance at the new-comers thus pointed out to me, and verily they are an ever fresh amazement.

How they have ever grown to be so big without bursting, I daily marvel. They surround "The Source" in the early morning and from five to six in the afternoon. They appear in all sorts of costumes, from the most gorgeous Paris toilets to a dressing-jacket and skirt, and, one and all, they drink, and they drink!

The system of treatment here is drinking, supplemented by baths; but the drinking is the chief thing, as the baths and massage are at Aix. If you are too thin, you drink; if your liver has gone crazy, you drink. If you have rheumatism, gout, paralysis, still you drink. You take a glass of the slightly warm, rather nauseous water, and then you walk for ten minutes, getting, meanwhile, what amusement you can from watching your fellow-sufferers. At the end of another ten minutes you drink again. Then you walk ten minutes more, after which comes your third glass; and then still again you must walk for twenty minutes or half an hour, and at the end of this final promenade you go in, extremely ready for the single roll and cup of coffee which constitute your breakfast.

The doctors are out in great force in these morning hours. They are dignified-looking creatures, in their black coats and their tall, shining beavers, which they seem to wear officially, as a priest does his cassock. They brood over one patient and then over another, and they smile, and bow, and congratulate you if you say you feel well, and if you groan with some recurring twinge assure you that you never do feel the real good of the treatment until afterwards; and so up and down they go, administering greetings and consolations.

Some of them speak a little English; my doctor does, for instance, and he is very proud of it. He is also the medical adviser of the English spinster, who is, alas, in a state of chronic discontent, and nearly drives the poor man wild with her doubts and her difficulties.

"*You* know Mees Blank?" he asks me. "*You* know Mees Blank. Yes?" and there is a touch of pathos in his voice.

"Yes," I answer.

"She is what you call in English an old girl, is it not?" and he smiles self-approvingly, quite innocent of any intentional slang, and persuaded that he has conquered an English idiom. I echo his self-approving smile, and then he sighs.

"She is, *is*, what in English you call — " He pauses. The occasion is too serious for his English, and he subsides upon French. "She is — *difficile.*"

"Yes," I say, "rather;" and I quite understand the undercurrent of pathos in his tone. Miss Blank is too good a woman for this unsatisfactory world. Her room is next to mine, and I wonder how many times a day she comes in to assure me that she never would have come to Brides had she not been misled into thinking it was bracing; "which," she adds tragically, "you *can't* say it is." As if, indeed, I were a lawyer enlisted for the defence of Brides, and determined to maintain its reputation at whatever cost to veracity.

The music troubles her. She had a room on

one side of the house, where the noise of the rushing torrent deafened her. She moved to the other side, and now the impertinent band *will* play under her window. They dance every night in the grand salon, and this she seems to regard as a personal injury. " Who wants to see them ? " she asks daily. " It's so uninteresting, you know, to see grown-up people dance. If it were children, now! It is pretty to see children dance."

Her opposite neighbors at table grieve her, because they are, as she says, "so common." Their French tongues wag too freely; their French laughter is too merry. The meat at dinner is too tough. The tea at breakfast is too weak. The whole world, in short, is out of joint. She approves the scenery sometimes, but her highest praise is to pronounce it " quite Swiss," as if the only hope for poor little Savoie were that it should resemble Switzerland. Am I wasting too much space over her ? If I were Howells or James I would put her into a novel.

I have had nothing to do with the bathing establishment at Brides. From an external point of view it seems to be a very good one. There are baths simple, Russian baths, vapor baths, douches; and the fat people who come here to be turned into sylphs soak in them, day after day. I think I see them already melting, as I look at them, morning after morning. They bathe, they drink the waters, they take incredibly long walks; in short, they undergo a system of training so vigorous that I am inclined to think, as soon as they get away and resume their usual habits of living, the too solid flesh will come back again.

Is Brides, then, of no use as a health resort? On the contrary, I have the highest esteem for it. I believe its waters have a great tonic power. Your physician will usually advise you to supplement them with the salt baths at Salins, where the water, he will tell you, " is the water of the sea quite entirely, and altogether fortifying."

Brides is surely the smallest watering-place extant. There is nothing here but " The Source," the hotels, and the doctors. When I first came there was precisely one shop, — a combination of grocer's and bakery. Later on a sort of summer-house was put up, where laces are for sale; and on the way to " The Source " some people from Moutiers have set up their transient tent, and offer you guide-books and stationery, and those familiar Swiss trifles of which you buy so many on a first visit to Switzerland, and which you are never tempted to purchase afterwards. You go to Moutiers — the nearest place of any size — for everything. Your food is brought from there, your medicines must be sent for to Moutiers, you go there for a paper of pins or a button-hook.

" What if one should be poisoned and want an antidote?" I asked. " I suppose one must send to Moutiers ! "

' But one never *is* poisoned here, madame," was the serious answer.

I thought, naturally, you could get everything at Moutiers, and being starved for an English paper, I sought one there during the last week of June.

No, in all Moutiers there was not an English newspaper, or even an English book.

"It is not asked for, madame," said the shopkeeper. "We have for English books and newspapers not the demand. But soon, yes, even on July the first, will the Hôtel des Thermes commence to take 'The Times of London.'"

And truly, on the morning of July 3 "The Times of London," dated July 1, made its appearance, and since then I know, even here, what happened three days ago.

I wonder why one likes this slow little out-of-the-world place, — for like it you do, as soon as you have become a little accustomed to its quiet. Partly, I think, it is that in that very quiet there is something soothing. The monotonous days and nights slip into one another, and you hardly know when one ends and the other begins. Then the place itself is very lovely, though the English spinster is fond of calling it "a hole." It is a tiny valley, over which the mountains stand sentinels. Through the midst of it the mad torrent tears along. The sun rises gloriously over the hill-tops in the fresh morning, and sets with a kind of lingering tenderness, leaving the sky bright with a rosy after-glow. I am not sure that I would come here out of the world merely in pursuit of pleasure, but I am sure that, having come here in pursuit of health, one finds plenty of pleasure also.

It is a short journey from Aix-les-Bains in point of distance, though we were seven hours on the way. It could be done in less time, however, by using, instead of the diligence, a private carriage. Two hours by rail takes you to Albertville, the nearest railway station to Brides, and at Albertville the deluding diligence awaits you and takes you in.

I think at least every fourth lady here is a *comtesse* or a *marquise*, and every fourth man is *décoré*. It seems a popular resort for the French nobility, as well as for the French *bourgeoisie*. One very stately *marquise* never condescends to sit at table d'hôte, but has her dinner in solitary solemnity in the very same room, at the very same hour, and not two feet away from the rest of us. The other titled people seem as friendly and simple as if they had no *de* to their names; perhaps more so. In spite of French novels, I believe the body of the French people to be singularly domestic. You see husbands and wives here who are as constantly together as were the Siamese twins in their day; mothers surrounded by their children as a hen gathers her chickens under her wings; and the few wives who are here without their husbands have an air of patient waiting which blossoms into hope, as Saturday draws nigh, when *mon mari* appears from somewhere to gladden the conjugal heart.

If you love quiet and monotony, and the cheerful clatter of the French language; above all, if you have found out that you have a liver, come to Brides.

LIGHTS AND SHADES OF TRAVELLING IN SAVOIE.

FROM Brides-Les-Bains I was to go to Les Voirons, in Haute-Savoie, a journey it would have been easy to make in a short day anywhere save in Savoie. Not so here. To begin with, Brides is twenty-four miles from Albertville, the place where I was to pass the night, and the journey must be made by diligence, unless you choose to take, at some frightful cost, a private carriage. I arranged to leave Brides at 2 P. M. Of course it was 2.30 before we fairly got off; but we arrived at Moutiers, our first stopping-place, only too soon, since the corresponding diligence for Albertville was not expected to depart until five o'clock. From 3.15 till 5 o'clock was long, with nothing to do in the empty hours.

It seemed to me that every third house in Moutiers was a café; but one cannot drink coffee forever, and there was literally nothing else to do, save to follow the example of 'Ziekel in Lowell's "Courtin'," who

> "— stood a while on one foot fust,
> Then stood a while on t' other,
> And on which one he felt the wust,
> He could n't a-told ye, nuther."

Of course the five o'clock diligence did *not* start till 5.45, and then there were twenty miles between us and supper. The driver assumed an air of breathless haste, just as if he had not been standing about and gossiping with his "pals" for three-quarters of an hour after he should have been under way. However, he was a very good fellow, as I found; for I took my seat beside him, the better to see the view. And what a lovely view it was, — beautiful enough to make up for small discomforts! The road leads through a valley, and on either side the high mountains climb toward heaven and lose their tops in the sky; and all the way beside you rushes on the swiftly flowing Isère, — a strong, turbulent, fascinating river, full of restless energy.

"How it hurries!" I said to the driver.

"Yes, madame, it goes all the way to Grenoble," — as if that were reason enough for its haste. And so on we drove beside it, on its way to Grenoble. The quaintest little peasant children came out and stood by the wayside to watch us, — grave little women, with their gray gowns as long as a grown-up person's, and the drollest gray caps on their heads. They had serious faces, — and, unlike the children in Italy, none of them begged. They seemed solidly independent and respectable, like their peasant fathers and mothers whom we saw working in the hayfields as we drove by, the women quite as busily as the men.

"The women work hard in Savoie," my driver said, as he saw me watching them. "I believe they don't work out of doors, the women in your country?"

"No," I answered.

"I suppose the summers are too hot," he suggested, as if no other possible reason had dawned upon his mind. And then he added, with innocent pride, " We have good wives in Savoie."

Had he ever been to Paris ? I asked him. No, he had never had the time. But he had been to Geneva. As Geneva is but a short distance away, his travels had not been extensive.

I made my appearance at the bureau of the diligence in good time. I had been told the night before that it would start at 8.30 ; but of course it was nine o'clock before we finally got away, and then we had not reached the other end of little Albertville before the driver dismounted for a glass of beer at a café where some of his friends were drinking at round tables in the open air. He and I and my luggage had the little diligence to ourselves, and, like most of the Savoie drivers, he turned out very well when once he had satisfied his thirst.

One would be hard indeed to please, whom the lovely Lake of Annécy should not delight. Its shores have not the rugged grandeur of outline that surround some of the Swiss and Italian lakes; but they are charming to the last degree. Soft hills which the green trees climb, fields smiling in the sunshine, bonny little villages, here and there a grand château looking down from some lovely height, and between these sunny shores the lake winding like a river, so that sometimes the very path seems closed before you. Ah, it is a delightful hour and a half that one spends in voyaging from Doussard to Annécy!

Annécy is a pretty town, where, if one were French, I should think one might live happily. Unlike the smaller towns in Savoie, it is fresh and bright and clean. Its position is lovely, on the borders of the lake, with the mountains watching over it like sentinels, and that gay little river, the Fier, wandering away from it through peaceful meadows; one could not ask for a spot more smilingly picturesque. And yet an hour's drive into the suburbs brings you to the wildest spot I know, the Gorge de Fier.

It was for the sake of this gorge that I had stopped over at Annécy, and within an hour of my arrival I was on my way thither. After I left the carriage, a few minutes of steep descent brought me to the entrance of the gorge. Of course there was a franc to pay, and of course a fat, garrulous old Savoyard guide trotted on with me, when I would much rather have gone alone; but there I was, in the very heart of the world. I have never before seen such a place. It looks as if some awful earthquake had rent the solid rock foundations of the earth asunder. There is little more than space in this passage for the narrow gallery in which you can walk single file, and over the railing of which you seem to look down into the under world.

How this frail, wooden gallery, at least half a mile long, was ever built midway up this steep, straight height of rock one can hardly conceive. But somehow the workmen were suspended from above while they made it, and the guide pointed out bolts driven into the solid rock for them to cling to. It seemed, even now that it was done, a frail and perilous pathway; but it is daily traversed by many feet, and one hears of no accident there. It would be perfectly hopeless to try to describe the gorge. It is as if the infernal regions themselves yawned underneath you, and in that narrow, sullen black stream far below you half expect to see the boat of Charon round the corner. High, high, high above your head the trees wave in the summer wind, and even to the solid rock ivy clings here and there, and hardy mosses have gathered on its sides.

But it was a grewsome place, and one was glad to leave it and climb to the cheerful light o' the sun, and drive back behind the strong little Savoie horse to a good dinner at that pleasant refuge of the traveller, Hôtel Verdun.

Travelling in Savoie is beset with as many hindrances as it is possible to contrive. Whether it is that the Savoyards are a stay-at-home people, and wish to show their disapprobation of gad-abouts, or whether in some forlorn hope that if they make it very difficult to get away you will stay on with them and spend all your money, I know not; but I do know that it requires superhuman energy to travel there. For instance, I wished to go, next day, to Les Voirons; and to do this I must meet the Les Voirons omnibus at Bon St. Didier at 1 o'clock P. M. Now, considering that the actual railway journey from Annécy to Bon St. Didier occupies rather less than three hours and a half, you would think, in common reason, that you could breakfast comfortably at Annécy, start from there at ten or eleven o'clock, and arrive at your destination in plenty of time. Not at all.

I consulted my landlady. The only possible way to arrive at Bon St. Didier in time for the Les Voirons carriage was to leave Hôtel Verdun at 3.45 o'clock in the morning, walk to the railway station, and take the 4.10 train. "Was madame, indeed, of such courage?"

"Madame must be of such courage. Could I have morning coffee?"

"But, madame, at that hour, so early, there will be no fires. No one shall be up but the porter, who will awaken you, and carry to the Gare your luggage."

Needs must, again. I submitted to my fate, went early to bed, and found myself on my feet at three o'clock next morning; and at 4.10 I was in the train, rubbing my sleepy eyes, and waiting for the sun to rise.

LES VOIRONS: A PARADISE ON A HILL-TOP.

TO leave the forlorn Restaurant de la Gare, at Bon St. Didier, is of itself enough to raise one's spirits, albeit the " Carriage of Les Voirons " turns out to be a queer little nondescript affair, with striped calico curtains and an entire absence of luxury. I mounted beside the driver. Josef, the " whip " of the Les Voirons Coach, is a good man and true, and properly proud of the beautiful country through which he conducts his passengers. I was ready to admire his favorite points of view to his heart's content, and soon we became excellent friends.

The ten miles which climb from St. Didier to Les Voirons occupy four hours. Looking up the mountain from the foot, it seems as if you must go up a ladder to reach the summit; but the road winds and doubles, and winds and doubles again: and now you face the east, now the west; now you are looking at Mont Blanc, and now, far down, at the blue waters of Lake Leman. And as you go on and up, wild-flowers thicken about your path, and you come into the sweet-breathed shelter of the great fir woods, and your spirits rise with the rising way.

LES VOIRONS: A PARADISE. 271

At five o'clock you come in sight of The Hermitage,— the solitary hotel on this mountain-top. The " Guide-Book to Savoie " assures me that this is " a magnificent hotel ; " otherwise I should have said it was the simplest one, to be fairly comfortable, that I had ever seen. But simplicity suits this shy spot, which seems quite apart from and above this world; though, truth to tell, you can reach it very easily from Geneva. Upholstery and gorgeous appointments would be as out of place here as a ball-dress in a whortleberry pasture. The view which the hotel commands is the great thing, and that must be a joy forever. On one side is the Alpine range, with Mont Blanc crowned king of the whole. On the other side you look down to the blue waters of the lake, and to Geneva, which seems like a toy village in the distance.

Many a legend is connected with the site of this hotel. It is called " The Hermitage" because it was formerly the retreat of certain hermits who founded a convent here. But its traditions go much farther back than the hermits. Long ago, when the world worshipped the gods of Olympus, — when Pan sat on a rock and tuned his pipes, and the wood-nymphs played in the shade of immemorial trees, — here, on this very spot, had the worshippers of Venus erected a temple in her honor. In this temple was an oracle, whose fame extended far and wide ; and long after Christianity had conquered the valley, Paganism still reigned on the height, and the mountaineers used to come to the Venus-berg to consult the oracle.

At last, however, a good bishop of Geneva was so scandalized by this idolatry that he led a band to overthrow the temple and break the statue of the goddess; and henceforth the oracle was dumb, and poor Venus lost her shelter. But Satan was not disposed to quit his old haunts: so he entered into the shape of a wild boar, and ravaged the country, and tore in pieces all the wayfarers who refused to deny and dishonor Christ and the Apostles. One day while hunting in the mountains, the pious chevalier, Amédée de Langin, encountered the Satanic wild boar. The boar devoured the servant of De Langin in a trice, and wounded the chevalier himself; whereupon the noble lord uttered a vow that if he were delivered from death he would build on the spot a chapel, and consecrate it to the Holy Virgin. This excellent offer was accepted by the higher powers, and the wild boar forthwith expired under the sword of the knight.

The Sieur de Langin erected the chapel according to his promise; and beside it he built a hermitage, whither he retired from the gay uses of the world, and passed the rest of his life in penitence and prayer. In the chapel he had set up a statue of the Virgin, of which the figure was black, while the face was gilded. This " Black Virgin," as she was called, worked many miracles; and people came to her from far and near to be healed, as they had come in other times to consult the oracle of Venus. The Black Virgin was particularly severe on Protestants. One of these sinners impiously took away the statue of the Virgin. She allowed him to convey her a little distance; then suddenly, so runs the legend, she arrested him and his wicked crew, and no efforts on their part could move the statue one inch farther. They turned their heads to look and wonder at this prodigy, and lo! they never could turn them back again; and to this day, if you seek long enough, you may find, in the neighborhood of Les Voirons, some of the descendants of these wry-necked men.

Another miracle was wrought in favor of a beautiful girl named Brigitta. Brigitta was a shepherdess, and, alas, one of the hermits saw and loved her, — for sometimes sin enters even into the abode of the holy. Brigitta herded her sheep near the hermitage,— which was a pity, for it was putting temptation in the poor hermit's way. Suddenly, one day, he rushed out, and caught her in his arms, and she cried aloud on the Black Virgin; and as she cried she took a leap — an awful leap — over the near precipice. The priests rushed forth in search of her, and, an hour later, they found her, quite unharmed; for the Black Virgin had sustained her in her fall, and deposited her gently in the ravine below. Do I not know that this is true, for I have seen the rock whence she flung herself down, and they call it, to this day, the " Saut de la Pucelle,"—the Maiden's Leap.

After this wonderful miracle the chapel was repaired, and the Black Virgin was set bravely upon her pedestal, and people came to seek her favor more numerously than ever. Hermits of high degree sought rest and peace in the hermitage, and prayed, and dozed, and died there; and all went well until 1769, when the monastery was burned. Then the hermits had to retire to Annécy, and the Black Virgin was taken to a church in Boëga, where, I believe, she still abides.

Since that time the mountain-top of Les Voirons has been given up to worldly uses, though there is a chapel here, near the ruins of the old one, and a good curé lives in his little house near by, and gathers from among the guests of the hotel a faithful few for his morning Mass.

Some years ago — I don't know just how many — Dr. Lombard, of Geneva, wrote a good deal about the great benefit for certain classes of invalids to be derived from mountain air, and called attention to Les Voirons, where he deplored the absence of accommodation for visitors. Thus it came about that one of the mayors of Boëga built the hotel called "The Hermitage," and threw open to the public this spot, which I think I have justly called " A Paradise on a Hill-top."

The view of Mont Blanc from Chamouny is not to be compared for beauty with the nearer one from Les Voirons. On the east is the mountain chain of which Mont Blanc is king; and the aspect of these various heights is never twice alike.

Sometimes the air is so clear that the mountains seem preternaturally near, and that means that a storm is threatened. Sometimes the lower mountains are covered with clouds, and you would fancy a great inland sea spread out before you, from which Mont Blanc lifted, like a strange god, his snow-crowned head.

I have risen to see the sunrise kindle these mountain-tops with sudden flame; and I have lingered to see the after-glow of the sunset flush them with rose-color as delicate as lines the heart of a sea-shell. I have seen them with a full moon bathing them in white splendor till they seemed like hills in Ghost-land. And morning, noon, and night their beauty thrills me with ever-fresh surprise.

The wonder is that people live here just as they live down in the lower world, and flirt and gossip, and play billiards, and smoke cigars, as if this were not paradise, and the heavenly gates did not open above the hills at night and morn.

For true lovers this might indeed be the veritable Garden of Eden. Paths lead duskily among the fir-trees, — paths soft with the fallen leaves of many a vanished year. The air is full of balsamic odor, and the climbing is just steep enough to give excuse for the constant pressure of a helping hand. Then there are seats on which to linger at ease, and dream, while the tempered sunshine sifts through the green boughs, and the happy, unafraid birds call to one another over your heads.

Bliss here is cheap, moreover. You have no need of the purse of Fortunatus. The terms of the hotel are reasonable, and you cannot spend money for extras, since the only thing you can buy here is a postage stamp. Shops and their commonplace temptations are of the lower world. Here — on the heights — you are neighbor to the sun, and to moon and stars, — the night's proud company.

HOW THEY CURE THEMSELVES
IN GERMANY.

MARIENBAD AND NUREMBERG.

IT is a far cry from London to Marienbad. We started — the Pretty Widow and myself — at 9.40, A. M., on a Friday. The Pretty Widow's soul was grieved because it *was* Friday. Some awful judgment, she thought, was sure to overtake us for tempting fate in this rash manner. I silenced her by telling her that, if we had left London on Thursday, we must have left somewhere else on Friday, and that would have been equally dangerous. We crossed from Dover to Ostend on a sea of glass, so smooth was it, — though the very name of the Channel frightened some timid souls into sea-sickness. At 4.30 o'clock we were speeding across level Belgium, catching sight of picturesque bits of landscape, with appropriate windmills, all trim and neat, as the Dutch painters like it. It was nearly midnight when we arrived at Cologne and drove to my old haunt, Hôtel du Nord, where, for the first time, I found a difficulty in obtaining rooms. The friendly porter recognized me as an old customer.

" You have not telegraphed from London — No? It was so great mistake! We have of the world mooch, at present. We turn away so many," —

with a widespreading gesture of the hands which seemed to indicate half the world, at least. "But I will give you rooms; yes. Follow me." And on he walked, like a shepherd leading a flock of sheep. It was not to an apartment in his own hotel, as his words had given us hope, that he conducted us, but through a large courtyard and along a silent street to another house, where we had a noble salon, and a landlady who spoke English "as she is taught" nowhere. We should have slept the sleep of the weary but for the beds. The beds in the Hôtel du Nord are very well; but those in the Hotel Braun were the regular German bed, lifted up at the head, like a steep inclined plane, and with a few feet square of feather bed for covering, which falls off every time you turn over. These curious beds are hard and rounded, and one needs to be an acrobat to perch judiciously enough on the very middle to escape the sensation of rolling down hill. We managed to conquer circumstances sufficiently to get a reasonably good nap, and then woke to realize how much better German coffee is than English. We went round, after coffee, to the Hôtel du Nord, and in its reading-room we heard some of our own country-folk discuss their plans with that charming frankness which characterizes the American on his travels. Hotels, pensions, banks, routes, dressmakers, — all were talked over and pronounced upon; and we were richer by the benefit of a good many personal revelations. Warned by the last night's experiences, we telegraphed for rooms to Hotel Bavaria, in Nuremberg, and at mid-day we were again on our way.

Much of our second day's journey was along the banks of "Father Rhine," as the Germans love to call their noble river. We saw the storied castles on the heights, the fay-haunted woodland paths climbing the green hills, the unutterable tranquillity of the landscape, all verdurous with summer, and with scarcely a sign of human life anywhere. Our train, rushing through its peace, seemed an impertinence for the sylvan gods to punish with their thunderbolts. When the sunset came, — when day was robed and crowned for dying, and her mourner, the dusky twilight, settled down over the solemn hills, — the beauty of it all seemed almost too much to bear. Perchance it was to escape its spell that the Pretty Widow went to sleep, and I — for we had a carriage to ourselves — sat and looked out into the gathering star-lighted darkness, and crooned to myself old ballads written by men long dead; and silent shapes came down from the silent hills, and they and I went on through the night together.

Again it was midnight when we reached our hotel at Nuremberg. Hotel Bavaria, like most of the other hotels in Nuremberg, is quite a journey from the railway station. The train stops where there seems to be nothing to invite its delay, and we drive across the long bridge over the river, and on and on into the heart of the sleeping town. Arrived at the hotel, we announce our names and see the good result of a telegram.

"Vera true, ladees; you have sent ze telegram, and ze chambers are ready."

So we follow the uniformed porter, who looks like a soldier, up the stairs and along the hall. He throws open two doors, he lights a cluster of candles in each room, bids us a kind good-night, invokes good sleep for us, and departs. The morning sun shirks his duty, and does not shine on Nuremberg. Instead, the rain pours, in a resolute, steady-going way, as if it were not in the least in a hurry, but never meant to stop. Nuremberg has always a curious charm for me. It is such a mysterious looking old town. Not a few of the houses have six, seven, and one or two even eight stories, in the roofs alone, represented by eye-shaped windows, which seem to watch you furtively from under their lids; for each of these eye-windows has a little projection over it, shaped like an eyelid. What goes on in those sky-chambers? What men and what women look out of those eye-shaped windows? It needs a Zola to climb up there and find out their secrets.

Before noon we were on our way again, speeding toward Austria-Hungary. The rain went with us everywhere, and the black roofs of the houses, as we neared Hungary, gave a singularly melancholy expression to the landscape. I kept thinking of a bit of dialogue from "Bluebeard:" —

"Sister Anne, sister Anne, what do you see from the turret?"

"I see the pump and the trivet, and the houses all in mourning, and the rain."

We, too, saw always "the houses all in mourning, and the rain," and we saw little else. Only twice during that day's journey was there any sign of human occupation, except at the infrequent railway stations. Once we saw a sort of carriage, old-fashioned enough to have been the resurrection of some fifteenth century vehicle, moving slowly across a field. It seemed to have come from nowhere, and to be going nowhere, and it only made the rainy landscape more desolate. And once we saw a melancholy peasant girl, in a deep blue cotton gown, and she, too, seemed to have come from nowhere, and to be going nowhere, and her unsheltered head was but an item of the general desolation of the scene, — a bit of the "composition" of the sorrowful picture.

The passage of the custom-house at Eger is a mere form, — no box or bag was unlocked. I think the Hungarians are only too glad to open their gates to the foreigner, with his British gold. From Eger to Marienbad is a lovely route when the sun shines on it; but with the rain falling still on the black-roofed houses, and the sullen, brooding clouds hanging low, it was by no means cheerful. When we arrived at our destination we found all the omnibuses of all the many hotels awaiting us. We asked for the Hotel Klinger, and the porter of that hotel came forward, — a tall, handsome fellow, with the melancholy Hungarian eyes. He saw to our luggage, and we were driven to the hotel and put into rooms which Lady Chatfield had been good enough to leave vacant that very day, — lovely rooms, looking out on the park, so that before our windows the fleeting show of Marienbad makes perpetual march. Beyond the park rise the beautiful hills, solemn with their dark groves of fir and pine, and the winds bring hither their healing balsam.

I should feel sure that I recognized in Marienbad the Garden of Eden, so long ago closed to the public, were it not for the absence of the four rivers which ought to flow through it. Indeed, the sole lack of the landscape is the absence of visible water. The Ancient Mariner complained of
"Water, water everywhere,
Nor any drop to drink."

Here the case is reversed. There is no water that eye can see; but the inexhaustible springs seem to hold enough for all the armies of the earth to drink. Perhaps the nymphs of the hills and the forests water the place by night; for one would think it had rained all night long, in the very face of the moon, to see the morning freshness of the whole green, beautiful world. It is a true hill-country, with scarcely a level stretch anywhere, and the deep charm of these forest-crowned hills holds one like a spell.

Said my German neighbor at table d'hôte, "I come when I am ill, to be cured. And I come when I am well, as now, that I may not get ill. So I come year after year. It is good always." And many others — English as well as German — come yearly, and gladly, as one goes back from the too busy world to the quiet of some early home.

It is in the northwestern part of Bohemia, this pleasant Marienbad, some two thousand feet above the level of the sea. It is not difficult of access, being but five hours by rail from Nuremberg and nine from Frankfort. High as it is above the sea, it is still in a ravine, sheltered and surrounded by mountains, on all of which are forests of fir and pine. Charming walks and drives — of which one might choose a different one every day for a month — lead over the hills to rural-looking cafés, where you can find the best of coffee and bread, the freshest of eggs, and the wholesome, sound wine of the country.

The air is said to be rich in ozone, and I suppose it is that which imparts to it its peculiarly stimulating quality, and makes the heart light within you.

When it is left to itself, in the long, snow-bound winter, Marienbad has only some two thousand inhabitants. In summer it is full of a countless, ever-changing throng. Grand people come from London, — Lady H——, for instance, has been passing some weeks here. She came with two

London doctors in her train, a courier, a *dame de compagnie*, two maids, and two or three men servants. She occupied, with her suite, twelve rooms of this hotel; but what she was here for only the London doctors knew, for she kept to her own rooms, of which the windows were never opened, — she neither drove nor walked, — and when she left, at last, scarcely a creature in Marienbad had seen her face. But it was a face that had looked on the world for seventy-seven years, and at seventy-seven one may be allowed, perhaps, to retire from view, — at least if one is a woman.

Lady Ashburton, whom all the peasants seem to adore, is here now with her nephew; and Sir Charles Russell, Q. C., and Lord This, and Lady That, and they go in and out among us, simply clad, and courteous, and eat their frugal meals in evident obedience to the rules of the cure. There are hordes of Germans — you hear their rather harsh tones everywhere; there are a few French — and, thank Heaven, there are but very few of the Polish Jews, with their rusty gabardines, and their long, oily black curls. It is at Carlsbad that the Polish Jews swarm like bees.

I should hardly dare to say how many hotels and lodging-houses there are here, — a good many more than a hundred, I believe, — and in June, July, and the first half of August, they are well filled. Hotel Klinger alone, where the Pretty Widow and I found shelter, includes three large and stately hotels under one management.

The only drawback to my complete comfort is the necessity of making known my wants in a tongue my knowledge of which is somewhat limited. This trifle does not discourage the Pretty Widow. Not one word of German does she know; but she declares she will make them understand English. To this end she speaks very loudly and clearly.

"I want some eggs, not much cooked."

"Me not know," says Bohemian Anna, with a pathetic glance of her dark eyes.

"I want some eggs, not much cooked," the Pretty Widow repeats, very emphatically indeed. Anna looks ready to cry with despair. I come to the rescue with my two words and a half of German, and all goes merrily again.

"I can make the good English language carry me anywhere," I once heard a venerable American lady say, in Italy; and my Pretty Widow shares that opinion. I hear her constantly making long speeches to uncomprehending German ears, with that slow emphasis we use for the benefit of those stupid people who don't understand our native tongue. Just now her fair face is troubled. I came in from a walk, and I laid my umbrella down on her bed.

"Oh, don't, don't!" she cried, almost turning white with terror. "It's such a bad sign to put an umbrella on the bed."

It seems that, in my ignorance, I am constantly defying the Fates, or whoever it is who avenges our disregard of omens — and what will become of us as a consequence, I'm sure I do not know.

. . . .

And now, alas, I am alone. Whether it was because we started for this place on a Friday, or because I put the umbrella on the bed, or in some other benighted manner affronted Destiny, I cannot say, but Dr. Ott, the wise man of Marienbad, decided that this "cure" would not do for the Pretty Widow, and sent her off to Kissingen. "Shall I go too?" I asked. He shook an oracular finger. "No, madam, you will not go. By just so much as Kissingen is better for her, by just so much it would be worse for you." So there was nothing to do but to part company, and here I am making the cure alone.

I get up at an hour I do not like in the morning. At six o'clock the music begins to play, and it plays till eight. This was very well,
"In summer when the days were long."
but just now, for the first hour, the music seems to address itself to empty benches. I don't aspire to get down before seven. I don't realize my aspiration usually till nearly eight. Then I drink a large glass of *Kreuzbrunnen* water, which a tall man in uniform, who salutes me in French, sometimes hands me, and sometimes a brown little peasant girl who smiles and says "Morgen," with a quaint little bob of her head.

Having drank the first glass, I walk up and down for fifteen minutes. Then another glass, then another walk of fifteen minutes, then a third glass; and then, if I obey orders, a walk of nearly an hour over the hills to some far-off café, where I get my morning meal. This morning repast consists of a slender stick of bread, a cup of coffee, and one soft-boiled egg. I don't always march over the hills to get it; but quite as often walk lazily to and fro, between the rows of shops in the park, and go to my own near hotel for the little feast which seems more delicious than any fine banquet elsewhere.

Then I may rest, or, as Dr. Ott says, "repose myself" with a book until eleven o'clock; and then comes my mud bath. I stay there for half an hour, and then a stout peasant woman appears, and I am rinsed off and put into a bath of clear water, and brought back to cleanliness again. And then I must "repose myself" for another hour.

After the two o'clock dinner, one must again "repose one's self;" but by four P. M. every one is astir. The streets are full of comfortable open carriages; but I, who am bidden to walk, seldom use one. Off over the hills one goes. Walking between the trunks of these tall trees, one feels as if in a cathedral, — one realizes how Gothic architecture came to be. And the religious suggestion is enhanced by the rude little wayside shrines you chance upon so frequently. Austria-Hungary is an intensely Catholic country; and the people seem to me to profit by their religion. They are good and simple and honest. I wonder, sometimes, if there are any criminals among them. I never think of locking up anything, and I feel sure that all my belongings are as safe as if I held them in my hand.

I began to say that at about four P. M. every one is *en route* for somewhere. In the regular season there is almost always an afternoon concert at some distant café to go to, so that your walk may have at once an object and a reward. At six o'clock until the end of August, and at half-past five, now that it is September, the band begins to play, and plays for an hour, in the little temple in the park; and the world of Marienbad, if not otherwise amused, gathers there, and the cure patients drink their afternoon glass of *Kreuzbrunnen* while they listen to the music.

Dr. Kirsch has written very exhaustively about the treatment here, and his list of the things for which one should come to Marienbad seemed to me to include nearly all the ills to which flesh is heir. I think that for weakness or fatty degeneration of the heart, for gout and rheumatism and neuralgia, for weakness of the nerves and a tendency to hysteria, Marienbad is one of the best places possible. Law lords come here to repair damages; barristers, worn out by hard work; everybody, in short, who wants his nerves strengthened. Marienbad is said to be the salvation of hypochondriacs, who go home feeling that they have been born again. The waters and the mud baths are also very restorative for anyone who has had one attack of apoplexy, and are said to prevent its return. I should think these things were enough for any bathing place to do, so I'll not make the list longer.

Strict obedience to the physician's orders is very important. Dr. Kirsch says that "moral emotions are to be avoided as much as possible." These are his very words. Precisely what they mean I don't know, — or whether the good doctor thinks immoral emotions less dangerous to the health than moral ones. Mental excitement is imperatively forbidden. One's reading must be of the lightest, since one's mental digestion should be as little taxed as one's physical. The system of treatment here seems to me sensible and thorough, — the place, as I have said, is a garden of Eden, — and it is no wonder that My Lord This and My Lady That come back here, year after year, to forget the world for a space, and to live a natural, simple, healthful life, in which system of living, no doubt, a great part of the cure consists.

. . . .

Before I left, "the season" had fairly closed. Most of the hotels had shut their doors for the winter. The shopkeepers "aus Prague," "aus Vienna," "aus Berlin," were packing up what were left unsold of their wares, and departing. The music played in a half-hearted way, and was about to stop altogether. On Saturday, September 17, there was a general exodus of most of the people whom I knew. I left on Monday, the nineteenth, and went to Nuremberg. Somehow, one is always going to Nuremberg. I arrived there in the afternoon, and discovered that I need not drive into the far-off old part of the town for a hotel, since, really, there is a very good one — Hotel Würtemberg — a rod or two from the station. I settled myself in a room there, and then walked about the old town till sunset.

To get really acquainted with a place, I perceive that you must walk. Hitherto I had only driven around Nuremberg, stopping at the most important churches and fountains, and regarding the place from the point of view of the guide-book. Now I wandered through the by-streets — stopped at a little shop for a bit of gingerbread, played with some children and their cat, lost my way over and over, and found it again, — wandered on, in short, at my own sweet will, while the furtive eyes blinked down from the lofty roofs on me, the solitary pilgrim from an alien land. During my whole long walk I never encountered one person who looked other than a German, or caught one syllable of any other tongue than *Deutsch*.

How beautiful the quaint old mediæval city — the finest mediæval city in all Germany — looked in the westering light! The river Pegnitz flows through the town, as the Grand Canal does through Venice; and, with the sunset glow on it, in some places where the balconied houses rose from the river's bank, and the trees bent low and looked at themselves in the clear water, it seemed as beautiful as Venice itself. One of the bridges over the river is copied from the Rialto; and from that, as from almost all the bridges that span the Pegnitz, you have such enchanting perspectives as might of themselves make Nuremberg seem worth the trouble of exploring, even without all else that renders it interesting.

The old town is still almost surrounded by the high wall, with towers and ditches, which fortified it so strongly long ago; and the interior has faithfully preserved the character of an imperial town of the middle ages, with its balconied houses, its glorious old Gothic churches, its fountains, and its squares. In one of these squares I came suddenly upon the great sitting statue of Hans Sachs, the cobbler poet. He looked like some gigantic old heathen god of feasting and laughter, ensconced in the silent place. He died in 1576, but his house is standing still, turned into a *Weinzimmer* (wine shop) now, — a not inappropriate use for the abode of this man, who drained so many deep glasses and sang so many drinking songs in his far-off time.

Nuremberg treasures loyally the memory of her great men, and she has had plenty of them to treasure. Albert Dürer, the sincerest of German painters, was born here, and Adam Krafft, the sculptor, and Peter Vischer, the bronze founder, and many another "cunning artisan," as Browning has it. About the year 1500 the prosperity of Nuremberg was at its height, and at one time there were more than fifty masters here of the goldsmiths' craft, — men who made of their craft an art.

The old town has at present a population of one hundred thousand, of whom three-fourths are Protestants, three thousand are Jews, and the rest Roman Catholics. The most beautiful of the Protestant churches is the Gothic church of St. Lawrence, with its great rose window, its wonderfully carven "Bride's door," and its high towers. Its noble Gothic interior, its wealth of sculptures, and its glorious old stained glass make this church worth a long visit. But stately churches are numerous in Nuremberg, and so are fountains which are works of art, and solemn old houses that seem to be nodding to each other, as their projecting windows almost meet across some narrow street. And, above all — literally above, since it overlooks all the rest — the very ancient castle, first mentioned in documents bearing the date of A. D. 1050. An old lime-tree stands in the courtyard, said to have been planted by the Empress Kunigunde in 1020. How many generations of men and women it has seen come and go, and what insignificant, butterfly creatures we must seem to its eight centuries of observation!

There are interesting pictures of Lucas Cranach's time, in the audience chamber of the old castle;

and in one room there is a collection of ancient instruments of torture, the very memory of which is a nightmare. The pentagonal tower of the castle is the oldest bit of architecture in venerable Nuremberg. In this tower a robber knight, Eppelin von Gailingin, was once imprisoned, and he escaped by a bold leap on horseback over the castle moat. Not so successful was the similar leap of the knight of Altenahr, in that most stirring of Kingsley's ballads, for —

"They found him next morning down there in the glen,
  With never a bone of him whole —
But heaven may yet have more mercy than men
  On such a bold rider's soul."

Nuremberg contains some of the noblest buildings and some of the finest works of art in all Germany; paintings, mellowed by time; wonderful old armor in which knights long dead did battle; portrait-statues of rare excellence, and — gingerbread! I mention the gingerbread because the guide-book declares that "the long-renowned gingerbread of Nuremberg must not be forgotten," and my sweet tooth remembers it gratefully. I can fancy passing happy months in Nuremberg, under the spell of its Old World charm; but somehow one always seems to be running away from it, as I did next morning.

1887.

TO AND AT CARLSBAD.

AS befits a lazy tourist, I came to Carlsbad slowly. I left London at 11 A.M., by way of Dover and Calais, reached Brussels at 7.30, and passed the night at the Grand Hotel. Next morning, at 10 o'clock, I was *en route* again for Cologne, where I arrived at about 4.30 P.M., and there was plenty of time to drive about the town, to see the cathedral, and buy photographs and *eau-de-cologne* before dinner.

I passed the next night at Frankfort, and went on, the third day, to Nuremberg. The old town, with its streets full of ghosts and of memories, had the same charm, subtle and powerful, which I find in it afresh every time I go there. The same eyes look furtively at me from the many-storied roofs; the old houses nod sagaciously at each other across the narrow streets. Hans Sachs sits in the market-place, near his favorite wine-cellar. It all seems as if it had been there forever, and as if it would be there, unchanged, when the last trumpet sounds, and the round world itself rolls together like a scroll. I did not want to leave it, after a single night there, to come on to bustling Eger, and then on again to Carlsbad.

Why am I here? Because the doctors commanded it. I suppose I should have been too happy at Marienbad, among the pine-crowned hills and with the same delightful companionship which made last year's August and September a joy to remember. Carlsbad always seems to me to have been built by a whirlwind. You see here and there houses standing cornerwise to the street. Nothing is harmonious or orderly in arrangement. The streets are impertinent, turning up where they have no business to turn, as if to look into somebody's window.

Yet — when I forget Marienbad and its associations — I can find here much to enjoy. It is a lazy place. I think one might live here a score of summers, and scarcely know that one of them had passed. One day is so precisely like another that you forget to name them by their names, and when Sunday comes it takes the Carlsbad people till one o'clock in the afternoon even to find it out, for none of the shops close until after that hour, and some of them not at all. I have never seen any one shopping on Sunday, but the shopkeepers look placidly out of their open doors, and the rings and bracelets glitter in the jewellers' windows, and the pretty wax girl behind the milliner's plate glass turns her brainless head over her shoulder, and smiles from under her new hat of the latest French mode.

Carlsbad seems to have been built and arranged for the stranger, and the Carlsbadians exist in the stranger's service, and on his gulden. Nature was very good to the place. The Tepl, bright river of healing, dances through it, and lovely, tree-clothed heights surround it, and over these heights footpaths lead through a soft mystery of greenness to mounts of vision, whence you catch glimpses of far-stretching beauty.

The Alte Wiese, or Old Meadow, on the west side of the Tepl, is the haunt of the shop-keepers from Paris and Vienna, who come here for the summer, and spread out their glittering temptations. Shopping, or at least looking into the shop windows, is as legitimate a part of life in Carlsbad as is drinking the waters.

I live on the west side of the Tepl, — on the Schlossberg, — the pleasantest part of Carlsbad. My hotel is the Victoria, and in connection with it is the King of England.

Madame Teller dispenses the hospitalities of the Victoria, while Monsieur, her husband, administers the affairs of the King of England.

"If you like these rooms not," said Madame, in her quaint English, when we were seeking for an apartment, "you shall live well in the King of England. Yes?"

The Schlossberg overlooks the Mühlbrunnen Colonnade, and in the colonnade an excellent band plays from six to eight in the morning, to cheer the water-drinkers in their imbibing.

The first morning I did not know from whence the music came, and rubbed my sleepy eyes with a vague notion that I was being serenaded. I concluded, however, that it must be my pretty neighbor in the next room, whose name is Maud, who was being invited to " Come into the Garden," and I turned over and went to sleep again. I behave better now.

When the concord of sweet sounds begins, I begin, too, and make my morning toilet in time to the music. Then out I go. I pass several springs on my way to the one whose waters are for my own healing, — the Felsenquelle. I struggle for a pathway through the motley throng surrounding each different spring, and finally reach my own place. There, inside the railing, are four flaxen-haired little Bohemian girls to dip up the water, and there, to watch over them, is also a bland policeman, who always touches his hat and says " *Good*-morning," with an Austrian accent, and a gentle pride in his knowledge of English.

Then I reach out my cup. First little girl takes it, and hands it to second little girl. Second little girl receives it, and puts it under the faucet whence the hot spring water is flowing; and then these two turn back to repeat this performance for a long line of other drinkers. My eyes follow my own cup. Third little girl lifts it up, full, and gives it to fourth little girl, who stands a step above her. Fourth little girl hands it to me, and with a parting bow from the bland policeman I move away, and drink slowly, as the doctor enjoins, my not at all disagreeable warm water.

There are fifteen minutes to dispose of before the next draught. They are passed in the lovely Kaiser Park, just at hand, watching the fountains toss their rainbow-tinted spray into the sunlight. Or I lean over the great odorous roses, lifting their scented beauty to the morning air, — and such roses, it seems to me, only Carlsbad knows. Fifteen minutes pass very quickly, and then back to the four flaxen-haired Bohemian girls, and the picturesque policeman, and the second cup of warm water.

This time I go across the Tepl, to the quaint, out-of-doors fruit and vegetable market, and see the droll little old women, in gay-colored peasants' clothes, sitting on the ground, and selling the most tantalizingly delicious fruit that ever was forbidden since the apples in Eden. For you must know that all uncooked fruits are interdicted to any one who is drinking Carlsbad water. Wild legends are fearfully whispered of rash people who have disobeyed, and who have swelled up and died an evil death, as if they had been poisoned. I don't think I quite believe these legends, but I respect them sufficiently to be proof against the beguilements of the market-women.

Such pears, such peaches, such raspberries, such blackberries — I flee from temptation, and hie me to the spring for my third and final glass. After that, I must walk yet an hour before breakfast is permitted.

"Madame has *much* letters this morning," says the red-cheeked Austrian boy, who is cashier in the queer little bank where I receive my mail; and madame walks away, contentedly reading. Next, a look in at the shop-windows, or a stroll off by a winding path under the trees, and a breakfast in some café on a hill-top, an hour away from home. Or I go to the Stadt-House, and order a donkey for an afternoon drive; or into the meat-market, and see the deft-handed women-butchers cut up their meat and arrange it on marble slabs.

Whatever I do, you may be sure that I know when my hour is up, and seat myself gladly for my out-of-doors breakfast. I have bought my bread on the way. All Carlsbadians buy their own bread, and carry it home in pink paper bags. You can count a thousand pink paper bags during your morning walk any time in the season.

My own pink bag contains "*zwieback;*" that is to say, rolls cut in two, and toasted until all moisture has been dried out of them. I order one egg, and a little pot of coffee. The egg is fresh and the coffee good, and I eat, oh, how slowly, that this slight repast may seem as much a banquet as length of time can make it.

Then I go home, answer my letters, read my book, rest a little, and, before I know it, it is time for a mud bath. I had made the acquaintance of mud baths in Marienbad. They sound uninviting, but really they are not so bad. The mud is clean mud,—perhaps it should be called peat rather than mud. It is first dried, then pulverized, then mixed with mineral water until it is of the consistency of a thick paste.

You feel a sort of horror, a kind of buried-alive sensation, as you sink into it for the first time; but you make your plunge, and soon you experience a curious sense of exhilaration. The bath stimulates the action of your heart, quickens your pulses, and brings a glow of the keenest life to your very finger-tips.

You remain in this dirty bliss not more than fifteen minutes, and then step from it into a fresh water bath, which is standing beside it, and soon you are as clean as ever, and much more alive. It is as if the earth of which we were fashioned had warmed us to fuller life in her dark bosom.

You go somewhere to dinner. Every one dines in the middle of the day, and scarcely any one dines at home. If you are energetic you may walk for an hour, out to the Freundschaft Salle (Friendship's Hall), or some other distant café, and dine under its trees among a crowd of friendly sparrows; but more likely you stop on the way at Pupp's Café Salon, as he calls it, and you get there a good though simple dinner,—delicious trout or carp, caught from the clear mountain streams, followed with mutton, beef, veal, or chicken, and any one kind of green vegetable, such as peas, beans, or spinach.

Between three and four o'clock you see crowds

of people starting for one of the out-of-doors concerts. These are from four to six o'clock, and the plaintive music seems the very voice of the sweet, dreamy summer landscape. Under the trees we sit and listen to it at our ease. Some of the ladies knit or sew; quick-footed Bohemian girls go to and fro, carrying little pots of afternoon tea and coffee, and the thin cakes called *Oblaten*. In the pauses of the music you sip your coffee and chat with your companions, but while the music plays no other sound breaks the stillness.

Six o'clock always comes too soon. With six o'clock the viol strings are mute, and the harpers cease their harping, and we go, in the gentle gloaming, back along the tree-bordered way, to eat a lingering but most abstemious supper, and then for home and bed.

Thus passes one Carlsbad day after another, except that sometimes you vary the programme by a donkey ride up the heights crowned with pines or beeches, or a drive to some of the beautiful environs of the town, where you will see views well worth a pilgrimage.

Your road will wind between fair fields among the hills, through which, perhaps, the goose-girl of the German story-books leads her flock of hundreds of white geese on to Strasburg; or, on the sunny harvest slopes, women in red petticoats bind the golden grain in sheaves. Bright little streams will dance by you down from the mountains, and broaden in the valleys below, and mirror sky, and trees, and the wind-swept grass, and your own face, if you stoop to look, happy with the placid happiness of Carlsbad

. . . .

"Just where *is* Carlsbad?" asks some would-be pilgrim. Carlsbad is in Bohemia, and Bohemia is part of the great Empire of Austria-Hungary. The town is in the narrow valley of the Tepl, near the Eger, and is surrounded by high hills covered with forests of pine and beech.

It is fourteen hundred and eighty feet above the level of the sea, and its very air is itself a tonic, so pure is it, and so invigorating.

It has nine separate springs, differing very much from each other in temperature, and somewhat, also, in the proportions of the different minerals with which they are impregnated. These differences are so important that it is considered necessary to see, as often as every third day, a physician, who observes the effect of the waters upon the patient, and prescribes at what spring and in what quantity he shall drink. As the cure progresses, he usually changes the spring.

Of these springs the Sprudel is the most remarkable. Its waters seem actually to boil. Over it has been built a spacious stone colonnade, a long hall, where hundreds of people march to and fro between six and eight in the morning, while the band is playing. As you approach the Sprudel, you can see its steam rising in clouds, and the noise of its boiling comes distinctly to your ears. Drawing nearer, its hot breath warms you.

Bare-headed Bohemian girls surround it, each with a long pole, at the end of which is a sort of tin mug, in which you place your own cup, which is thus let down into the seething waters and filled. You take it gingerly by the handle, when it comes up again, and drink the hot water through a glass tube.

The Sprudel petrifies whatever vegetable growth it touches. I have seen ears of corn which were turned to stone by it, and one of the industries of Carlsbad is to make carvings and mosaics from these petrifactions.

Next to the Sprudel in interest is the Mühlbrunnen, also a hot spring, and also under a long stone colonnade, where a band plays from six to eight every morning during the Carlsbad " season " — that is to say, from the first of May to the first of October.

Carlsbad has its guests, however, out of season, and even in the winter, for the waters are said to be equally beneficent in their effects at all times of the year, though I can hardly conceive of the place except under a summer sun and glowing with roses. The diseases for which the Carlsbad waters are most frequently prescribed are gout, rheumatism, and troubles of the liver and the kidneys.

Of the nine springs, the most frequented are the Market-brunnen, the Mühlbrunnen, and the

Schlossbrunnen; and it is impossible to approach any of these in the early morning except by forming a so-called " queue," — a sort of procession in which people march, two by two, slowly and solemnly, each pair pausing to get the glass cups — which they usually wear hung round their necks on leather straps — filled by the busy little nymphs of the spring, the lint-haired girls of Bohemia.

During the " season " Carlsbad gives itself up to " the stranger within its gates." The city has twelve thousand inhabitants of its own, and nine hundred houses. But, as long ago as the season of 1885, there were twenty-eight thousand visitors, and the number is said to increase with every year.

It is thronged by all sorts and conditions of men, especially by Polish Jews, who seem especially to thrive here. Each man of them has a sleek, oily ringlet, evidently the result of curl-papers, hanging down on either cheek. Each man of them, too, wears a long, robe-like black coat, or gabardine, which comes quite down to his heels. Some of these garments are of the richest satin and lined with costly fur, and others of humble black camlet; but all are precisely alike in shape.

Here are a larger number of enormously fat women than ever, surely, were collected together anywhere else, — even at Brides-les-Bains. You see, also, hundreds of pretty, bright-eyed, rosy girls, who look as if no ache or pain could ever have found them out, and they drink the waters, and laugh their happy, girlish laughs between their sips.

Here, too, are prosperous, comfortable-looking husbands and wives, who go about arm-in-arm, each with a drinking-cup, and chatting cheerfully. Handsome young men come here for their vacations, and tone up their tired livers with Schlossbrunnen or Kaiser-Karl.

But also, among these holiday-makers, you see a sadly large percentage of invalids, such as no kind soul could look upon without a pang. Wilkie Collins's blue man is here; and there are several quite green, and one of a vivid, livid orange, who somehow seems to me the most pitiful sight of them all. Here are half-crippled sufferers, with pallid, ghastly faces, limping to the springs on crutches, and looking as if their next step would be into their graves.

The "cure" lasts from two to six weeks, according to the special needs of each special patient. Three weeks was the term prescribed for me. One of my friends was sent away at the end of two weeks, and others were detained for six.

Life here is simple and quiet to the last degree. The wildest dissipations are only prolonged till ten o'clock, and, as a rule, Carlsbad is in bed and asleep as early as nine. This regularity and simplicity of living are, no doubt, of great assistance to the waters, but it is certain that the springs themselves are important curative agents, and also that, taken at random, they may be very powerful for harm.

The peasantry round about show their fáith in the cure by hurrying to Carlsbad whenever they are ill, and Austrian priests and nuns are numerously represented among the guests.

It is a good lesson in contentment for a woman to come to Carlsbad. She sees how much worse her lot might have been had she been born here. I have often wondered what part of the hard work the men do.

To be sure, many of them wear uniforms, and I suppose that fact releases them from other labor; and then men drive the horses, and beat the donkeys, and play in the bands, and blunder in the post-office, and change money in the banks, but they seem to do nothing that requires much strength or exertion.

I have seen only women working in the fields near Carlsbad; and besides being butchers and fruiterers and vegetable-mongers and shop-keepers, they are literally hewers of wood and drawers of water, and they carry, in great baskets on their poor bent backs, burdens which a well-cared-for Yankee horse would resent. Yet, in spite of this, they are a blithe-looking, happy set, and they laugh and chat with each other as if life were good and toil a pleasure. Everything in this Happy Valley is bright and sweet and peaceful enough to put the veriest grumbler to shame. It is not so lovely here as at Marienbad; but then, what other place is so lovely as Marienbad? Comparisons aside, this other "Bad" is good enough for anybody. It is almost the only one of the important European watering places which the much prowling Roman does not appear to have found out. Tradition attributes the discovery of the healing springs to Emperor Charles IV. At any rate, he gave the place its name and its charter.

After his time a long succession of royalties came here, and among them was George III. of England, then crown prince. He gave a grand entertainment to the inhabitants of Carlsbad, at which he himself put on livery and waited on his guests. Augustus, King of Poland, came here also, and he, too, gave an entertainment, — a grand ball, — at which he showed the charming playfulness of his disposition by having Sprudel water conducted in pipes to the ball-room, and when the dancing was at its height, ordering it turned on his guests, giving them a thorough drenching. Peter the Great of Russia came here in 1711 and 1712, to be cured of rheumatism. His doctor told him to take three glasses of the water before breakfast. He got the idea that it was to be three large pitchers full. He had taken one, and was struggling with the second, when the opportune appearance on the scene of his physician stopped the performance.

But the royal person whose visits to Carlsbad most interested me was that king of poets, —

Goethe. He came here first in 1785, when he was thirty-four years old, and he subsequently passed here many of his happiest and most productive seasons. He made fourteen visits here in all, and the different houses in which he resided are marked with marble tablets. It is believed that Carlsbad did much to prolong his life and his vigor of both mind and body. His very last visit here was in 1823, and, though he was seventy-four then, his heart was as good as new, for he fell desperately in love with a charming young lady, — Fräulein von Levetzov. He proposed marriage to her. She declined the proposal; but, having been honored by the love of Goethe, she never married any one else, and when his bust was unveiled here, in 1883, she, — think what an old heart to remember so freshly, — she, whom Goethe had asked sixty-two years before to be his wife, sent a wreath of roses to be laid on the pedestal!

In 1791 the other great German poet, Schiller, came to Carlsbad with his wife, whom he had married the year before; and he speaks in his letters of his sojourn in this Happy Valley as the pleasantest period of his life. The cure-books at Carlsbad bear the names of Bach, Beethoven, Catalani, Sontag, Paganini, Schopenhauer, Chateaubriand, Auerbach, Turgenieff, and many another distinguished author or artist.

The absolute literalness of the German handmaiden is as amusing as it is vexatious. I am about to leave, therefore cure rules are somewhat relaxed for me; and as I had a slight headache last night I thought I would take a little longer rest in the morning. "Teresa," I said, "I don't want to get up at 6.30 to-morrow. Don't call me. Order a warm bath for me at eight o'clock, and call me then." "Yes, ma'am, at eight o'clock." She departs, and as she goes out of the door, I call again, "Not until eight, Teresa." She vanishes with a final "Yes, ma'am." I read late — I am to have a good long sleep in the morning. Has morning come when my door opens? It is so dark I can hardly see Teresa.

"Is it eight o'clock, Teresa?" "Oh, no, ma'am; it is half-past six." "But I told you not to call me until eight o'clock." "But I don't call, madame" — and such a hurt look comes into her eyes — "I only bring the hot water that madame has said was always to come at half-past six." What could I answer? I had not remembered, when I told her not to call me, to add, "Teresa, I don't want my hot water until eight o'clock." Faithful, yes — much more faithful than the sun, who only shines here when he pleases; but of a placid stupidity it would be hard to match. They are honest as the day, these *Mädchen.* They will even carefully pick up and restore to you the rubbish you have thrown away. But a French maid, who might put her hand in your pocket, would do it gracefully, and make you a hundred times more comfortable.

I don't think the Germans quite understand what comfort means, while the French understand it a great deal too well. To walk, especially to walk up hill, is a large part of every German cure. You must hurry out of bed in pursuit of the lark, and you must earn your breakfast by an hour and a half of preparatory walking. In Aix-les-Bains, you remember, they carry you in a sedan chair to your morning bath, and then carry you back again to your bed for a half-hour's delicious rest, and then the maid brings your dainty little breakfast, and you eat it, and dream again, or read and write your letters, and get up when you get ready. No such lazy fashions prevail in Germany or in Hungary. If you get any good here, at least you will have worked for it. I am rather inclined to think the German fashion is best; and yet there are people who go, year after year, to Aix and other French cures as faithfully as Lord Odo Russell came to Carlsbad for forty years; as faithfully as the present Prince de Rohan arrives here every year on May 4, at four o'clock in the afternoon.

1888.

FROM CARLSBAD TO PARIS.

I LEFT Carlsbad in the 11.20 A. M. train, and reached Frankfort about ten o'clock that evening. I was very tired with this eleven hours of railway, and glad enough that I had telegraphed to the Englischer Hof for a room and for some one to meet me at the station. By a happy intuition their hotel clerk stood before the door of my railway carriage as the train stopped, and before I knew it my luggage and myself were on a cab, whirling through the gas-lighted town. It seems to me that travellers write singularly little about Frankfort; perhaps because they usually treat it, as I had hitherto done, as a mere railway junction, a place to stop in for the night and go away from in the morning. This time I resolved to stay over a day, and make the town's acquaintance, and I was richly rewarded.

It was one of those brilliant days, warm as summer, and yet with a certain autumnal freshness in the air. There was an atmosphere of brightness and beauty which would have lent charms to a less charming place. Tired with my journey of the day before, I rose rather late, and spent the time until the one o'clock dinner in some of the well furnished shops near the hotel, shops as tempting as those of Paris.

Dinner over, I took a cab and proceeded on a solitary sight-seeing expedition. I saw Lessing's monument, and Schiller's, and Goethe's, and Goethe had a wreath in his hand with which one felt quite sure he would have had no hesitation in crowning himself. I saw also the cathedral, with its beautiful stained glass; and the oldest house in the town, enriched with such wonderful wood-carving as would set a modern wood-carver crazy with jealousy. And then I went into the town-hall where are the portraits of centuries full of German emperors; and among them was Albrecht II. of the early fifteenth century, who looks so much like Wilson Barrett that I am inclined to believe that the emperor of centuries ago is reincarnated in the actor of to-day. Many of these old emperors, from the great Charlemagne down, were handsome men. What a set of fighters they were! and yet, one after another, Death, the stoutest warrior of all, laid them low, each one.

I drove back and forth across the Main, and looked up and down the beautiful river, and then into the old street of the Jews, and saw the humble house where was born the founder of the great Rothschild family, Charles Meyer de Rothschild, who died in 1855, and whose splendid monument is in the new Jewish Cemetery. My driver pointed to the old house where the Rothschilds began, and made a significant gesture, pointing to the ground. "So little then," he said, "and now big as the world, and high as the sky."

He had his own opinions, this driver. Nearly opposite the cathedral he pointed out to me Luther's house, with the picture of the fat, jolly, well-fed-looking reformer over the door. "Catholic there," he said, pointing to the cathedral — "not Catholic here," pointing to Luther. "And which do you love?" I asked. "I love not Catholic," he answered, with energy. "You will see the house of Goethe?" he suggested; and of course it was the place I wanted to see above all. It is quite worth while to stay over a day at Frankfort, were it only to see that house. There was Goethe born, and there he passed twenty-seven years of his life. He was of gentle blood, and the coat of arms of his father is over the door. In his mother's chamber, under a glass case, were two little silken jackets and a pair of tiny shoes that she had worn when she was a child of two, — how long they had outlasted their wearer! How strange it seemed to linger in the room where the mighty master first saw the light!

It was yet more interesting to go into his study. I sat down at his great capacious desk and wrote my name in the visitors' book, dipping my pen in his own inkstand. All round were traces of him. Here was the manuscript of a novel, there of a poem, and there were pictures of him at almost every age. The last was a full-length oil portrait, painted when he was eighty, and this portrait won my heart for Goethe as nothing had ever done before. It was such a noble, benignant face, with such power, and yet such goodness, in the eyes. I felt sure from it that he grew spiritually nobler as he grew older, and I saw, too, how becoming old age can be to a man. Alas, I don't think it ever is to a woman. Looking at this picture, I wondered that when he proposed marriage to Fräulein von Levetzov at Carlsbad, she did not make haste to accept him. He was only seventy-four then.

The beautiful picture of his beloved Lili was on the wall; and there hung the presentments of various others of those fair human flowers he wore briefly in his heart, as a man wears a rose in his button-hole. There was an engraving of Werther's Charlotte, too, and her marriage contract — not a copy of it, but the veritable contract itself — framed under glass. There were treasures innumerable, of all sorts; and the roly-poly old German *Frau*, who showed them to me, seeing that I really cared for them, gave me a leaf from the wreath with which some loving hand had crowned the poet's bust, in the chamber where he was born.

I went from the Goethe house to the Statuary Museum, to see Dannecker's "Ariadne." What a graceful statue it is! The lithe loveliness of the limbs, the beauty of every curve and line, would hold one captive but for the head. The head is pretty enough, with its curls and wreath; but it is the prettiness of a successful circus rider. You are sure that the tiger has been tamed to figure in a show, and that the lithe rider is waiting for the plaudits of the amphitheatre to break forth.

Having driven till I was tired, I walked about for a little while, and then I thought I would try a Frankfort street-car, which was going by me, on its way to the Palm Garden. Street-cars in Frankfort are not like street-cars elsewhere. You pay everywhere from two cents to five, according to the length of your ride, and the conductor hands you a ticket on which he has marked the amount of your fare, and as he hands it to you he says "Please," or at least the German equivalent for please, and when you hand him the money he says "Thank you;" and when a lady got out he civilly helped her, and then touched his hat by way of adieu. I wish this conductor, or his like, lived in America; but it would be his fate to be misunderstood. Perhaps they would shut him up in an insane asylum.

One day was far too brief a time in which to see Frankfort. There is a picture gallery, and a theatre, and an opera house which cost over a million and a half of dollars. The performance there begins at 6.30 P. M., and it is quite the fashion to come over from Homburg to the opera, and go home again to supper. From an historical point of view, Frankfort is interesting. Charlemagne had a palace here, and held a council within its walls in 794, more than a thousand years ago. Later on it became a free city and the seat of the German Diet, and remained so till 1866. In 1871 Prince von Bismarck and Jules Favre signed, in the Hotel Swan, the treaty of peace between Germany and France. So you perceive its historical associations, which began with the time of Charlemagne, did not end there.

The town has a delightful climate, and ah, how well I like the simple, kindly, courteous people who live there! I came away from it with real regret; and I want to go back again, and see whether the sun always shines on it,—whether it is always as bright and glad and homelike and pleasant as I found it.

What a different impression Strasburg makes on one!—the sad, solemn strong city, as it seemed to me, when I drove about it. It did not look as if any one could really amuse himself there; though it has a large theatre, and a magnificent new opera house. But there was no air of gayety anywhere. Nobody lounged, nobody was in a hurry. There were no shadows, no tender lights. A sort of pitiless glare pervaded it. Its cathedral spire is the highest in the world. The next highest thing of man's erection is one of the pyramids of Egypt; but the pyramid stopped some fifteen feet short of what the spire afterward attained. I wish I were a good climber. I should like to go to the top of that spire some night, and see if I could establish a bowing acquaintance with the man in the moon.

After the cathedral, the most imposing thing in

Strasburg seems to me to be the Germania restaurant. It is a superb palace, where you can buy a tall, foaming glass of beer for six cents. But it is the cathedral which makes Strasburg worth visiting. What pains they used to take, those men of long ago! The edifice was begun in 1277, and only finished in 1601. Over three centuries went to its making. Generation after generation of men worked on it, and died, and were buried, and nobody so much as remembers one of their names; but the great fane they builded survives them all, and looks as if it might endure forever. Its stained glass is wonderfully rich and beautiful; but its spire and its clock are the two things in which it surpasses all other churches. I have been to the cathedral several times, but I have never chanced to be there just at high noon, when the grand show of the clock takes place, — when the cock crows, and all the images are set in motion.

The second most interesting church in Strasburg is that of St. Thomas, which contains the monument to Marshal Saxe, erected by Louis XV., and which contains also the ghastliest thing I have ever seen, — two bodies in glass cases, said to be those of the Count of Nassau and his daughter, of which the flesh and the clothes have been preserved in their present state for over four hundred years.

On my way to Strasburg from Frankfort the only occupant of the carriage " For Ladies Only " was a young Englishwoman, so pretty and so charming that she reminded me of Henry James's remark in his pleasant volume entitled "Portraits of Places," that the capacity of an Englishwoman for being handsome strikes him as absolutely unlimited. My travelling companion was one of the most shining illustrations of Mr. James's theory, — and as piquant and original as she was beautiful. She had been in Homburg for the season, and she was discussing certain German characteristics. She said, quite seriously: "I have been thinking, while I was at Homburg, how thankful I ought to be that I was not born a German. I might have been, you know." "Would you have liked better to be born French?" I asked. "Oh, no!" with the prettiest little shudder. "Oh, I should be sorry not to be English." I thought of the man in "Pinafore," who,

"In spite of all temptations,
To belong to other nations,"

had "remained an Englishman;" and, really, I don't blame our English cousins for being aware that there can be nothing on earth pleasanter or more desirable than to be born into the higher circles of English life; but when one descends from these higher circles I should prefer to have been born elsewhere.

From Strasburg to Paris you will, if you love comfort, take the "Oriental Express." You pay $2.40 in addition to your first-class fare; and, in return for this extra charge, you make the journey some three hours more speedily, and you find yourself in the same train with a well-managed restaurant, where you can get an excellent mid-day meal which you will call luncheon if you are English, dinner if you are German, or breakfast if you are French.

The afternoon was wearing late when I reached Paris, — this Paris radiant withSeptember sunshine. The sun was low, and the soft rose of the western sky, the delicate light that rested on everything, made on me a swift impression of indescribable beauty. It seemed incongruous that the place should be so noisy; and I think I had never quite realized how horribly noisy Paris is until now, when I came to it straight from sedate Strasburg. The clamor seemed to me fairly deafening. The sense of all-pervading noise comes largely from the habit the Paris cab-drivers have of perpetually cracking their whips. I should think the poor horses would go mad; only, as a rule, they are so ill-fed that they have no more energy than suffices to hold themselves together and plod along. But, noise and all, a fresh sense of the abiding charm of Paris came to me as I drove to my hotel through the air brilliant with sunset.

AT WIESBADEN, AND AFTER.

WHAT ONE DOES AT WIESBADEN.

THE sky when I left London was dark with clouds. They broke into rain before I reached Dover, and the four hours by sea from Dover to Ostend were not a joy. The rain poured still as the train bore me through level Belgium on to Brussels. Even the windmills had a dejected air, and turned slowly and heavily, as if they were saying to themselves, "What is the use of whirling round and round and playing at life in such outrageous weather?" When I reached Brussels the streets were like shallow brooks, in which the people seemed afloat. I waded to the hotel omnibus, and presently I was under cover for the night. I had bought my ticket of Cook, and the Cook man had advised me to go to the Grand Hotel, for its convenience to the station. I am afraid he gives this advice to a great many people, for the hotel was crowded, and I could only get a room on the topmost floor. And in the morning the lift did not work. I suppose it had had to carry up so many people the night before that it struck, as the hands do on American railways. But to fall in the world is easy, and the descent from my perch was easier than the climb to it would have been. I got down stairs in good season, took my morning coffee, and was off on the ten o'clock train for Cologne.

It rained its best, or its worst, all day, and I was glad to find myself at five P. M. in the friendly shelter of Hôtel du Nord. In the morning I was *en route* again. Cook's man had told me to leave Cologne at nine o'clock A. M., but I found the best train left at 8.45, and I was barely in time for it. Just as it began trembling, as a train does, with the thrill of departure, a young man and a girl sprang on board, the guard banged the door after them, and we were off. I looked at my young neighbors with that vague curiosity you feel about the people with whom you are shut up in the small space of a railway carriage. I should think they had just come from their wedding. Everything was spick and span about them. The cotton in their ears — why do so many Germans wear cotton in their ears? — was as white as snow. Their clothes were absolutely and aggressively new; so was their hand luggage. They were evidently planning a very long wedding journey, for their two books of railway coupons, which the bridegroom offered to the guard's inspection, were thick volumes. Diamonds as big as hazel nuts, and of exquisite quality, hung from the fair bride's cotton-stuffed ears. She had a pretty gown and a dainty little hand, and if her teeth were too emphatic for beauty, that was at least not her fault. The dapper little husband, in in his speckless new gray suit, did not look like the hero of a novel, but he was as much in love as the exigencies of the most sentimental novel could require. I remembered the young French lovers, —the bridal pair who travelled with me one day last May, when I went from Milan to Basle. I do not think the French sweethearts were one whit less in love, but they at once accepted me as a part of their programme. Their joy overflowed on me and warmed my day. I did not feel myself an intruder, but rather as if I were the appreciative spectator to whom the love-birds were not unwilling to coo; and we parted almost with emotion, as if we had been old friends. My German bridal pair, I could see clearly, regarded me as a nuisance. I had settled myself in the railway carriage before they came near it; yet I believe they regarded me as an unjustifiable interloper. I think they were glad, and I am sure I was, when they left the train at the first stopping-place, and betook themselves and their luggage and their innumerable railway tickets to another line.

I steamed on, quite alone, toward Wiesbaden, and how beautiful is this railway journey along the left bank of old "Father Rhine!" I longed for the guide-book I had been so careless as to leave behind me, for I wanted to know the name of every castle, and what legend haunted it. Lacking the book, however, I invented the legends for myself. Is the Rhine the very loveliest river in the world? I almost think so, when you add to its beguiling curves, its tranquil depths, its overhanging castles, the dignity of history and the charm of romance, — for all these belong to it, and are part of it. I reached Wiesbaden at thirty-five minutes past twelve, and the Rose Hotel at one P. M.

Wiesbaden is by far the largest watering place in Germany, and one of the largest anywhere. It is a town of stately dwellings, and the "cure" itself goes on all winter, though the most fashionable months here (for it is a very fashionable place in the season) are September and October.

May and June are also good months, and even the winter is pleasant. In July and August, on the other hand, it is too warm for comfort, for Wiesbaden is in a valley of the Taunus Mountains.

It is the famous hot springs which attract the invalid world, and the place has been made fashionable by the visits of many royal patients.

The beloved old Emperor William used to make a sojourn here every spring, and he gave to the town theatre the name of the Royal Opera House.

The Empress Augusta, the late Emperor Frederick, Prince Charles of Prussia, the kings of Greece and of Denmark, and many other "royalties" besides are familiar to these quiet streets. Prince and Princess Christian are here just now, and there are plenty of Austrian, Russian, and Polish princes and magnates from I don't know how many other countries besides.

I know few cities fuller of beautiful private

residences than is Wiesbaden. Hundreds of lovely villas crown the heights and border the streets; and as for hotels, you can count them by the score. There are forty-five mentioned in the "Guide." I looked at several of them before settling myself at the Rose, which is a home-like place, and but a few steps from the principal spring, the Kochbrunnen; so that, after you have rubbed open your sleepy eyes and jumped into your morning toilet, you have scarcely to do more than go down stairs before you find yourself under the roof of the Drinkhall, at one end of which the Kochbrunnen is steaming like a gigantic caldron of boiling broth.

The water is somewhat salt. You hate it savagely for the first day or two, but after you get used to it you do not mind taking the three or four cups you will be expected to quaff, as though they were nectar, within an hour. If you get up early enough, the band — a very good band — will cheer you while you drink, and you can march to its music between your cups.

But the band plays from seven to eight o'clock, and it is not so easy to be down at seven o'clock in the autumn as it was in summer, when the days were long.

In the Drinkhall and the surrounding garden you see everybody you know, and everybody you don't know, and there are flower stalls, where all the gay young men buy roses for all the pretty girls, and sometimes even for those who are not pretty.

In the middle of the forenoon you take your bath, and the Rose is one of the few hotels into which water is conveyed from the Kochbrunnen itself.

The centre of social life in Wiesbaden is the "Kurhaus." Concerts are given in its grand salon in winter, or when the weather is unpleasant. At present the music is out of doors, in the lovely grounds of the Kursaal, and there you see a yet larger crowd than surrounds the Kochbrunnen in the morning, as a large proportion of the guests of the different hotels and pensions are not themselves "cure" patients, but only the wives, the sisters, the cousins, and the aunts of those who are here for their aches and pains.

In winter they say the Kursaal is even gayer than in summer.

There is an excellent restaurant there, where people like to dine or sup; masquerade balls are given there, charming and artistic concerts, private theatricals, — entertainments of every sort. There is a room for chess, and there are in the enormous reading-rooms some three thousand papers and journals, the largest portion of which are German, though I found the "Chicago Tribune," the "New York Herald," and one or two other American papers.

There is a guide to Wiesbaden, and I have seldom seen a funnier specimen of English as she is written by German pens than this same guide.

The soil here is sandy, and, judging by my boots and the hems of my gowns, I should say that Wiesbaden, with all its charms, is certainly a dusty town.

But the "Guide" assures me otherwise. It asserts that, "By the complete absence of dust, and the protected situation, there is, even in winter, plentiful opportunity of being in the open air. The use of the Kochbrunnen raises the appetite, and the general state of the system becomes for complete reconvalescence. Also will one find abundance of suitable and stirring occasions which generally are only to be found in very large cities."

Farther on, "pleasant social realition" (whatever that may mean) with your doctor's family is mentioned among the attractions of the place.

There is a good picture gallery in Wiesbaden, and an interesting museum, and I hardly know any place from which you can make more agreeable excursions. At the theatre — the "Royal Opera House" — something is always going on. Usually there is a play one night and an opera the next.

The great industry of this part of Germany is vine-growing. A week ago, when it was cold, I said to the house porter, who is supposed to be on intimate terms with the clerk of the weather: —

"Do you think we shall have any more warm weather this year?"

"Why, we must," was the answer, "or what would become of the vines?"

And he said it with an air of conviction, as if there could be no power in any world that would interfere with this chief interest of German life.

It is something, I think, on which to congratulate myself, to have made the acquaintance of Wiesbaden's venerable poet, Herr Friedrich von Bodenstedt.

A German friend of mine, who lives half the year in London, brought the poet to see me the day after I arrived here.

Picture to yourself a tall, handsome, active man of seventy-two, with gray hair, with eyes full, still, of the keen fire of youth; with the grand manner which belongs to the high-bred gentlemen of his generation, and the gift to please and to charm which is not always the dower even of a poet.

Herr von Bodenstedt speaks English — as he writes it — like a scholar; without priggishness, yet at the same time in a fashion more literary than colloquial; and it certainly seems to me that a foreigner has very seldom written in English with such grasp of the possibilities of the language. But English is only one of the many languages which the German poet has at his command.

Friedrich von Bodenstedt has had a life full of variety and of incident. He has seen many lands, and his experiences have brought forth fruit abundantly. In his early youth he travelled widely in the far East; and a few years ago he visited America and heard the waves of the Pacific Ocean break on the shores of California. The Caucasus and the Rockies are alike familiar to him. Between these two extremes he has been almost everywhere.

He has written books so many and so varied that I will not undertake to enumerate them; but he is, perhaps, best known as the author of "The Songs of Mirza-Schaffy," that wonderful volume of lyric poems which has been translated into almost every written language in the world, and of which Herr von Bodenstedt has presented me the one hundred and thirty-third German edition. I think no other work of any living German poet has reached so many as one hundred and thirty-three editions.

The poet took the name of Mirza-Schaffy from an old Persian teacher of his (who himself never wrote a poem in his life), because he wanted a distinctly Persian name, and because he held in honor the character and attainments of this Mirza whose name he borrowed. For some time the reading world supposed the book to be a volume of translations, and wondered greatly why no one had ever heard of Mirza-Schaffy before; but after a while it became generally known that it was the original work of the young German poet, and from that time Von Bodenstedt's position in the German Olympus was assured.

There is something in these lyrics — warm with the love of life and the love of love, perfumed with the roses of the East — that reminds me of Tom Moore. Here is one from the songs to "Zuleika":—

> "My heart adorns itself with thee,
>   As Heaven with the Sun is bright.
> Thou art its glory; wanting thee,
>   It would be dark as darkest night.
>
> "So fades the fairest pomp of Earth,
>   When Darkness holds its cheerless sway;
> But when the smiling sun looks forth,
>   Its beauties spring to meet the day."

I must give you one of his quatrains. To write a good quatrain is an art by itself. See how well Mirza succeeds in it:—

> "Who would make friends of all men
>   Is bosom friend to none;
> She who would please the million
>   Will never please the one."

The poetry of Shakespeare has been one of the absorbing interests of Herr von Bodenstedt's life. He translated Shakespeare's "Sonnets" into German, and achieved the noblest and most perfect translation of them that has been made in any language. Later he translated ten of the most important of the plays, and had the rest translated under his supervision, so that there is now in German a complete edition of the works of Shakespeare, called "The Bodenstedt Edition."

His character is not less worthy of praise than his achievements. A man who knows him well wrote me that he had never met any one who united to such vast knowledge and wide experience such large-heartedness, such warm sympathies, and such perfect modesty and simplicity. His seventieth birthday was made a festival, not only in Wiesbaden, but throughout Germany; and gifts and letters and telegrams came to him from America, from England, from Asia, from Japan, from Africa, from far Australia, — in short, from every quarter of the world. I have seldom seen so many interesting curios in any house. If he had chosen to form an art museum, he would have had a very good foundation for it in the gifts that came to him on that one day. But he said, half quaintly, half pathetically: "It upset me a good deal. Perhaps, at seventy, one is too old even to be happy with impunity." [1]

A charming world lies round about Wiesbaden. With two friends who joined me here, I have been exploring the neighborhood. We went one day to Biebrich on the Rhine, and on another we took the long drive to Schwalbach and Schlangenbad, — two more of the noted "cure" resorts of this region of mineral waters. We started at 10 A.M., and drove on through the beautiful forest toward Schwalbach.

Last spring, when I saw at the New Salon in Paris a picture, "La Religieuse," by Paul Hoecher

[1] It was in 1890 that I had the pleasure of knowing Von Bodenstedt. Alas, he has died since then, and all Germany mourned for him, as all Germany had honored him.

of Munich, I half thought it untrue to nature, because the grass beneath the trees was dappled with spots of opaline light, in which the hues of rose and green and violet seemed to blend and change, even while you looked at them. Now I beg the artist's pardon for my lack of faith. I saw the very same effects on the grass under the trees on that drive to Schwalbach. It is only that Hoecher had seen his German forests in all lights, and I had never seen them in this one before. I fancy there was still dew upon the woodland grass. Anyway, the strong September sun poured down through the thick tree-boughs and dappled the turf below, just as in the picture.

We reached Schwalbach at a few minutes after twelve, and had nearly an hour before dinner in which to ramble about the little place.

In the time of the Romans Schwalbach (which literally means Swallows' Brook) was celebrated for its sulphurous springs, and the old conquerors of the world used to come here then, just as people come now, in some wild hope to be cured of all their ills. When they got cold, and ached worse than ever, I suppose the doctors told them, just as they tell us now, that it was only the effect of the waters, which bring all ills to the surface, in order to drive them out forever, — as the saints of old used to drive out the devils from those unhappy men who were possessed of them.

Alas! the modern devils of gout and rheumatism do not always yield to the invocations of saints or of doctors.

At present the most important feature of Schwalbach is its iron spring, the Stahlbrunnen, first discovered about one hundred years ago. It is the resort of people whose vital forces are low, and who need a tonic, — for to drink these waters is one of the safest ways of taking iron; and the place offers the additional advantages of fine air, and quiet almost as deep as that of the castle behind the thorn hedge, where the Sleeping Beauty passed her one hundred years of repose. Perhaps Americans do not like quiet. I saw few of them at Schwalbach, but there were plenty of Russians and English, and not a few Germans.

The drive from Schwalbach to Schlangenbad is a delightful one. Sometimes you are in the depths of the enchanted forest; sometimes you come out into the open, and from some lofty coign of vantage you see the vine-bordered Rhine far below, with its brooding castles or its gay little cities. And Schlangenbad itself, — ah, how beautiful it is! I wanted to move over there the next day, " bag and baggage;" but the doctor forbade. Twenty-five baths from the Kochbrunnen were necessary to frighten away my rheumatic demon, and I had had only ten!

Schlangenbad means, literally, the Serpents' Bath. Once upon a time there was a heifer, — I would prefer to say a princess, but I must confine myself to facts. Everything disagreed with this unfortunate but amiable creature. The more her mother licked her hide, the rougher it became; and the more she ate, the thinner she grew. She got so rough and so thin that not even a fly of the forest would bite her; and the sleek, handsome heifers — her former companions — would have nothing at all to do with her. She was very unhappy, and after a time she disappeared from the herd.

They thought — at least I think they must have thought — that, wounded by their slights, she had gone off to die alone.

But no. After a few weeks she came back, carrying her head high, her skin as sleek as that of a grain-fed mouse, her eyes sparkling like a deer's, and her once gaunt ribs covered with flesh. And day by day her beauty became more conspicuous, till at last a herdsman was so devoured with curiosity that he resolved to watch her; and, so watching, he discovered that each evening she stole off into the forest till she came to a hitherto unknown spring of water. From this spring she drank long and deeply, and then came back to her mates.

This marvellous story grew old, and so did the herdsman who had made the discovery. He did not see or hear so quickly as of yore, but one day he pricked up his ears, for he heard them talking about a young lady of Nassau who seemed to be afflicted with the very same symptoms that he had seen in the heifer in the long ago time when he was a lithe young herdsman; and he told again the old story. As in the song, " physicians " had been " in vain," and there seemed no hope for the fair maid of Nassau. So at last, in very desperation, her parents consented that she should try the spring which had proved a spring of healing in the case of the heifer.

Proudly the old peasant led them to the fountain of whose existence he only knew; and the maiden drank of its waters, and from that time her health began to mend, and presently she was the fairest of the fair.

The legend adds that it was afterwards discovered that the efficacy of this marvellous spring was due to the presence of large serpents in the waters near their source. I have read a fifty-years-old book, the author of which said that he himself had seen the creatures swimming about near the fountain's head. I cannot hear that any one has seen them since then. I hope not, for I like Schlangenbad, and I don't like serpents.

It is a forest village, — this beautiful Schlangenbad, — nestling among wooded hills. Enticing paths wound up and away through the green depths of the wood. The air was balmy with the breath of firs and pines. I was sure there was healing in every breath.

But it is not healing alone for which one goes to Schlangenbad; the waters are said to give one back one's youth again, and to make one beautiful forever. I think the guests I saw there must have been newly arrived, and had not, as yet, begun the " cure."

We drove reluctantly from this happy valley,

where Rasselas might have been content; but the day was wearing late. For reward we had the charming drive to Wiesbaden, with its varied views of castles on the heights and villages nestling in the valleys, and at last of the Neroberg, crowned with its temple, from which the view of town and forest is as beautiful as anything I have seen here, unless it be the wider panorama one sees from the base of the Niederwald monument.

You go by rail from Wiesbaden to Rudesheim, unless you prefer to go to Biebrich, and there take a steamer. We went by rail, and at Rudesheim we took the cog-wheel road that carries its passengers to the summit of the mountain, where stands the Niederwald monument, erected in memory of the victories and the heroes of the Franco-Prussian war. The foundation stone was laid by the old Kaiser William on the 16th of September, 1877, and, thank Heaven, he lived to see the glorious monument unveiled on September 28, 1883. One could hardly have borne that any other than he should have been lord of Germany on that day of days.

On the front of the statue's base is sculptured Germany's own national song, " The Watch on the Rhine."

She is a gorgeous creature, this bronze Germania, the embodiment of German pride and power. She is thirty-six feet in height, and her head measures four feet from brow to chin. She looks forth over the splendid Rhine, up which surely, while she watches there, no enemy will dare to sail.

I chanced to be here on the 2d of September, the anniversary of the Sedan victory. When I went down to the Kochbrunnen at the hideously matutinal hour on which my German doctor insists, I saw the streets gay with bunting. Flags were everywhere, and in the spaces between them hung wreaths on wreaths of artificial flowers. And already the people had on their holiday clothes, and the bells were ringing from the steeples as if they had all gone mad together. I thought, at first, that it must be the Emperor's birthday; but I inquired, and was told that it was the anniversary of Germany's triumph. There is nothing quite like it in America. The small boys make plenty of noise on Fourth of July, and the bells (what there are of them) ring, — they don't chime, because they can't; and we fire cannon, and send off fireworks, and play that it is a holiday, — at least those of us do who have not run away from town to escape it: but it is all commonplace and uninteresting when compared with this Fest of Germany.

When my doctor came to see me in the forenoon, he told me I must not fail to go to the Neroberg (Hill of Nero), where the true festival, with games and music, would be held. And at two o'clock, through the town marched a grand and gay procession: drums were beating, flags were flying; at every turn new people fell into line, and it really seemed as if no one were indoors and the whole town were out on a pilgrimage of joy and triumph. I did not start until four o'clock, when, having found a London friend for companion, we took a comfortable landau, and set forth to see the fun. But first we saw something better, something serious yet glad, solemn yet gay; for we took the long drive through the forest, — the beautiful, deep forest, its paths softly silent with their covering of dead leaves. It was an enchanted wood, and I could fancy that all the wood nymphs of the old German legends haunted it, though we saw no one, on all our winding way, save on one bench, under a low-growing tree, a young man and a young girl; and perhaps they, too, had been enchanted like the wood, and would linger on there and grow old with the trees, — who knows?

All Wiesbaden, except ourselves, had taken the short, straight path to the Nero height, to get there as soon as possible; and when we reached the hill-top the wayside was walled with empty carriages, and all the pleasure grounds about the restaurant on the summit were so crowded that there seemed scarcely a path for two unprotected ladies among the throng. My friend, however, though she lives in London, was born in Germany, and she soothed the crowd with pleasant little sentences in their own tongue as we struggled on, among the hundreds of tables, in search of one little spot where we could take our afternoon coffee. At last two kind strangers lent us their seats for a few minutes; we prevailed on one of the flight of waiters, who were darting hither and thither like busy bees, to get us our Mocha, and as we drank it we looked about us. You could see just such a sight nowhere but in Germany. If I were asked to name the two most prominent German characteristics, I think I should say beer-drinking and domesticity. These groups that surrounded the innumerable tables seemed almost all to be family parties. You would see a father and mother and five or six children seated at a single table, and each one with a tall glass of beer. And as they drank, the band played gay, triumphant, clamorous martial music. "And so we beat the French!" it seemed to peal; and then the beer glasses were set down for a moment, and thousands of hands would clap, and a shout — a wild, exultant shout — arose, at which the birds, high up in heaven, would pause on their swift wings to listen in wonder. I never saw a hundredth part as many glasses of beer at one time. I never saw a denser crowd, and I have hardly ever seen one more kindly, even in Italy; and I have always thought an Italian crowd, at carnival time for instance, the gentlest the sun shines on.

At a farther distance from the restaurant, games of all varieties were in progress. It made one think a little of some French holiday in the garden of the Tuileries or at the seaside, only the French people amuse themselves more gayly. It is the difference between beer and wine. Here at the Neroberg, as in France, was the merry-go-round, — but it seemed to me the lads and lassies rode on it as if they were at work, rather than at play; and here were chances to shoot at prizes, and to pay your pfennigs for a " grab " in a basket of paper parcels. The crowd took all their pleasures, however, with a sort of solemn earnestness, doing with their might what their hands found to do. I think the Germans are more capable of an " orgie" than of a " lark."

We stayed on the height until the sun was low, and a soft rose, like a filmy veil dropped out of heaven itself, fell softly on the summits of the Taunus Mountains, and then we drove down to the town again, and this time by the short path, hedged on each side with returning pleasure-seekers. Among these I saw one funny sight, characteristically German. A young peasant husband was escorting his young wife, and the wife, if you please, was carrying their little child. This was not so strange, — among the same class in England it is always the wife who carries the baby, — but the droll thing was that the young fellow was playing at gallantry, and had offered his wife his arm, in honor of the holiday, and she held it proudly, though she had a hard struggle to manage the child with the one arm remaining to her. But why should one laugh at them on whom the gods smiled? for they were young and happy, pleased with themselves, their offspring, and each other; and, after all, in this disobliging world we can be young but once, and, for the most part, when we are young we do not appreciate our blessings, and the cry goes on forever, " Oh, if youth would; or if age could!" It is something to have had one real festival day, full of light-hearted mirth, even if the baby on one's arm was heavy, and the man at one's side ought to have carried it, and did not.

I like to linger of an afternoon in the beautiful garden of the Kursaal. There, in the lovely lake, a combat goes on daily. There are two stately swans, with snow-white bodies and long black necks, who consider this lake their own special domain. They are rearing there their family, — their little cygnets. When I first came to Wiesbaden, a month ago, the parent swans used to take their little ones on their backs and swim about the lake with them. Now the cygnets can swim unaided, but their papa does not relax his vigilance. In the lake are also quite a number of ducks.

Some one said the other day of the Emperor of Germany that (like Prince Albert in his time) he believes that the world contains only two classes of people, — royalties, and those who are not royalties, — and if you are not a king, or the wife or son or brother of a king, it matters very little, really, whether you are a count or a counter-jumper.

The papa swan evidently feels about the ducks much as the German Emperor is said to feel about the rest of mankind. How these " low-down trash," the ducks, made their impertinent way into the lake over which he rules is an abiding puzzle to him. Their very existence he regards as an insult, and when they snatch a bread crumb of those that are so liberally thrown into the water, then he considers that insult has become outrage.

Majestically, but very swiftly, he sails to and fro, driving the ducks before him as some great general would drive a routed army.

I admire the swan, but I pity the hungry ducks, and I try to throw my bits of bread where they can get some. It is of no use. Papa Swan sees me, and bears down on them like a steam launch, and instantly my crumbs are carried in his bill to the cygnets, who are watching the combat in the sheltering neighborhood of their mamma.

I shall be sorry to part with the swans when I leave Wiesbaden, and I shall grieve, also, to part with the beautiful goldfish that dart to and fro in the transparent water like live jewels; but I shall leave with decided relief some of the busiest denizens of this place, — to wit, the mosquitoes.

The Duke of Nassau comes no more to his fair Castle of Biebrich, because, forsooth, he took the side of Austria in the war; and many another noble lord has retired from German view, because, in 1866, he fought under the wrong banner. But evidently the mosquitoes were not the allies of Austria; so they stay on in Germany.

I have passed two " cure " seasons in Carlsbad and two in Marienbad without ever having heard, in either place, their war cry, or seen their too swift wings. But here in Wiesbaden they sing me to sleep every night; and when they have sung me to sleep, they stab me and quaff my blood as it were wine. Perhaps without them one would be tempted to linger too long in this happy valley among the Taunus Mountains.

1890.

TO PARIS, BY WAY OF FRANKFORT AND METZ.

THE Fates or the mosquitoes drove me away from Wiesbaden at last. Once more I went to Frankfort, which is only an hour's journey by rail. I never miss an opportunity to pass a day or two in gay and pretty Frankfort, — one German town where certainly the stranger can well amuse himself.

I was here this time over Sunday and Monday; and on Sunday afternoon, like everybody else, I went to the Palm Garden to hear the music. All the year round there are two concerts a day at the Palm Garden, — one from 4 to 6 in the afternoon, and the other from 7.30 to 10.30 in the evening. During the cold months the concerts are held in the great hall of the Casino in the midst of the Garden; but in summer, and in these beautiful autumn days, only the musicians are under cover. The band is in a sort of pagoda, roofed over, but open at the sides, and the audience sit at little tables on the terrace of the Casino, and drink their afternoon coffee, or else they walk to and fro within sound of the music.

There are fountains here and there, flowers, palm-trees, ferns; and in addition to all the other attractions of the place, the band is one of the best in Germany. I was alone, but I sat at the table with some gracious and graceful German ladies, and I amused myself by watching the constantly changing crowd that marched past me, and inventing characters and histories for them as they came and went.

The Palm Garden is well patronized on most days, but on Sundays all the rank and fashion of Frankfort is to be found there.

It is loveliest of all on a soft summer night, when all the lamps are lighted, and the fountains plash in the gentle dusk, and the music sounds like music in a dream.

Monday was a sun-bright day, and full of pleasant occupation. One always wants to see the Goethe house again, and to dream of the old, old days when the author of " Faust " was young, and full of hope and life, and pride and power, — he who has been dead so long now. It may be that Walter Besant is right when he thinks that, if death were abolished, all that is noblest in life would be abolished, also; but I wish that when a great genius is born, — a Goethe or a Shakespeare, — he could linger on in the world somewhat longer than other men.

I went once more to see that pert, self-conscious young person, the " Ariadne," as Dannecker sculptured her. I don't believe that he divined her aright, and I think if there are such things as trials for libel in Olympus, she could make him suffer some immortal penalty, — though, to be sure, her back is beautiful, and the lines of her figure are, perhaps, charming enough to reconcile her to his presentment.

I drove across the Main, over the oldest bridge of all, to the oldest old Frankfort. Half-way across, at the middle of the bridge, stands Kaiser Karl, watching forever the river that he loved. He must have thought it beautiful this night. It was just at sunset, and the rippling water reflected the pageant of the west. Every ripple seemed alive with golden glory, and boat and barge were mirrored in the sun-kindled stream. Then I drove away from the river, and to and fro through streets so narrow that there was barely room for the carriage to pass, and the quaint old houses seemed to nod at each other across the way as if they were saying : " You and I know what becomes of these butterflies that are here to-day and gone to-morrow. Let them stare at us while they can." Over the door of one old beer shop, that looked as if it were hundreds of years old, I read the legend, " In the New Paradise," — so even that had been new once.

I think Frankfort is like a charming woman. You come here for a day, and you see the Palm Garden, and the Goethe house, and the self-satisfied " Ariadne," and the shops full of pretty things, and you think you know the place by heart; but linger on for a few days, and you find a deeper, tenderer, more suggestive side, touched with the light of memory, sad with the pathos of long ago, — a Frankfort to which I could return year after year unwearied.

I hated to go away, — how is it that one hates to go away from almost everywhere, unless it be Long Branch or Saratoga? It required stern resolution on my part to start off for Paris in Tuesday's early morning. I came by way of Metz, without any hope of finding the place interesting (for I had often been told that it was not so), but simply because I had been so many times by Cologne, and also by Strasburg, that I thought I ought to see what a new route had to offer.

I left Frankfort at eight in the morning and reached Metz at two in the afternoon. Some one told me to go to the Hôtel de Metz, and to the Hôtel de Metz I came. I went into the dining-room for a hurried luncheon before starting out to explore the town. There was a long table at which the mid-day table d'hôte was in process. I sat at a little table by myself in a corner, but I glanced at the long one with curiosity. It was almost full of officers in uniform. They were talking so boisterously that I thought at first they were quarrelling; but I soon saw that the loud talking was only the military habit. Everything is military in Metz. The manager of the hotel told me that twenty-two thousand German soldiers are quartered here at present, and the number is seldom less. When the Germans captured the place in 1870, they made up their minds to hold it. It ought not to take so many troops to do this, however, for Metz is one of the most strongly fortified towns in the world. I took advantage of my afternoon there to drive all about the fortifications, as well as all about the heart of the town. My coachman was French. A German friend of mine, who knows Metz well, told me that when Germany took possession of it, such French people as could afford it went away, but the working-people, and those who had no money for experiments in home-making, stayed on here. So it happens that almost all those whom a traveller comes in contact with are French. When my coachman found out that I sympathized with the dispossessed race (on the principle, perhaps, which draws one's sympathies to the under dog in the fight), he begged me to go to the cemetery and see the soldiers' graves. There were several monuments to individual officers, but the most imposing was a large one "erected to the memory of 7,203 French soldiers who died in the ambulances at Metz." The cemetery was as French as Père-la-Chaise itself. There was scarcely a tombstone that had not its wreath made of horse-hair, or of black and white beads strung on wires, in true French fashion. In the rare instances when you saw a German name on a tombstone, you felt as if here were a dead intruder who ought to be warned off the premises.

There is, all through Metz, the most curious combination of French and German. On every street corner, so far as I observed, are two signs, — one, the old, long-ago sign in French, and above it the new sign, the translation of the French name of the street into German. A shop window would tell you in both languages what was for sale within. Every place of business in the town — bank, dentist's, milliner's, bakery, everything — made its appeal thus to both nations. I never saw in any one place so many habitations for soldiers. It seemed to me the barracks almost outnumbered the houses of the ordinary citizens. But, in spite of all this incursion of German soldiery, Metz still seems like some old town in Normandy or in Brittany, — intensely French, and intensely provincial. It has, however, one of the most glorious Gothic cathedrals of northern France, — for one thinks of it as French still, when one speaks of this noble monument of architecture which French hands reared. The cathedral was begun in the fifth century, and was finished about the middle of the sixteenth. It is rich in carving, both without and within, and it has sumptuous windows of that glorious old stained glass that no modern art has been able to rival. There is devotion in the very air of a solemn old cathedral like this. If I lived near one, I think I could find in it some strange peace — some hope born not of this world — which would make life nobler. Here and there in a dark corner knelt some peasant at her prayers; and when a young girl rose from kneeling long before one of the altars, it seemed to me one could read in her pure eyes that she had found the grace for which she had prayed so fervently.

I went back to the hotel in time for the six o'clock dinner. The mid-day table d'hôte seems to be the favorite with the military, for at six o'clock only two men in uniform lent distinction to the motley company. I had a pretty room, with lovely old-fashioned furniture, and mirrors enough to content a New York belle; but I had such a little pitcher of water that I was reminded again of the hotels in rural Normandy and Brittany; and when I rang for hot water, a little pot of it was brought me, hardly the size of the family teapot. I recalled the Frenchman in the story, who said, "I have English habits; I bathe — my face." That was certainly as much as any one could do at the Hôtel de Metz.

I was off again in the morning for Paris. Metz is situated on the banks of the Moselle; and during the first two or three hours of my journey the railway skirted that beguiling river. I believe there are impertinent steamboats on the dear Moselle in the neighborhood of Coblentz; but from Metz to Frouard it is, thank Heaven, not navigable for the *bateaux à vapeur*, and anything more peacefully lovely than the gentle stream and the scenery along its banks one can hardly imagine. I saw little islands in the river, on which clumps of pollard willows grew. I had a hundred glimpses of just such misty loveliness as Corot used to paint; and sometimes, when a herd of dappled cows came down to drink, there was a " Troyon " all ready for framing. I think that the French landscape is the secret of French art, — at least of French landscape art. There is nothing glaring or obtrusive about it. It is full of softly beautiful effects. The green of the willow-trees is subdued and tender. There are slopes more often than hills, and the sentiment of it all is dreamy and melancholy, rather than passionate and startling.

I thought, as I journeyed on, what I would do had Heaven but made me an artist; and the pictures I planned still linger in my memory.

It was the late afternoon when my journey ended, as so many of my lazy tours have, at the only Paris, — the gayest, brightest, yet most tragic city on which the far-off stars look down.

AN ENGLISH "CURE," AND A GLIMPSE OF YORKSHIRE.

TUNBRIDGE WELLS.

I HAVE been making a visit to Tunbridge Wells, as charming a place to-day as it was in the old time when Beau Nash used to saunter through its fashionable walks. One reaches it from London in a little more than an hour; and I only wonder that it is not crowded enough to spoil its pleasantness, — for very pleasant it is. With the exception of Bath, it is the most noted of the inland watering-places of England. It has always been associated with royalty and nobility. In fact, it was first discovered by Dudley, Lord North, a young nobleman no better than he should be, — I ask the pardon of his high-bred ghost, who, very likely, may be looking over my shoulder at this moment. Ghost-world has been brought so near of late that one may not even gossip about the past without saying, "By your leave," and dropping a courtesy.

Dudley, Lord North, was a gay young fellow in his long ago time, and he fell into a consumption when he was only twenty-four years old, in consequence of having pleased himself too much. He belonged to the court of King James I., or rather to that of King James's son, Prince Henry. He was a very energetic young man in the pursuit of his pleasure, and sad indeed was he when he could no longer catch up with the object of his pursuit. Eridge House belonged then, as it still does, to Lord Abergavenny; and to Eridge House he was sent, to try the benefit of change of air, and the cessation of his accustomed amusements. This was in 1606, almost three centuries ago. The gay young lord was extremely bored at Eridge House, and finally he resolved to take his life in his hands and go back to London. On his way through the forest he noticed a stream of running water in a wooded hollow, — a stream of very peculiar appearance, with a shining mineral scum upon its surface and a yellowish deposit in its depths. Perhaps it was his ancestral *dæmon* who whispered to him that this water might be of use to him in his debilitated condition. Any way, he had a quantity of it bottled up, and carried it to the most noted physicians of London. They examined it, and pronounced it to be just what he needed. So he returned to Eridge House, drank the waters, was restored to health, went on his evil, light-minded way, and lived to be eighty-five years old, — eighty-five years in which he had enjoyed himself hugely, and done as much harm as most men of his time. And with him began the fame of Tunbridge Wells.

Of course Lord Abergavenny was much interested in the new spring of healing thus discovered at his gate, and he set to work to clear the surrounding ground, sink wells, and turn the spot into a regular watering-place. The high repute that Tunbridge Wells had acquired early in the 17th century is evident from all the chronicles of that time; but the first really great event in the history of the place was the visit of Henrietta Maria, the queen of Charles I., which took place in the year 1630. During her sojourn of six weeks, undertaken with the view of re-establishing her health after the birth of Prince Charles (afterward Charles II.), she and her suite dwelt in tents, pitched on Bishop's Down Common. Though she sojourned in a tent, she had no lack of amusement, but was entertained by masques, pageants, and dancing, — all on a regal scale.

After this royal visit they began to build houses at Tunbridge Wells, and the famous Tunbridge Walks were laid out in the year 1638. In 1652, as John Evelyn records in his well-known Diary, he brought his wife and her mother to Tunbridge, and stayed with them "in a very sweet place, private and refreshing." On his journey to London, — that journey which we make now by train in a little more than an hour, — Evelyn was robbed by two "cut-throats." His Diary recounts the excursions made from Tunbridge Wells two centuries ago, and we go over the same ground to-day, and look at the ghost-haunted places, — at Clanrickarde House and Penshurst, and the rest, — and say to ourselves as we look : —

"Where are the snows of yester year?"

In the summer of 1664 King Charles II., with his queen, Catharine of Braganza, visited Tunbridge Wells, and in a review of the favorite watering-places of England at the period between the restoration and the revolution of 1688, Lord Macaulay speaks of the great attractions of Tunbridge. The Count de Grammont wrote in his "Memoirs":—

"Tunbridge is at the same distance from London that Fontainebleau is from Paris. All the handsome and gallant of both sexes meet here, in the season, for drinking the waters. The company is always numerous and always select, and as those who seek only to amuse themselves are always more numerous than those who resort hither for health, everything breathes pleasure and joy."

At that time the visitors were lodged in little dwellings, "clean and convenient," and there is still to be seen in the British Museum Library a warrant dated March 19, 1669, providing for the erection of tents at Tunbridge Wells for the entertainment of the Queen. After this period stately houses began to be built, and with every year the Wells grew more and more in favor. Beau Nash, who was born in 1674 and died — a very old beau of 87 — in 1761, became at about the year 1735 the first king, or arbiter, of Tunbridge Wells, — an office which he had previously held in Bath. Under his *régime* it was expected that every visitor should live in public. The lodging-houses were merely to be used for eating and sleeping. The rest of the time was to be passed on the walk then called "The Pantiles," now "The Parade," or in the Assembly Rooms, or in pleasure excursions. This sort of life went on not only while the old Beau was alive, but long after he had withdrawn from society into the discreet seclusion of his grave.

Every person who is familiar with the story of the 18th century knows that one met at Tunbridge all the celebrities of the time, and that one was wont to find them, sooner or later, on "The Pantiles." There walked Mrs. Elizabeth Carter, the woman who could talk Greek faster than any one in England; there was the novelist Richardson, Dr. Johnson, Colley Cibber, Garrick, and all the rest of the brilliant company who adorned those much-talked-of days.

Thackeray pictured them, as only Thackeray could, in "The Virginians." "There was," he says, "a great variety of characters. My Lord Chesterfield came by in a pearl-colored suit, with his blue ribbon and star, and saluted the young men. 'I will back the old boy for taking his hat off against the whole kingdom, and France either,' said my Lord March. 'He has never changed the shape of that hat of his for twenty years. Look at it; there it goes again. Do you see that great big, awkward, pockmarked, snuff-colored man, who hardly touches his clumsy beaver in reply? His confounded impudence! Do you know who that is? It's one

Johnson, a dictionary-maker, about whom my Lord Chesterfield wrote some most capital papers, when his dictionary was coming out, to patronize the fellow. I know they were capital. I've heard Harry Walpole say so, and he knows all about that sort of thing. Confound the impudent schoolmaster! That fat man he's walking with is another of your writing fellows, a printer,— his name is Richardson; he wrote "Clarissa," you know.'" Richardson was accustomed to be adored. Enraptured spinsters flung tea leaves around him, and beguiled him with the coffee-pot. Matrons kissed the slippers they had worked for him. There was a halo of virtue about his nightcap. All Europe had thrilled, panted, admired, trembled, wept, over the pages of the immortal little, kind, honest man with the round paunch.

Tunbridge was a great place for match-making in those gay old days. A letter, dated April 1, 1724, sets forth how a young Kentish yeoman, who had one thousand pounds a year to his fortune, ran off from the Wells with a young lady who had five thousand pounds, and that on the very day he made her acquaintance. "And," the letter slyly adds, "they say there are not less than twelve or fourteen ten-thousand-pound young ladies in the town who would be glad to go off on the same terms."

From first to last, I should think more royal personages had frequented Tunbridge Wells than almost any other watering-place in England.

Before Victoria came to the throne, she and her mother had passed two seasons there, and the Princess Louise and the Marquis of Lorne, in the summer of 1871, spent a long time at the Calverly Hotel, and were so charmed with the neighborhood that they bought an estate there, which they have since resold. The Queen herself and the Prince Consort honored the Calverly Hotel by staying in it, and Queen Marie Amélie, the widow of Louis Philippe, lived at the Chancellor House for several summers before her death.

Since the beginning of the present century Tunbridge Wells has been growing more and more into favor as a permanent abode. It has some thirty thousand all-the-year-round inhabitants, and the whole neighborhood is full of pleasant residences. For transient guests the "season" extends from Easter to the late autumn, but is at its height during August and September. It is a charming place to go to. There are plenty of good hotels, and of convenient and reasonable lodgings; and for lovelier scenery or more enchanting walks and drives no one need wish.

IN YORKSHIRE.

BY way of contrast to Tunbridge Wells we thought we would try Yorkshire.— The "Flying Scotchman" flies fast on its northern way. We left King's Cross, London, at ten o'clock of an August morning, and were at York, one hundred and eighty-eight miles distant, at a quarter before two o'clock,— one hundred and eighty-eight miles in three hours and three-quarters, including stoppages!

From York we drove ten miles across country, to Stillington Hall. This part of Yorkshire is almost as level as a Western prairie; but the landscape is softer and more luxuriant than anything I know in America. The trees, in love with the earth they sprang from, grow so low that their boughs almost touch the ground. Instead of wooden fences or stone walls, all the fields are separated from the highway and from each other by hedges, whose lush green is a rest to the eye.

Stillington Hall is a haven to rejoice in. One must carry a heavy heart indeed, not to be happy there. It has belonged for centuries to the Croft family, and it has all the charm bestowed by antiquity on a stately place where generations of men have lived and died. The house is full of old pictures, old books, and old furniture. The park — two thousand acres in extent — is the home of trees so venerable that one can fancy them shaking their boughs in derision at us, poor weaklings of a short-lived race, who come and go while they live on.

One especial interest the place had for me was that for years of his life the author of "Tristram Shandy" was the rector of Stillington and the adjoining parish of Sutton. Laurence Sterne in the pulpit! I suppose no one has ever accused him of being a religious man; but preaching was his profession, and he followed it according to his lights. For his sermons, no less than for his fiction, he sought suggestions from actual life; and his keen eyes overlooked the doings of his parishioners, and found in them the basis for his discourse. Whatever a man did during the week was very likely to confront him on the next Sunday. Did "doughty deeds" the rector please, due credit was given to the doer of them; for the Reverend Laurence was a fighting parson, and despised cowardice. On one occasion a well-known pugilist came to Stillington, and, vaunting himself on his prowess, sounded the trumpet of his own fame and challenged all the parish to fight with him. For three days Parson Sterne waited, in hope that some one of his stout parishioners would arise to maintain the honor of Stillington. On the fourth day, seeing that the prize-fighter waxed proud in his unchallenged might, Sterne himself went forth and fought with him. I am thankful to say that the fighting pastor won the victory and the pugilist limped off well beaten. The next Sunday Sterne announced as his text, Judges, fifteenth chapter and eighth verse: "And he smote them hip and thigh with a great slaughter." He crowned his own achievement with the laurels that were its due, and the strong men of Stillington were put to shame.

To one going from the noise and confusion of London the stillness of Yorkshire seemed almost solemn. Sometimes a bird sang, and sometimes, if you listened with attentive ears, you caught the sough of winds conferring among the trees; but other noise there was none. There was no sound of wheels grinding the pavements, or of hawkers crying their wares in the street, — nothing to suggest the toil and turmoil of the far-off town. But even Adam and Eve had to leave their paradise, and it was for a breath of sea air that we had come to Yorkshire.

All English artists conspire to praise the beauty of the Yorkshire coast. In discussing places of summer resort with English friends, ninety-nine out of a hundred suggested this region; but all the artists said, "Go to Whitby," while all the fashionable people said, "Go to Scarborough."

We consulted maps and guide-books, and found that Scarborough and Whitby were within less than two hours' drive of each other, and decided to see them both.

After leaving York, the character of the landscape changed. We were no longer in the midst of gently rolling fields. High hills rose abruptly everywhere, and we were constantly reminded of our own White Mountain landscape.

Arrived at Whitby, we drove to the Royal Hotel, a stately house, high on a cliff, overlooking the German Ocean. As we wound up this cliff, we took in something of the varied and picturesque charm of the town.

We saw the quaint houses with their red-tiled roofs, the bathing-machines, the donkeys "all saddled and bridled and fit for the fight," as the old rhyme hath it.

I thought at first that I wanted to ride on one of these little beasts; but they were *so* little — so much smaller than myself — that I resolved to refrain from such cruelty to animals. I was consoled a moment after by a sight of the funniest tiny open carriages, driven — if one may call such an arrangement driving — by the gayest-looking postilions, seated magnificently on the backs of their horses.

When we reached the hotel and were shown to our room overlooking the sea, the almost magical loveliness of the place began to dawn on us. Opposite the great cliff whereon our hotel stood, another headland jutted out into the sea, on which are the ruins of Whitby Abbey; and to the Abbey we made our way next morning.

Down into the town we went, across a bridge

and up one hundred and ninety-eight steps, till we stood on the east cliff of Whitby and before the ruins of the Abbey, — ruins as noble as those of Melrose or Dryburgh. The Abbey was founded by St. Hilda in the seventh century, but the oldest portion of what one now sees was erected not earlier than the latter part of the eleventh century.

According to Sir Walter Scott, the sea-fowl flying over Whitby used to bow themselves, and do homage to the saint.

The monastery at Whitby, like many others of that date, was meant as a home for monks as well as for nuns, the two sexes living in separate portions of the convent, and meeting only at the hours of prayer. The most noted of the monks was Cædmon, who is called the father of Saxon poetry, and is said to have received the gift of song by direct inspiration.

This story has been beautifully rendered by the English poet, Philip Bourke Marston. We are told how Cædmon was dumb with shame when others sang, and how once, in his humiliation, he retired to the lonely place where the oxen were kept, and laid himself down to sleep among them.

So sleeping, he dreamed a dream, in which a celestial presence appeared to him and commanded him to sing, bestowing, with the high decree, the power to fulfil it, touching his lips with flame and filling his soul with the ecstasy of song.

Among the ruins of this old Abbey one seemed

to go back to another world, where life was simpler and grander — where men were contented to pray and praise and build temples and pass away and be forgotten.

That afternoon we drove to Robin Hood's Bay. I cast longing eyes at the gay postilions with their little open traps; but I followed my friend's lead into a more substantial vehicle. We drove through miles of beautiful country, the fields "dressed in living green," as the old hymn says, which contrasted vividly with the rich dark hawthorn hedges.

At last we paused on the brow of a hill so steep that the driver seemed reluctant to drive down it.

Pointing far below with his finger, he said, "Yon's the village."

We saw no village, and said so; but he informed us that we should see it soon, if we went on; and sure enough we were presently in the midst of the strangest village it has ever been my fortune to behold.

The houses are perched one above another, so that the roof of one might easily be the doorstep of its neighbor. Some of the houses on the upper tiers are accessible only by steep, narrow flights of stone steps, running up between the lower houses.

Down through the midst of this quaint village we plunged. We knew it stood upon the sea, but we saw only the narrow street and the odd little stone houses with their red-tiled roofs.

There was but one shop, about as large as a Saratoga trunk. One half of its one window was filled with little stone ink-bottles, and the other with neck-ties. The place swarmed with children, and we asked one of them where was the sea.

"Round yon corner," he answered; and we turned the corner, and, sure enough, there was Robin Hood's Bay; but it would require another art than that of the pen to make you see the superb red-chalk headlands shutting in this tranquil shining German Ocean, which can be so deadly and so treacherous, though it smiled very tranquilly in the August sunshine.

The next morning I realized my ambition at last, and had a drive after a postilion. A very gorgeous fellow he was, to be sure, — the most splendid, I am proud to say, of the whole band.

We passed the afternoon in climbing up and down the steep, narrow streets of Whitby. The chief business of the place seemed to be in jet.

"*Real Whitby Jet*" is a familiar label in every jeweller's in Boston or New York; and here we were, in the very midst of it. Nearly every other shop was a jet shop, and we visited them all. I think that by night we knew the resources of every establishment in the place. When I see your sleeve-buttons, or your necklace, or the earrings in your dainty ears, I shall know whether they came from Bryan's, or Chapman's, or Wilson's. I know but few things well in this world, but Whitby jet is one of them.

The next day was our last in Whitby, and we improved it. We had learned that within a reasonable drive were moors, — real moors, such moors as the author of "Jane Eyre" and her gifted sisters used to wander over,— and we determined to see them.

We were not disappointed. They were all we had dreamed. For thirty miles or more they stretched away, all purple with heather and gorse, — a sight never to be forgotten.

They looked pathless to us; but our driver assured us that there were dalesmen in those parts who could traverse them, for all their miles of length, with never a misstep, guided by landmarks quite imperceptible to the unpractised eye.

In the afternoon we drove to Runswick Bay; and here, it seems to me, the glory and beauty of the Yorkshire coast reaches its climax. Again, as at Robin Hood's Bay, we were sent plunging down a steep declivity in search of a village where literally the roofs of one row of houses form the footpath of those above them.

All the way down through this village we could see the ocean, and coming up again, we turned midway for one last glimpse of the semi-circular bay, shut in by its noble cliffs, whose headlands jut far out into the sea; and suddenly we beheld, glorified by a burst of sunlight, such a sight as I never expect to see again.

At the extreme end of the red-chalk headland on the right appeared a gigantic face upturned to the sky. It looked like a child's face, and a bit of cap-frill could be seen above the forehead. The features were clearly defined, the lips seemed actually to smile as the sunlight kissed them.

So clearly was it cut that we thought it must have been fashioned by human hands to enhance the attraction of the scene. A peasant was coming down the path we were climbing.

"You see that face?" I asked.

He nodded; Yorkshire men do not waste words.

"Did any one about here make it?" I inquired.

He looked at me in half-reproachful surprise before he answered: —

"It's God's makkin, yon; nobbuddy else ever put a hand to it."

We were told afterwards that the face is frequently quite invisible; we had chanced upon the moment of vision.

The next morning we left the Royal Hotel, — which the Whitby guide informed us, in guide-book English, was "replete with accommodation for visitors," — and betook ourselves to Scarborough, the place which bears the proud title of "The queen of English watering-places."

It is indeed a town quite beautiful enough to justify its fashionable prestige. We settled ourselves at the Prince of Wales's Hotel, situated, like the Royal Hotel at Whitby, on a cliff overlooking the sea. Directly beneath it are the grounds of the Spa, and there is an almost perpendicular railway which takes you down to them and up again. It is absolutely frightful to stand at the foot of this railway and watch the passenger-car almost at the top of it. You can't help expecting to see it tumble down; but I think no accident has ever taken place. The cars are moved, I believe, by water-power.

Scarborough boasts its ancient castle, a picturesque ruin enough, but not half so beautiful as the Abbey at Whitby. We reached the place on mid-day on a Saturday. We lunched, and then we went out to look about us, and found Tony Weller, the veritable Tony Weller of the "Pickwick Papers."

He had a vehicle which seemed as if it had shared the sorrows of several generations; but we preferred it to all the smart carriages in Scarborough for the sake of its driver's honest and good-natured face.

We spent much of our time inside that disreputable-looking vehicle. We drove about the town, — to the Castle, to Oliver's Mountain and the Park, — also we drove out of town to make excursions along the coast; and at every step we said to each other, "If we had not seen Whitby, how beautiful we should think Scarborough!"

But Scarborough, unlike Whitby, is gay; it moves to music. Down there in the midst of the Spa there is a pavilion, and there the band plays from eleven in the morning until one P. M., and from seven to nine at night.

At night the scene is wonderfully brilliant,—

more like a bit of open-air Paris than anything belonging to sober England. There are lights everywhere among the soft foliage; there is a little temple, open on all sides, where perpetual ices and sherbets are eaten; and the throng of pleasure-seekers walk and talk, or lounge under the trees and listen to the music; and the sea comes up softly, with a low murmur, and looks on, and retreats again.

All the features of the English watering-place are in full force at Scarborough: bathing-machines, donkeys, bath-chairs for invalids, salt-water bathing establishments for those who shrink from the actual embrace of the sea, — all are there. By Monday night we felt that we knew it by heart, and determined to spend the last night of our happy week in York, and give the next morning to the cathedral.

I knew, of old, this cathedral, with its wonderful beauty of architecture and its superb stained glass; but this time it seemed more beautiful than ever. It was a glorious day, and the windows shone in its light like mighty jewels.

We went to morning service and heard the little white-robed boys chant their morning anthem; then we wandered away among the ruins of St. Mary's Abbey, and there only the birds sang in the sweet summer day, while a gentle wind waved the tree-boughs in and out the great crumbling arches of gray stone.

By the way, everything is of stone in Yorkshire.

Such a thing as a wooden house I did not see in the whole of this journey. The smallest little shepherd's hut would be of gray stone, with red-tiled roof. Flowers and stone are universal. I scarcely saw one house in the neighborhood of Whitby that did not have its yard and its windows aglow with brilliant blossoms.

I suppose they are blooming still. Shall I ever see them again? Who knows?

THE END.

www.ingramcontent.com/pod-product-compliance
Lightning Source LLC
Chambersburg PA
CBHW032032220426
43664CB00006B/449